BREAKING THE BONDS OF FATE

Epicurus (341–270 BCE)

Breaking the Bonds *of* Fate

Epicurus and Marx

by JOHN BELLAMY FOSTER

MONTHLY REVIEW PRESS
New York

Library of Congress Cataloging-in-Publication data
available from the publisher

978-1-68590-123-3 ISBN cloth
978-1-68590-124-0 ISBN eBook trade
978-1-68590-125-7 ISBN eBook institutional

Typeset in Bulmer MT

MONTHLY REVIEW PRESS, NEW YORK
monthlyreview.org

5 4 3 2 1

Contents

To John Mage

Preface

The origins of *Breaking the Bonds of Fate* go back twenty-five years to the writing of my book *Marx's Ecology* in 2000. In 1999, I published an article on "Marx's Theory of Metabolic Rift" addressing Karl Marx's theory of ecological crisis. However, as soon as that article was completed, I was presented with a major dilemma. How did Marx develop the depth of theoretical insight that led to such a radical ecological critique going well beyond his time, and in many ways, beyond our own as well? Neither his critique of political economy nor his considerable knowledge of nineteenth-century science seemed capable of explaining this. The answer, I concluded, lay in the roots of his materialism.

The resulting research into the foundations of Marx's materialism led me back to his doctoral dissertation on Epicurus. Marx's thesis on the *Difference Between the Democritean and Epicurean Philosophies of Nature* had generally been treated in the Western Marxist philosophical tradition as an immature product of his early Hegelian idealist phase. Departing from the dominant tradition in this respect, *Marx's Ecology* presented Epicurus's materialist philosophy as the nascent basis on which he had begun to work out a materialist dialectic, inverting G. W. F. Hegel's idealist system. It was this fundamental reinterpretation of Marx's materialism that constituted the theoretical foundation for *Marx's Ecology*. Hegel's dialectic, in Marx's conception, was the single greatest achievement of speculative philosophy. In contrast, Epicurus's system, with its immanent dialectic, pointed beyond speculative philosophy to materialism, the intellectual birthplace of socialism.

After completing *Marx's Ecology*, I planned to pursue the analysis of Marx and Epicurus further. However, a much more pressing challenge stood in the way. *Marx's Ecology* ended with the deaths of Charles Darwin and Marx in 1882 and 1883, respectively. The question inevitably arose: What was the fate of the materialist conception of nature and ecology after Marx and Darwin? Within the Marxist tradition, this was wrapped up with the issue of the "dialectics of nature" associated primarily with Frederick Engels. It took twenty years before I was able to carry the story begun in *Marx's Ecology* all the way forward to the rise of the modern environmental movement in my book *The Return of Nature: Socialism and Ecology*, published in 2020. One of the startling aspects of this history was the way in which it traced an Epicurean as well as Marxian thread running through the entire development of ecological materialism.

At this point, it seemed possible to return to the issue of Marx's treatment of Epicurus's philosophy, which Marx stated he had made his "object of *special* study."[1] Although there were numerous partial treatments of Marx's doctoral thesis, no comprehensive work on the theoretical connections between these two thinkers had ever been attempted. In 2023, I drafted a chapter on "Marx and Epicurus" for a book being edited by classicists Tristan Bradshaw and Ben Brown at University of Sydney.[2] In late February 2024, I delivered a keynote address on this topic to the Critical Antiquities Network. Having arrived at this point, I decided to continue on to write the full assessment of Marx and Epicurus that I had long envisioned.

It soon became apparent, however, that my overall perspective had shifted over the decades. I no longer saw the task as simply one of explaining the Epicurean materialist roots of Marx's analysis. Epicurus's historical and theoretical stature had grown in my conception to the point that I saw it as rivaling in his own time that of Marx in his. What I had originally thought of as an inquiry into *Marx and Epicurus* turned into an exploration of *Epicurus and Marx*, with Epicurus's philosophy as the actual starting point and a crucial part of the millennia-long struggle for human freedom. If Epicurus in antiquity sought to "break 'the bonds of fate,'" this was a task that Marx would consciously take up and carry forward under very different historical conditions in modern times. In this view, Epicurus's philosophy had a lasting significance for historical-materialist theory and the practice of sustainable human development. *Breaking the Bonds of Fate*, *Marx's Ecology*, and *The Return of Nature* had thus turned into a dialectical trilogy, with each of the works constituting a "moment," reinforcing the others.

A note on the sources and translations used in the text is in order here. In references to classical sources, I use the Oxford abbreviations from the *Oxford Classical Dictionary*, fourth edition. Where English translations of Greek and Latin texts are employed, the particular translations are indicated. In the case of Lucretius's *De rerum natura*, of which innumerable translations are available, I have relied mainly on the 2003 verse translation of Walter Englert (Hackett). However, Lucretius, because of his influence on philosophy and science, is also frequently translated in prose editions that allow for more exactness. Here I have relied chiefly on the 1924 prose translation of W. H. D. Rouse from the Loeb Classical Library (Harvard), supplemented by R. E. Latham's 1951 prose translation (Penguin). The main source for Epicurus's extant writings is Book 10 of Diogenes Laertius's *Lives of Eminent Philosophers*. However, quotations from other works not included in Diogenes, such as the *Vatican Sayings* and Book 25 of Epicurus's *On Nature*, rely primarily on A. A. Long and David Sedley, eds., *The Hellenistic Philosophers* (Cambridge); and Brad Inwood and L. P. Gerson, eds., *The Epicurean Reader*. In numerous instances in this study, where the context demands it, translations from Epicurus and Lucretius are taken from Marx and Engels's *Collected Works*, and from noted Epicurean scholars such as Cyril Bailey, Norman DeWitt, Benjamin Farrington, George Thomson, and Simon Laursen.

The present book would not have been possible without the constant inspiration and help offered by my close friend John Mage, to whom it is dedicated. John has seen me through all the works of my materialist-dialectical trilogy, and he has contributed most directly to this latest volume. His knowledge of the Greek and Latin classics and the history of antiquity, not to mention his familiarity with Marx and the Marxian classics, helped guide me throughout this complex literary detective story. I owe many of my insights on the contemporary debate on Epicurus's conception of free will and determinism, related to Book 25 of Epicurus's *On Nature*, to John's inspired input.

The nineteenth-century papyrological discoveries from the charred remains found in the Villa of Papyri in Herculaneum, and the resulting philosophical revelations associated with Epicurus's *On Nature*, all began with the extraordinary work of Theodor Gomperz in the nineteenth century. I am grateful to Anita Mage for translating from the German on my behalf a number of essays by and about Gomperz, which proved indispensable for this study. Joseph Fracchia translated a crucial part of Roland Daniels's *Mikrokosmos: Entwurf Einer Physiologischen Anthropologie* (*Microcosmos: Outline of a Physiological Anthropology*). Jacopo Bergamo sent me a copy of Jean Fallot's *Il piacere e la morte nella filosfia di Epicuro*, allowing me to address that important work.

In my youth, with the encouragement of my father, I studied Plato's *Dialogues* and Greek history and culture along with introductory Latin. As an undergraduate at the Evergreen State College in Olympia, Washington, I was formally introduced to Aristotle's *Politics* and the Greek dramatists. Later, in graduate school at York University in Toronto, I was fortunate to have the opportunity to delve extensively into ancient Greek political philosophy and history under the tutelage of Ellen Meiksins Wood and Neal Wood at the time that they were writing their *Class Ideology and Ancient Political Theory: Socrates, Plato, and Aristotle in Social Context* (1978). My own interest was primarily directed at Artistotle and specifically at the question of "Aristotle Discovers the Economy," as raised by Karl Polanyi. In subsequent studies related to ancient philosophy, noted classicists Richard Seaford and A. A. Long, each responded to inquiries. Don Konstan, whose work influenced much of the discussion of Epicurean physics in this study, was an invited commentator for my Critical Antiquities Network keynote on "Marx and Epicurus" in February 2024. Thomas Nail and I had some useful exchanges on Epicurus, Lucretius, and Marx, and I found his three books *Lucretius I: An Ontology of Motion* (2018); *Lucretius II: An Ethics of Motion* (2020); and *Marx in Motion: A New Materialist Marxism* (2020) to be helpful in some of the later phases of my research.

Brett Clark did an initial copyedit of this whole book. Our shared interest in Epicurus goes back to the time I was writing *Marx's Ecology* and is evident in all of our subsequent coauthored works. Brett and I have therefore talked through this book nearly every step of the way. Others at *Monthly Review* and Monthly Review Press who have aided and supported in the writing and publication of this book in various ways include Hannah

Holleman, Michael Yates, Martin Paddio, Intan Suwandi, Jamil Jonna, Sarah Kramer, Camila Valle, Rebecca Manski, Fred Magdoff, Victor Wallis, and the late John J. Simon.

Over the last five years or so, I have explored many of the philosophical questions raised here in an informal seminar with three gifted philosophers—Kenny Knowlton, Chris Shambaugh, and Oscar Ralda—who were working on their PhDs in philosophy, focusing on studies of Hegel and Marx, at the University of Oregon. As my *MR* research assistants, Chris helped me obtain materials while Oscar fact-checked the entire book.

István Mészáros never ceased encouraging me to go forward with my work on Epicurus. Robert W. McChesney has offered his friendship and thoughts during this entire journey, as he has with respect to all of my efforts over the last fifty-plus years. Ian Angus has been a fountainhead of support, sharing with me his own interest in ancient materialist philosophy. Brian Napoletano and I corresponded on many of the philosophical issues involved in this work numerous times. My son Saul Foster and I have discussed Epicurus and Marx in the context of the meaning of life. Helena Sheehan has been at the forefront on all questions related to dialectical materialism and is a constant source of inspiration.

Carrie Ann Naumoff and I have talked about Epicurus's philosophy of enough, his discussions of freedom and necessity, his principle of emergence, and his notion of love dancing around the world over all the years we have known each other. Epicurus, it came out in our discussions, brought something vitally necessary to Marx, socialism, and ecology. Carrie Ann was thus for me the final *Energeia* behind this book, the reason for it eventually seeing the light of day.

—EUGENE, OREGON
JULY 22, 2024

Introduction

We always hold fast to what is possible.

—EPICURUS

This book is about the historical and theoretical connections between the ideas of two of the greatest materialist thinkers, separated by millennia of development and change: Epicurus, writing in Hellenistic Greece at the end of the fourth and the beginning of the third century BCE, and Karl Marx, writing in mid-nineteenth-century capitalist Europe.[1] The ideas of each of these thinkers are treated here as having roughly equal standing in relation to their times. They both deeply affected the ages in which they emerged, giving rise to revolutionary new views that attracted numberless adherents. Both sought to "break 'the bonds of fate.'"[2] Epicurus stood on the shoulders of the entire Ionian tradition before him. Marx stood on the shoulders of Epicurus—as well as on those of the German Idealists, British political economists, and French utopian socialists.

Epicurus was the foremost materialist philosopher in antiquity, whose work extended from epistemology, to physics, to ethics. He introduced a new, if limited and defensive, praxis aimed at human survival, sustainability, and happiness. Marx, in the age of the dual industrial and political-economic revolutions in nineteenth-century Europe, developed a materialist conception of history, complementing the earlier materialist conception of nature. Here human beings, as in Epicurus, were conceived as both corporeal and social beings. Both thinkers were concerned with underlying material conditions; the alienation of essence from appearance; the sensuous nature of existence and knowledge; human freedom and determinism; historical contingency; the emergence of new forms and powers; and the reconciliation of humanity and nature. Epicurus was seen by Marx as the Enlightenment figure of antiquity, while Marx was himself both a child of the seventeenth- and eighteenth-century Enlightenment and its most revolutionary critic.

What Epicurus and Marx taken together provide us with is a conception of a complete materialism—ontological, epistemological, and practical—associated with the struggle for human freedom and the creation of a new relation between humanity and nature. Building in part on Epicurus's emergent materialism, Marx was able to develop an analysis that neither denied the objectivity of nature, nor the active relation of the human subjects to nature (and to each other) through production. On this basis, he built a thoroughgoing materialism that began with the active, sensuous relation of human beings (and of life in general) to the universal metabolism of nature of which they were a part. Human beings, as both corporeal beings and historical beings, transformed via their production—not entirely as they pleased, but under conditions inherited from the past—their material relations to both nature and society, allowing for an ongoing process of human development.[3]

In the materialist view, the *emergence* of new levels of reality, with new creative powers, through the organization of matter/motion (energy) does not generate a one-way, unilinear movement but has as its counterpart *disemergence*.[4] All that emerges is subject to dissolution, as explained in Book 6 of Lucretius's great poem, *De rerum natura*. Everything that exists in the material world is transitory and thus historical in nature.

Nevertheless, it is characteristic of Epicurean philosophy that while commencing with "death the immortal" as a materialist proposition imposing determinant limits, it swerves away from all teleology, mechanistic determinism, and fatalism. Nothing comes from nothing and nothing being destroyed is reduced to nothing. The universe is infinite. Matter and motion continually lead to new organizational forms in the phenomenal world. The reality of the world is characterized by material limits imposed by both nature and society. Attempts to pursue endless riches or to achieve the final conquest of nature only lead to disaster. Hence, it is necessary in the end, in the Epicurean view, to seek self-sufficiency, qualitative human development, and friendship/community, leading to *ataraxia* (literally untroubledness).[5] Justice is based on reciprocity and changing material conditions. All of this is conceived as within reach of human freedom. Epicureanism, while holding on to causal determinism, emphasized contingency and avoided all fixed determinism or divine power that would remove the realm of human freedom. It is here that Epicurus's notion of an infinitesimal swerve, or *clinamen*, a declension from the fall in a straight line of the atom, enters into his philosophy. It introduces a degree of indeterminacy and chance/contingency that stands for the *possibility of freedom*.

It was Marx who first emphasized that Epicurus's swerve formed the basis of a philosophy of freedom. In the early twentieth century, partly as a result of developments in physics with the introduction of Werner Heisenberg's uncertainty principle, classicists and specialists on Hellenistic philosophy began to take seriously Epicurus's swerve, which had long been dismissed as nonsensical. This occurred independently of Marx's dissertation, which was not published until 1902 in Germany, and not made available in an English translation until 1967. By the late twentieth century, following up on the work of Theodor Gomperz in the late nineteenth century and successive translations of fragments from Book 25 of Epicurus's *On Nature*, recovered from the Herculaneum papyri, it became possible to explore more fully Epicurus's complex philosophy of mind. This revealed his sophisticated conception of the emergence of mind from an "original constitution," by means of internal development/production of mental characteristics within each individual, responding to social interactions, and thereby establishing the basis of human reason, agency, and freedom.[6] Here Marx's early nineteenth-century analysis of Epicurus's conception of materialism and freedom finally came into its own—although the significance of this was generally lost on Western Marxism, which failed to recognize advances in classical scholarship in this area.

The more complete materialism that results, through the long march from Epicurus to Marx, and then down to the present, allows for a more synthetic development of the materialist philosophical views of nature and society, and thus of ecology, necessary for our time. The immanent dialectic that Marx found in Epicurus was multifaceted, providing a complex, dynamic conception of the material world. Aspects of Epicurean materialism had been incorporated into almost all seventeenth- and eighteenth-century Enlightenment materialism. It was Epicurus, as Marx repeatedly noted over the years, who introduced the concept of the *social contract*, along with the whole historical approach to the development of society.[7]

Although idealist philosophers emphasized human action and free will, starting always from the mind, Epicurus, as the culminating figure in the whole Ionian materialist tradition, introduced a philosophy of development and human freedom in which nature was its own cause, and in which freedom arose not out of an ideal realm—that is, from above, like Athena from the head of Zeus—but through contingent struggles associated with human existence itself. In the *last instance*, Epicurus wrote, what we choose is "up to us."[8]

Praxis: Ancient and Modern

In terms of praxis, or the dialectic of theory and practice, the contribution of Epicurus's philosophy was affected by the fact that he was writing at a time of an "empire of chaos" that ensued during the Wars of the *Diadochi* (or Successors) over Alexander's Empire, and the related demise of the polis.[9] Nevertheless, his emphasis on contingent freedom was an important break from the fatalism of his time. Although he advised his followers to avoid where possible any serious engagement in the political life of the time, he also supported taking direct actions on behalf of friends who were victims of injustice. In a famous case, Epicurus, and his follower Metrodorus, intervened in support of their friend the Syrian Mithres when he was imprisoned in Piraeus, reflecting the fact that in Epicurean philosophy the distinction between Greek and "barbarian" had been dissolved. Epicurus was well known for providing aid, in the form of bushels of food, from his limited means, to those in distress.[10] In general, the social praxis promoted by Epicurus in the Hellenistic Age was one of defiance of the state (astral) religion, accompanied by a relatively distant relation to the polis itself, focusing instead on creating self-sufficient communities rooted in friendship, the reconciliation of humanity and nature, egalitarianism, and *ataraxia,* or contentment. The emphasis was on internal human development, cultivation of philosophy, and an atmosphere of reciprocity and "mutual exchange."[11] "Nothing is enough," Epicurus wrote, "for those for whom enough is too little."[12]

The significance of Epicurus and Epicureanism for an understanding of classical historical materialism and for the renewal of Marxism today should be readily apparent. The one-sided Western Marxist philosophical tradition, for all of its immense contributions, was based from its beginning in the 1920s on a rejection of materialist dialectics, or the dialectics of nature, and thus of natural science. This translated into the negation of any meaningful materialist conception of nature. Yet, without a thoroughgoing materialist perspective it is impossible to perceive the relation of humanity to nature, of which we are a part. In terms of Marx's later analysis, this requires recognizing how the labor and production process constitutes the specific human "social metabolism" within the "universal metabolism of nature." The relation of freedom to necessity, peculiar to our time, demands a dialectical perspective, one that refuses to divide nature from society, while recognizing the contradictions imposed by capitalism in that respect.[13]

In any attempt to address Marx's materialism, his "genetic exposition" of Epicurus's philosophy, exploring its "objective logic," is of decisive importance given its *genetic* relation to his own materialism and dialectical method.[14] Reduction of historical materialism to a purely *social* dialectic, excluding the *natural-material* realm, has robbed Marxian theory of its *earthly* basis, including any understanding of the relation of freedom and necessity. The result is to negate the whole larger conception of revolutionary struggle as aimed at the creation of a society of sustainable human development. Here the "associated producers" would "govern the human metabolism with nature in a rational way, bringing it under their collective control . . . accomplishing it with the least expenditure of energy and in conditions most worthy and appropriate for their human nature."[15]

Epicureanism is often seen as constituting a merely contemplative materialism, characteristic of natural science, rather than a philosophy of praxis as such. However, the requirements of praxis change with changing historical conditions. As noted, Epicurus's philosophy arose during the early Hellenistic Age in a time of internecine conflict and imposed tyrannies associated with the collapse of the Greek polis, which had largely succumbed to Macedonian rule, followed by the Wars of the Diadochi, the successors to Alexander's empire. Political life was no longer centered in the Greek poleis but encompassed a wider Hellenistic world. In this context of an *empire of chaos*, Epicurus developed a materialist philosophy that emphasized corporeal existence and sense certainty as the basis of knowledge against an idealist approach to knowledge, often seen as purely contemplative. His philosophy saw inescapable mortality as the key to affirming life itself. Self-sufficient community and friendship provided a basis of mutual accord that offered the best protection to whole communities. This philosophy of material existence and the pursuit of a common life secured by equality and reciprocity spread rapidly throughout the Hellenistic and then Roman worlds, having its greatest influence in the East beyond Greece itself. Epicureans were known, on at least one occasion, as recounted by Lucian, to have courageously organized *en masse*, risking death, in defiance of the inimical mystical-religious domination and repression of Alexander of Abonoteichos (also known as Alexander the False Prophet).

Although Epicurus himself seldom referred directly to other philosophers in his extant works, Epicureanism was at all times a *critical philosophy*, which was evident in his *On Nature*.[16] Numerous Epicurean works, written by Epicurus's early followers, were aimed at criticizing both Platonic idealism and Academic Skepticism.[17] Aside from certain aspects of

Democritus's philosophy, Skepticism was mainly connected in third century BCE Athens with the Second or Middle Academy of Arcesilaus, although it was often traced back in part to Socrates.[18] In Epicurus's Garden, Metrodorus, Hermarchus, Colotes, and Leontion all developed critiques of the leading idealist and skeptical philosophers.[19]

The most famous of these critiques, of which we have extensive concrete knowledge, was Colotes's *On the Point that Conformity to the Doctrines of the Other Philosophers Actually Makes It Impossible to Live*, which took material life and the world as its criterion of judgment, arguing that the dominant philosophies were removed from the most basic aspects of everyday existence, divorced from physical needs and limits. So influential was this work that it was still being favorably quoted by the Epicurean Diogenes of Oenoanda in the second century CE, some five hundred years later. Writing hundreds of years after Colotes, in the late first century/early second century CE, Plutarch was to devote two works—*Reply to Colotes in Defense of Other Philosophers* and *That Epicurus Actually Makes a Pleasant Life Impossible*—to a "polemical counterblast" to Colotes's work.[20]

For Marx, Plutarch's attempt to prove in response to Epicurus and Colotes that it was actually possible to live in this world in conformity with the views of the idealist and skeptical philosophers entirely backfired, only demonstrating the strength of the Epicurean critique that it had sought to disprove.[21] Marx strongly identified with Colotes's criticisms of Socrates for failing to acknowledge that his continual disingenuous profession of ignorance, coupled with his skeptical and idealist positions, generated a philosophy that contradicted the conditions of his own material existence. In this way, Epicureanism displayed a critical spirit with respect to idealism and skepticism that was later to be reproduced in Marx's own materialist philosophy.[22]

Hellenistic Epicureanism versus Eurocentrism

The Hellenistic philosophies, Marx observed, were the means by which Greek culture was transmitted to Rome.[23] Epicureanism, however, was unique within Greek philosophy in the degree to which it went eastward as well, where it was to find its greatest number of adherents. At the outset, it migrated throughout Alexander the Great's Hellenistic Empire, while, after the lapse of a century, it also took up residence in Rome. Epicureanism thus was geographically a Hellenistic rather than simply a Greek or European philosophy, penetrating into Asia Minor, including Syria, Judea, and Egypt, as well as further to the east. Diogenes Laertius wrote that Epicureans were "so many in number that they could hardly be counted by whole cities."[24]

In the early second century BCE the Epicurean philosopher and mathematician Philonides from Laodicea in Syria produced a commentary on Book 8 of Epicurus's *On Nature*, along with well over a hundred books in all. He attracted throngs of followers in Antioch, the capital of the Seleucid Empire, with Epicureanism attaining something like the status of a court philosophy. Zeno of Sidon, head of the Epicurean school in the late second century and early first century BCE, came to Athens from Lebanon. Philodemus left Gadara in what is now Jordan ca.75 BCE to teach Epicurean thought in Italy.[25] As already noted, in the second century CE, Alexander the False Prophet, in the Roman province of Bithynia and Pontus in modern-day Turkey, seeking to expand his mystical religion, found himself confronted by entire cities of organized Epicureans standing in his way.[26] In the late second century CE, Diogenes of Oenoanda in Lycia in what is now southwestern Turkey, constructed his "immense inscription" of Epicurean writings, "which, like an opened roll of papyrus, offered to its readers column after column on the walls of a porch of the city of Oenoanda."[27] Epicureanism was a vital, living philosophy for seven centuries, reaching the peak of its influence in the second century CE and entering a slow decline in the third and fourth centuries, eventually, it is thought, overcome by Christianity.[28]

As Martin Bernal demonstrated in *Black Athena*, Greek culture was never as removed from Asia and Africa as the later "Aryan myth" propagated in Europe supposed.[29] This was particularly the case with Greek philosophy, which originated in the Ionian cities on the western coast of Anatolia in present-day Turkey. Hence, the influence of Egyptian, Semitic, and Persian cultures on Greek thought was enormous. Democritus was a great explorer constantly in search of knowledge, which took him far to the East. Plato took many of his ideas from Egyptian thought. Pyrrho, the great skeptical philosopher, and proponent of a calm and indifferent life, was deeply affected by his encounter with Eastern philosophies, particularly Buddhism, in India, while accompanying Alexander's army as far as Afghanistan. He carried back to Greece ideas that influenced subsequent Hellenistic philosophy.[30]

Epicurus grew up in the Athenian settler colony on the island of Samos, near the ancient region of Ionia on the Aegean coast of Asia Minor. Here Persian cultural influence (the island had been ruled only decades before by a Persian satrap), as well as that of the Ionian Greek cities nearby in Asia Minor, were undoubtedly substantial. After completing his military service in Athens, he returned to live with his parents who, as a result of Athens's loss of Samos by Alexander the Great's decree issued shortly before his death, were then residing in the Ionian city of Colophon. After years of further study, Epicurus opened schools first in Mytilene on the island of Lesbos, where Aristotle had taught for several years, and then in Lampsacus, near the Hellespont—a wealthy

Greek city that had drawn close to Persia prior to Alexander's crossing of the Hellespont.

Due to this rich historical and cultural background, it is undoubtedly the case that fourth-century BCE Ionian Greek and Persian culture, as well as the new Hellenistic ethos introduced by Alexander, impacted Epicurus's philosophy, which he carried to Athens when he set up his school there in 306 BCE. If the philosophy of Plato was quintessentially Athenian (though inspired by Egyptian thought), Epicurus, while also an Athenian citizen, was a product of the much more diverse and varied Hellenistic civilization that followed.

Epicurus's philosophy thus reflected both the harsh political realities and the wide cultural sphere of the end of the fourth century and the beginning of the third century BCE. Rather than centered on the declining polis, it was rooted in an "association of friends," constituting a necessary response in a climate of continual warfare and political decay.[31] Consequently, its reach expanded well beyond Greece. As Norman DeWitt explained in *Epicurus and His Philosophy*, Epicureanism "flourished among the Greeks and barbarians alike in Greece, Asia Minor, Syria, Judea, Egypt, Italy, Roman Africa, and Gaul."[32] Its gradual demise during the late Roman Empire is believed to have been due to the triumph of Christianity. "Epicureanism," DeWitt continues,

> was the only missionary philosophy produced by the Greeks. At its inception it stood to the dominant Platonism as Buddhism to Brahmanism in Asia. Nonconformity, as opposed to orthodoxy, is prone at all times to be militant. Platonism, strange though it may seem, was orthodoxy; its front was to the past and not to the future; it was a theoretical continuation of a political experience that had served its purpose and come to a halt. It kept ethics, religion, and the intellectual life all tied together in a political

> context. Epicurus socialized the virtues and divorced ethics from religion and politics. While a man could be an active Platonist only in a Greek city-state, a hedonist, as Cicero acutely observed, could go where he chose and still remain a hedonist. A barbarian could hardly be naturalized in a Platonic city but he could readily become an Epicurean. Multitudes of them did so. Cicero informs us, with grudging frankness, that Epicureanism "had a sensational influence not upon Greece and Italy alone but also upon the whole barbarian world."[33]

The numbers of extant images of Epicurus and of his early followers, Metrodorus, Hermarchus, and Colotes, in the form of images on rings, cups, paintings, busts, statues, and statuettes, far outnumber those of other ancient Greek and Roman philosophical schools (though extant rings with profiles of Socrates, who cannot be seen as a member of any particular philosophical school, outnumber those of Epicurus). Although it would be hazardous to draw any hard and fast conclusions from numbers of extant images in archaeological finds, which are in many ways the product of chance preservation and discovery, these artifacts do point to the outlook expressed by Titus Pomponius Atticus in Cicero's *De finibus bonorum et malorum* (*On the Ends of Good and Evil*): "I am not at liberty to forget Epicurus, even if I want to, since we Epicureans have his image not only in our paintings but also on our cups and rings"—and this in spite of Epicurus's own recorded indifference in this area.[34]

Due to its countless adherents and its epistolary literature, which served to hold its scattered communities together, a method later adopted by the early Christians, Epicureanism was to come into direct conflict over the centuries with Christianity, especially following Christianity's adoption as a state religion in the later Roman Empire. As Marx observed in *The German*

Ideology, "Among all church fathers, from Plutarch to Luther, Epicurus has always had the reputation of being the atheist philosopher *par excellence*. . . . Clement of Alexandria says that when Paul [in 'The Acts of the Apostles' in the New Testament] takes up arms against philosophy he has in mind Epicurean philosophy alone."[35] Rooting its ethics in the materialist notion that "death is nothing to us," Epicureanism was a philosophy of life rather than afterlife, defying all organized religion, and the extremely oppressive political life of the day.

Epicureanism died out completely after the fourth century CE, around the time of the fall of Rome. However, it was rediscovered in the West during the Renaissance, when it became a key element in inspiring the development of the modern scientific view and Enlightenment thought in general. A major figure in reviving the Epicurean historical perspective, as conveyed by Lucretius, was the eighteenth-century Italian philosopher Giambattista Vico in *The New Science*, who famously argued that we can understand human history because we "made it."[36]

In his influential work *Eurocentrism*, on culture and imperialism, Samir Amin explicitly defines modernity, in line with Epicurus, Vico, and Marx, as "the claim that human beings, individually and collectively can make their own history. This marks a break with the dominant philosophy of all previous societies, both in Europe and elsewhere." Although modernity in this sense triumphed in the Renaissance, Amin saw a foreshadowing of this shift taking place among the "secular Hellenistic philosophers," beginning in the third century BCE, of which Epicureanism was the epitome. Secular Hellenism provided a "philosophy of nature" that was materialist in character. It paralleled in many ways developments occurring at the same time in India, with the development of Buddhism with its quasi-secular metaphysics, and China, with the emergence of Confucianism and Daoism. Amin noted that while in the Euro-Arab world secular "Hellenism gave way to religious formulations, both Christian and Islamic," this did not occur in the case of Confucianism in China. Still, the three great religions, Judaism, Christianity, and later Islam, he argued, were to arise out of the humanistic context provided by Hellenistic culture.[37]

In a similar fashion, and prior to Amin, Joseph Needham, the great Marxian scientist and Sinologist, saw Epicureanism and Daoism, along with Confucianism, as reflecting analogous critical perspectives toward the world, constituting an early dialectical and organicist approach to modernity.[38]

For Amin, the relation between these different organicist philosophies was not simply a culturalist phenomenon, as in contemporary religious and idealist interpretations of the "axial age" in the first millennium BCE, as first articulated by Karl Jaspers.[39] Rather, critical modernity, for Amin, was a result of struggles that emerged simultaneously in the high tributary mode of production, often at the point of social crisis and collapse. Modernity, seen as a conception of humanity as the self-mediating being of nature, was a product of the more advanced tributary societies, before capitalism (with Western feudalism constituting a backward peripheral tributary formation in this respect). It was only with the further development of the means of production, however, that the conception of humanity as *homo faber*, which had its roots in Hellenism, was fully to come into its own, though distorted by Eurocentrism. This had a lot to do with the rediscovery of Epicureanism during the Renaissance.[40] All of this suggested, for Amin as well as Needham, that modernity was not simply a Western product, although it was to have an early efficacy there, but in its more radical philosophical forms had roots in late antiquity across the globe, with Hellenism playing a key role in the Middle East and the West.[41]

For Epicurus, the discovery that humanity was part of the *natural world*, while equally part of the *social world*, and that no transcendent forces governed either, lay at the very core of his materialist philosophy of causal determination, contingency, emergence, and freedom. Here materialism, when brought together with humanism, represented a true universalism, in which the supreme value was friendship. Indeed, for Epicurus, as Marx said, "the world is my *friend*."[42]

It was no doubt something like this that the young Marx had in mind when he insisted on the reconciliation of the social world of humanity with the world of nature, and therefore humanity with itself, as the precondition of the transcendence of the alienation of essence and existence. In this view:

> Communism as fully developed naturalism, equals humanism, and as fully developed humanism equals naturalism; it is the *genuine* resolution of the conflict between man and nature, and between man and man, the true resolution of the conflict between existence and being, between objectification and self-affirmation, between freedom and necessity, between individual and species. . . . Society [in its developed communal form] is therefore the perfected unity of man with nature, the true resurrection of nature, the realized naturalism of man and the realized humanism of nature.[43]

More than a distant echo of Epicurus can be heard here in Marx's declaration of the dialectical unity of humanity and nature. If Marx was the first to penetrate to the essence of Epicurus's philosophy, the study of Epicurus enables us to uncover the essence of Marx.

CHAPTER ONE

Epicurus and Hellenistic Athens

Epicurus was a citizen of Athens of the *deme* (political division) Gargettus, descended from the family of Philaidae and thus of noble heritage, but nonetheless coming from what was often characterized as a declassed, plebeian background, belonging to the educated poor. He was born in early 341 BCE on the Greek island of Samos near what was then Ionia, on the western coast of Anatolia, where he lived until age eighteen. He had three brothers: Neocles (the eldest), Chaeredemus, and Aristobulus, with Epicurus likely the second-oldest of the siblings. Their father, Neocles, and mother, Chaerestrate, were poor Athenian citizens who had emigrated in 352–1 to Samos as part of a contingent of two thousand settlers who joined the *cleruchy* that had been established there in 365.[1]

A cleruchy was a Greek form of settler colonialism in which a group of settlers, or cleruchs, drawn mainly from the indigent population of a city-state, were given allotments of land in a colony while retaining their citizenship in the "mother country." The cleruchies also served as garrisons meant to secure a colony. Although drawn primarily from the poorest sectors of the overcrowded Athenian citizenry, cleruchs included individuals from various trades such as farmers, shipwrights, carpenters, and sailors. Each cleruch took over a residence formerly occupied by a local family as well as an allotment of land.[2]

The island of Samos (the ancient city-state on the island had the same name) is about 183 square miles in area and has several large plains, mainly in the eastern part, and rocky regions to the west. It is separated by only a mile of water from the mainland of Asia Minor. It was situated in antiquity near a number of old Ionian city-states on the mainland, including Miletus, which had for centuries been an important cultural and commercial center. Samos itself was an important Greek city-state in the sixth and fifth centuries and a leading naval power allied with Athens, occupying a strategic location in the Aegean. It had fertile soil and was famous for the olive oil it produced. In 440 BCE Samos was able to maintain and equip fifty triremes, marking it as a wealthy city-state. With an Athenian-style democracy, it was Athens's most steadfast ally in the Peloponnesian War (431–404 BCE). Following the Athenian defeat and the overcoming of Samian resistance, the victorious Spartan general Lysander threw out many of the citizens—Xenophon claims that all citizens were removed, though this is unlikely—and put the island under oligarchic rule.[3]

Samos regained its independence in 391, which was reinforced by the King's Peace between Persia and the Greek states in 387. Nevertheless, the Samian democracy was never fully restored. Along with other Greek islands in this period, it was subject to the continual rivalry between Athens, Sparta, Thebes (then aligned with Persia), and Persia itself. The old Ionian states on the mainland had fallen under Persian suzerainty and Samos, due to the terms of the King's Peace, lost its territory (the *Peraea*) on the mainland in Ionia. Samos was gradually drawn into the Persian orbit. This occurred at a time when Athens, which had begun to form the Second Athenian League in 378 on the model of its earlier Delphian League, was seeking to restore its former naval hegemony in the Aegean. The Second Athenian League was to consist of around sixty states. Yet, due to Persian influence, Samos was noticeably absent from the League. It fell entirely into Persian hands sometime after 371 and was ruled by Cyprothemis, a Greek, most likely Samian, renegade and mercenary commander, who was put in place by the Persian satrap Mausolus of Caria.[4]

In 366, the Athenian general Timotheus "liberated" Samos after a ten-month siege. He was able to accomplish this without actually breaking the King's Peace, since the installation of the Persian garrison on the island, which was then ruled by a mercenary commander imposed by a Persian satrap, had violated the terms of the peace, in which the islands of the Aegean were to remain autonomous. However, rather than treating Samos as an independent city-state after "liberating" it, as in the case of the members of the Second Athenian League, Athens introduced a cleruchy in Samos in 365, exiling the Samian citizenry, numbering perhaps in the thousands. They were then replaced by Athenian settlers. Many of the Samian exiles likely went to Ephesus, the closest sizable polis on the Ionian coast. A second contingent of cleruchs was sent to Samos in 361 to further reinforce Athenian colonial control of the island.[5]

In 364–63, the Theban hegemon Epaminondas courted Chios, Rhodes, and Byzantium in an attempt to lure them away from Athens and break the Second Athenian League, with the aim of establishing Theban naval supremacy in the Aegean. Epaminondas died at the Battle of Mantinea in the Peloponnese in 362. But in reaction to Athenian creation of the cleruchy in Samos and the increasingly dominating role of Athens, Chios, Rhodes, and Byzantium overthrew their democratic governments in 357 and broke with the Athenian League, declaring war on Athens and the League in what came to be known as the Social War (357–54). Samos was immediately besieged by the anti-Athenian alliance but was defended by the cleruchs and the siege ended with the arrival of an Athenian fleet. Nevertheless, the Social War was a disaster for Athens. Philip II of Macedonia took advantage of the open hostilities to capture states in the Aegean region, while Persia, by threatening war with Athens, forced the disintegration of the Second Athenian League. Athens, meanwhile, was bankrupted by the war.[6]

Athens was able to retain its cleruchy on Samos following the Social War. It reinforced it in 352–51 with two thousand additional cleruchs that included Epicurus's parents. In 338 BCE, three years after the birth of Epicurus, Macedonia defeated a Greek alliance led by Athens and Thebes at the Battle of Chaeronea, establishing its domination over all of Greece. Athens was treated leniently, due to Philip's interest in using its navy in his planned conquest of Persia. It was also allowed to retain its cleruchy on Samos. In 335, Thebes recklessly revolted against Macedonia and was defeated, with six thousand Thebans slain in the final battle. Philip's heir, Alexander III of Macedon (Alexander the Great), sold thirty thousand Thebans into slavery and burned the city to the ground, creating "a paroxysm of horror and fear in the other Greek states."[7]

The situation of the small Athenian cleruchy on Samos, only three decades old at the time that Alexander's conquest of Persia began in 334, was obviously an extremely precarious one. It consisted of a few thousand settler colonists in a hostile world. Samos had been placed under siege in the Social War around twenty years before, and the legitimacy of the cleruchy there was widely questioned. At the time that Alexander the Great was commencing his war on Persia at Miletus only about twenty miles by sea from Samos, Epicurus was beginning his elementary school studies. The seven-year-old Epicurus may have witnessed

Alexander's fleet as it passed through the Samian Strait on the way to the siege of Miletus. A decade of continual warfare followed as Alexander's army pushed continually east. Alexander's death in 323 left behind a Hellenistic empire extending to three continents and covering over two million square miles, stretching as far east as Taxila in contemporary Pakistan.[8]

Schoolmaster's Son

It was in this larger political and social context that the life of Epicurus commenced. His father Neocles had obtained a land allotment as a member of the cleruchy, but he also received earnings in Samos and probably later in Colophon as a schoolmaster, teaching sons of wealthy free-born citizens. Greek education excluded slaves, metics (free, usually Greek non-citizens), and, in the Athenian case, if not all Greek poleis, women. The schooling of children prior to age of six or seven was usually carried out by private tutors. Between the ages of seven and fourteen or sixteen, boys were taught simple arithmetic, music, history, and ethics under a writing master or *grammatistes*. Comprehensive physical training was carried out in the *gymnasium*. Some went on to *ephebeia*, or secondary education, until the age of eighteen, when they became *epheboi* and entered military service. During the secondary stage the curriculum advanced to philosophy, rhetoric, and advanced mathematics under a *grammatikos*. Those who could afford it paid for their sons to study with a sophist/philosopher, specializing in dialectics and rhetoric.[9]

In ancient Greece, schoolmasters were held in low esteem, since they worked with children, and were paid at very poor levels. In some cases, it appears, a grammatistes received no more compensation than that of an ordinary sailor. Neocles was a grammatistes who had his own elementary school, which would have had the effect of declassing his entire family. Indeed, some of Epicurus's detractors, including later Stoics, were to refer to him as a schoolmaster's son, while labeling Epicurus too as a schoolmaster, since he had worked with his father at his school for a "pitiful fee," suggesting a low-class background. These aspersions of ignobility of birth and inferior class position were leveled at Epicurus in his own day, causing his closest follower, Metrodorus, to write a book, *On Noble Birth*, defending Epicurus in this respect. Metrodorus traced Epicurus's descent to the noble Athenian family of Philaidae, which included Militades, one of the two Athenian generals responsible for defeating Persia in the Battle of Marathon. The Philaidae family traced their origins back to the mythological Philaeus, son of Ajax. Nevertheless, it is clear that Epicurus's parents were poor members of the Athenian *demos* prior to their emigration to Samos in search of a better life. Neocles's decision to join the Athenian cleruchy on Samos together with his role as a schoolmaster indicated that Epicurus's family had faced difficult times, which were to worsen again in 322 with the end of the Athenian cleruchy on Samos.[10]

Less is known about Epicurus's mother, Chaerestrate. Later opponents of Epicurus, seeking to emphasize his low-class background, and pointing to his being a schoolmaster's son, also directed aspersions at his mother, referring to Chaerestrate as a person who visited small cottages to "perform purification rites and read charms," accompanied by the young Epicurus. The attempt was to present Chaerestrate as a pious, superstitious, and lowly seller of charms. However, this may partly reflect the negative views with respect to women healers in general, which has been pervasive over the entire history of Western culture. Equally important, omens, charms, and superstitions were associated with the beliefs of ordinary people and thus signaled low-class position within the demos.[11] According to Plutarch, who undoubtedly had access to biographies of Epicurus, Chaerestrate "had the joy of living to see her son ensconced in his little garden," that is, his school in Athens, after it was established in 306.[12]

Epicurus's early education was undoubtedly at his father's school. He was precocious and seems to have moved on to secondary education under a *grammatikos* early, where it is clear that the curriculum included Hesiod and Homer. It is recorded that he turned to philosophy at the age of fourteen when the *grammatikos* could not explain to him the meaning of "Chaos" in Hesiod's line "At first Chaos came to be." Epicurus may have had some knowledge early on of Democritus's atomism, which had no need for the notion of Chaos, connected as it was to creationism. Epicurus asked out of what Chaos was created and how it was created. The schoolmaster is reported to have replied that the answers to such questions lay with philosophers, leading Epicurus to answer that he would then seek out the philosophers.[13]

The first philosopher that Epicurus studied with was the Platonist Pamphilus in Samos. Epicurus was to deny that Pamphilus and the other philosophers he worked with were at any time actual mentors, insisting that he was "self-taught." Nevertheless, his encounter with varied systems of thought was significant. The choice for him to study with a Platonist was no doubt made by his parents, who would have preferred that he work with an established, orthodox figure in the immediate vicinity. The association with Pamphilus may have lasted as much as four years, until he turned eighteen. Epicurus would have been exposed at this time to the typical Platonic mode of education, which focused on geometry, rhetoric, and dialectic. His philosophy was to be opposed to all aspects of Platonism, particularly the Platonic dialectic and its "four assumptions," as stated by Norman Wentworth DeWitt in his *Epicurus and His Philosophy*: "First, that reason was the criterion, second, that sensations were undependable, third that phenomena were shifting and deceptive, and fourth, that the only real and eternal existences were the ideas." Epicureanism was to develop primarily in response to Plato, to whose ideas Epicurus had been exposed in his first serious philosophical encounters.[14]

The Downfall of Athens

In 324 BCE, Alexander decreed that all the exiles from the Greek cities would forcibly be returned to the poleis, with the intention, as Diodorus Siculus explained in his *Historical Library*, of ensuring that he had "in each city many personal supporters to counteract the risk of revolt," as well as to enhance his own glory. Some twenty thousand exiles gathered at the Olympic games where Alexander's decree was announced and greeted it with shouts of praise. The decree related particularly to the Samians exiled by the Athenians in 365 and signified Alexander's intention to remove the Athenian cleruchy. Faced with the prospect of the loss of their colony along with other causes, Athens began preparing for war. Immediately following Alexander's death in 323, most of mainland Greece revolted, forming a new Hellenic League, with Athens at its head, in an attempt to throw off Macedonian domination, leading to what came to be known as the Lamian War.[15] Aristotle, who had been teaching in Athens at the Lyceum since 335, fled the city after Alexander's death in the face of the growing anti-Macedonian sentiment, and with fears of being charged with impiety and facing the same fate as Socrates. He died the following year in Chalcis on the island of Euboea in Greece.

Amid these events Epicurus left Samos in late summer 323 at age eighteen for his two years of military training as an *ephebe*, or cadet. By the time Epicurus's class of cadets reported for service in Athens, Alexander's death was common knowledge, and the city was engaged in mustering an army. Given that the primary *casus belli* was the decision of Alexander to remove the Athenian cleruchy on Samos, which would mean the exile of Epicurus's family and entire community and the loss of the only home he had ever known, he was undoubtedly strongly sympathetic with the war that ensued upon his arrival in Athens.

Aristotle's *The Constitution of Athens*, written only a year or two before Epicurus's military service, explained the nature of the military training that the *ephebi* received. It started with establishing the cadet's claim to citizenship and his physical fitness. This was followed by a tour of all the surrounding temples. Following this, the ephebi were distributed among training schools and were instructed in fighting in the heavy armor of the hoplite, how to use a bow and the javelin, and how to discharge a catapult. Such direct military training took up the first year. In the second year the class of cadets, who were now considered drill-ready, performed a military tattoo before the Athenian Assembly at the festival of Dionysus, followed by the presentation of each ephebe with a shield and spear, and a military cloak. This signified the initiation into full citizenship. The cadet was then assigned to garrison duty for the remainder of the year. In the case of Epicurus's class, this garrison duty took place during a major war between Macedonia and the Hellenic League, with Athens increasingly in peril.[16]

The Athenian-led war of the Hellenic League against the Macedonians under Alexander's general Antipater was conducted by the able Athenian commander Leosthenes. After the Hellenic League defeated the Macedonians near Thermopylae, Antipater withdrew his forces to the small Thessalian city of Lamia (hence the term Lamian War), where they were besieged. Leosthenes, who refused to consider Antipater's request for terms of surrender and instead insisted on unconditional surrender, was killed in a skirmish near the besieged city, while the arrival of Macedonian reinforcements forced the Greek coalition to lift the siege. With his enlarged Macedonian army, Antipater's forces defeated the Hellenic League at the Battle of Crannon in August 322. Meanwhile, an ostensibly smaller Macedonian fleet twice severely defeated the Athenian fleet, which, although physically having a larger number of triremes, was grossly outnumbered because of the inability to find sufficient crews for all of their ships.

Antipater refused to negotiate a general peace but offered the Greek states individual terms of surrender, causing the Greek coalition, divided within itself, to crumble. Soon Athens and the Aetolians were all that was left of the Hellenic League. Recalling Leosthenes's demand for unconditional surrender, Antipater now demanded the same of Athens, which was forced to submit. The leading Athenian orators backing the war were given death sentences for high treason and were executed by Antipater, except for the great orator Demosthenes, who, having fled to Calauria, committed suicide with poison in the temple of Poseidon in order to avoid capture. A Macedonian garrison was placed in the fortress in Piraeus, the seaport of Athens, and a heavy war indemnity was imposed on Athens, which was also forced to give up its navy, along with its overseas territories. Meanwhile, Antipater replaced the Athenian democracy with an oligarchic government, with two-thirds of the Athenian citizens disenfranchised by a property requirement. This marked the downfall of Athens, which after its total defeat in the Lamian War was never again to be a major power.[17]

In 322, the entire cleruchy on Samos, which included Epicurus's parents, was forcibly removed by Perdiccas, regent of Alexander's empire, to whom the question of its continued existence had been referred. Epicurus's parents were relocated, presumably with the rest of the Athenian cleruchy from Samos, to Colophon, not far away inland on the Ionian mainland, about fifteen miles northwest of Ephesus.[18]

All of these events occurred while Epicurus was undergoing his military training in Athens. Two former disciples of Epicurus, who became disenchanted and exhibited real enmity toward him, Timocrates and Herodotus, wrote a book titled *On the Training of Epicurus as a Cadet*. All we know of that work is that it sought to challenge Epicurus's position as a genuine Athenian citizen, given his birth in the cleruchy in Samos. However, it is clear from Diogenes Laertius that Epicurus was in some sense accused of disloyalty, which would have been touched on in this work as well. It is likely that Epicurus at some point expressed criticism and even bitterness about the Athenian conduct in the Lamian War and the defeat and downfall of Athens, along with the exile of his parents and the Athenian cleruchy from Samos.

The ignominious surrender forced upon Athens must have left a deep impression. There is little doubt that Epicurus recognized that the disastrous defeat of Athens in the Lamian War was a historical turning point, symbolizing the downfall of Athens as a great power. He therefore sought to adapt his philosophy to the emerging world of Hellenistic civilization, rather than to the Greek polis as such.[19]

Timocrates and Herodotus accused Epicurus of questionable loyalty to Athens, since he honored Mithres the Syrian, the minister governing Lampsacus for Lysimachus ruler of Thrace, while Epicurus was establishing his school there. The fact that Mithres was not a Greek seems to have been the sole basis of this accusation against Epicurus. Epicurus was to remain loyal to Mithres after leaving Lampsacus, honoring him in one of his works (*Of Diseases and Death*) and later coming to his aid with the help of Metrodorus when Mithres was arrested in Piraeus.[20] In Epicurus's Hellenistic philosophy the distinction between Greek and "barbarian" was dissolved.

Epicurus's years in Athens during his training as a cadet would have left him with considerable time to get to know the city and its culture. He would undoubtedly have taken part in the Panathenaic festival in 322, as well as the Dionysiac festivals, and would have been introduced to the Eleusinian mysteries, the most famous secret religious rites of Greek antiquity. Menander, the poet and "New Comedy" playwright, was an ephebe in Epicurus's same class, and they likely knew each other. Epicurus may have seen the production of Menander's first play in 321. He would have heard the philosopher Xenocrates, who had studied under Plato and was head of the Academy beginning in 339. Xenocrates had friendly relations with both Philip and Alexander and was sent to Antipater as an Athenian ambassador to Macedonia in 322 to negotiate the freeing of Athenian prisoners from the Lamian War. Xenocrates was the first to divide philosophy into three parts: logic, physics, and ethics. Epicurus would doubtless also have been present at some of the public lectures of Theophrastus, now head of the Lyceum. Theophrastus's real name is thought to have been Tyrtamaus. However, Aristotle is said to have renamed him for the excellence of his speech, as the word *theophrastus* means "speaking like a god." It is reported that as many as 2,000 people would attend his lectures. It is also almost certain that Epicurus would have heard some of Demosthenes's orations in support of the Lamian War, no doubt coloring Epicurus's views of rhetoric and political life in his age.[21]

Epicurus in Ionia

Although Samos was listed by Herodotus, the fifth-century BCE historian, as part of the Ionian League, the culture that Epicurus had grown up with in the cleruchy on Samos was more Athenian than Ionian, though undoubtedly Ionian and Persian cultural influences lingered on the island. However, in joining his parents at Colophon, after they had been expelled from Samos, Epicurus was now directly confronted with Ionian culture, which had given birth to Greek philosophy, and where older, more materialist Greek philosophical traditions remained relatively strong. Colophon had been the birthplace of the poet and philosopher Xenophanes, who flourished in the late sixth century and early fifth century, known for his criticisms of the Greek conception of the gods as presented in Homer and Hesiod. Xenophanes was also credited in antiquity with the view of the earth as the *archê*, or first principle of all things. Traces of his philosophy might have been kept alive in Colophon in Epicurus's day.[22]

For a decade, following his cadetship in Athens, from 321 to 311, Epicurus seems to have lived with his parents and brothers in Colophon. These years when he was twenty-one to thirty-one were the most formative ones in his development as a philosopher. He studied for a while with the atomistic philosopher Nausiphanes in Teos, a city-state a short distance to the west of Colophon on the Aegean coast. Teos had provided colonists for a refounding of Abdera, the home city of Democritus, and the connections between the parent city and the colonists no doubt explains the persistence in Teos of the then fading atomistic philosophy. Nausiphanes, though a follower of Democritus, had studied with the skeptic Pyrrho. Epicurus was always asking for information on Pyrrho, who had written nothing himself. In this, he was no doubt interested in Pyrrho's notion of *adiaphora* (indifference) with respect to conventional values and his encounters with Eastern philosophy while present in Alexander's military campaigns in Persia and as far as India. There is some speculation that Nausiphanes had taken part in Alexander's campaigns, through which he got to know Pyrrho. Of secondary interest for Epicurus to these Eastern influences in Pyrrhonism would have been Pyrrho's skepticism, or the proposition of the impossibility of definite knowledge, a view that Epicurus was to reject. Although in many ways deterministic, Democritean atomism also contained an element of skepticism, in which the atoms and the void were seen as eternal natural reality, while all else, including the evidence of the senses, was doubtful or existed merely by convention.[23]

Nausiphanes is known for having provided an epistemological canon referred to as the Tripod, though concrete knowledge of it is unknown and all we know is the title.[24] It may have influenced Epicurus's own famous Canon, with its three legs of sensation, preconceptions, and feelings. However, what distinguished Epicurus's epistemology at the time was the elevation of nature as its basis, rather than reason, the criteria for which could be found in the later research of Aristotle and his school and their investigations into zoology. It was unlikely that this was present in Nausiphanes. What seems fairly certain is that Nausiphanes and Epicurus were to have a falling out, with the young, still hotheaded Epicurus casting various calumnies on Nausiphanes. This was undoubtedly due to Epicurus's conflict with Democritean Atomism over questions of free will and the ethical task of philosophy. Not only did Epicurus reject Democritean determinism, but he also denied that the earlier atomist, Leucippus, could be properly ranked as a philosopher, presumably because Leucippus was concerned only with physics and not epistemology or ethics.[25]

It can be assumed that in these years Epicurus extended his studies of philosophy in all directions, including the Presocratics, Plato, and Aristotle. His favorite thinker among the Presocratics was Anaxagoras (ca. 500–428 BCE), who wrote a work titled *On Nature*, fragments of which survive. Born in Clazomenae in Ionia, he spent much of his life in Athens. He propounded a materialism in which the universe was characterized by a form of Mind, or life force (*nous*), made up of an infinite number of particles or "seeds," each of which contained an element of everything existing, a unity of opposites. He wrote that "there is a portion of everything in everything." However, there was one exception to this in the case of Mind, the lightest of seeds and unmixed, penetrating others and setting them in motion: "No thing," Anaxagoras wrote, "is generated or destroyed." Rather, it would be correct to call "generation mingling and destruction dissociation." Anaxagoras had settled in Athens in the time of Pericles but was charged with impiety since he regarded the moon and the sun not as gods but physical entities. He therefore fled to Lampsacus on the Hellespont, where he spent the last few years of his life.[26]

Although it has long been assumed that Epicurus was mainly, perhaps exclusively, familiar with Aristotle's early *exoteric* works in his Platonic phase, there is now clear evidence that he had some knowledge of the later, *esoteric* works of Aristotle. Thus, a fragment of a letter by Epicurus, "To the friends of the school," preserved by Philodemus, refers to Aristotle's *Physics*, along with his *Analytics*.[27]

In 311–10, after a decade in Colophon, Epicurus attempted to establish a philosophical school in Mytilene on the island of Lesbos, where Aristotle had taught for several years prior to going to Macedonia to occupy the post of Alexander's tutor. It is on Lesbos that Aristotle is said to have commenced his zoological studies. The dominant philosophical influence in Mytilene at the time seems to have been Aristotelian but Platonism was also present. As elsewhere in the Greek poleis, philosophers in

Mytilene would seek out pupils in public *gymnasiums* where youth and young men gathered for their physical exercise and training. The gymnasiums were rectangular in shape, open and sanded, and characteristically marked off by colonnades, partly shaded by trees. These properties were under the supervision of officials known as *gymnasiarchs*. In aggressively seeking to promote his philosophy in Mytilene in this public context, Epicurus soon came into conflict with the more orthodox Aristotelian and particularly Platonic philosophers. This created friction and Epicurus appears to have been driven out of Mytilene against his will on charges, whether officially lodged or merely threatened, of sacrilege and impiety.

There is some indication that Antigonus the One-Eyed—one of Alexander's former Macedonian generals or *Diadochi*, who contested his empire after his death, controlling most of Asia Minor and the Aegean, including both Colophon and Lesbos—may have been involved in Epicurus's removal at the request of orthodox philosophical schools and gymnasiarchs. The expulsion occurred during winter, a dangerous time for a sea voyage in which normal navigation was suspended.

However, despite failure in his attempts to establish a school in Mytilene, Epicurus gained one important follower in Mytilene, Hermarchus, who came from a poor plebeian background but may have been a student of rhetoric in Mytilene. Hermarchus did not immediately take up philosophy and was only reunited with Epicurus when the latter established the Garden in Athens. After that he would remain with Epicurus for the rest of his life and became the head of Epicurus's school of the Garden, following Epicurus's death in 270. Some of his works included *Against Plato*, *Against Aristotle*, and *On Sciences*. However, his most important work was undoubtedly his *Against Empedocles*, published in twenty-two books.[28]

In departing Mytilene, Epicurus chose Lampsacus as his destination, and as the location of a new school. His forced departure from Mytilene and arrival in Lampsacus coincided with the end of the Third War of the Diadochi (315–311) in which the other Diadochi, Ptolemy, Lysimachus, Cassander (the son of Antipater), and Seleucus had combined against Antigonus to prevent him from reuniting Alexander's empire under his rule. Athens at that time was under Macedonian rule headed by the pro-Macedonian governor Demetrius of Phalerum, appointed in 317 by Cassander, who gave Demetrius the title of *prostates* (one who stands before). Demetrius was himself a leading Peripatetic philosopher from Athens, who had studied under Aristotle and Theophrastus, and had written over fifty works on such subjects as Homer, philosophy, politics, rhetoric, and the interpretation of dreams. He was the most accomplished philosopher in all of Greek antiquity to rule a state. Some 360 statues were erected in Attica in his honor. He provided strong political and financial support to Theophrastus, who continued to head the Lyceum. Given Epicurus's conflict with Peripatetic philosophers in Mytilene and the despotic rule of Demetrius of Phalerum, he no doubt decided that relocating himself in Athens, despite his Athenian citizenship, would be unwise, causing him to choose Lampsacus instead.[29]

Located on the eastern side of the Hellespont (Dardanelles), Lampsacus was under the control of Lysimachus, who ruled Thrace, and thus was outside of Antigonus's sphere. It was a wealthy, commercial city, which had its own gold coinage in the fourth century BCE and became the location of one of Alexander's mints. Its strategic location on the Hellespont made it a crossroads. It had been a part of the Athenian Delian League but revolted against Athens in 411, and was put down by force. In the fourth century, Lampsacus drew close to Persia. This ended, however, with Alexander's crossing of the Hellespont in 334.

Lampsacus had originally been a colony of Phocaea and Miletus. The connection to Miletus was significant in that it was considered to be the birthplace of Greek philosophy, beginning with Thales (ca. 625–547 BCE). The reverence for Ionian philosophy no doubt remained strong as not only had Anaxagoras fled from Athens to Lampsacus in the time of Pericles, when accused of impiety, but after his death a memorial to Mind and Truth was set up in the marketplace in his memory. When Epicurus arrived in Lampsacus, an annual holiday was still being held in Anaxagoras's memory. Given the warm reception that Epicurus received in the four years in which he spent in Lampsacus, it is clear that the city was relatively free of what were then the dominant Greek philosophical traditions of the Academy and the Lyceum.[30]

Although Lampascus was then the capital of Lysimachus's Thrace, Lysimachus was engaged elsewhere in the wars of the Diadochi when Epicurus arrived in the city. Epicurus's first step was to secure himself and his school by appealing to the Syrian steward Mithres, who was then in charge of the city. Thus, Epicurus, arriving as a destitute refugee, approached Mithres as a suppliant and may have managed to establish himself on the margins of the Hellenistic courtly circle at the time, for which he was later criticized by his Greek detractors.[31]

The substantial impact that Epicurus's philosophy had on Lampsacus can be judged by the numbers, quality, and faithfulness of his adherents within his "Lampascene circle." His first converts included Idomeneus and Leonteus, together with the latter's extraordinarily talented wife, Themista. Idomeneus was likely introduced to Epicurus by Mithres, and was an important official under Lysimachus, who, as was common in Macedonian regimes, would have been amply rewarded for his role. He was the main financial benefactor of Epicurus, from beginning to end. Idomeneus was himself highly educated and defended Epicurus in a work called *On the Socratics*. He also wrote *On Demagogues*, on Athenian politicians.[32] Leonteus's importance was highlighted by Strabo, viewing him as a major thinker in his own right and a backer of Epicurus. Themista is known to have written on the vanity of fame. Her standing as a writer and a philosopher, admired also for her style, was so great as to lead Cicero centuries later to refer to her in a speech before the Roman Senate, using the phrase "wiser than Themista." Her extensive correspondence with Epicurus was published in their day, in line with the candor and frank criticism that characterized the school, in which nothing should remain hidden. Cicero later ridiculed those who devoted "bulky volumes to Themista." Nevertheless, Epicurus's school stands out in antiquity for including women and giving them the full status of philosophers and writers, breaking with the rest of Greek philosophy in this respect. Leonteus and Themista were to name their son after Epicurus.[33]

Epicurus's foremost recruit on Lampsacus and his most talented follower, sometimes referred to as a "second Epicurus," was Metrodorus. He clearly came from a high-ranking family as his sister married Idomeneus. Among the numerous works by Metrodorus were *On Wealth*, *Against the Physicians* (three books), *On Sensations*, *Against Democritus*, *Against the Sophists* (nine books), *Against Plato's "Gorgias, Against Plato's "Euthyphro," Against the Dialecticians*, *On Noble Birth*, and others. Fragments from *On Wealth* and another of his works, either *Against the Dialecticians* or *Against the Sophists*, have been found in the Herculaneum papyri. Metrodorus never left Epicurus once he met him, except on one occasion, for six months. Although recognized as the heir to Epicurus's Garden, he died in 278 BCE ahead of Epicurus. In honor of his friend, Epicurus wrote a work titled *Metrodorus*, in five books.[34]

The accomplished mathematician Polyaenus, who, it is believed, had studied with Eudoxus, a forerunner of Euclid, also joined Epicurus's Lampascene circle, and later was to become one of the principal philosophical guides in the Garden, alongside Metrodorus and Hermarchus.[35]

Pythocles, a youthful follower of Epicurus, had the role of the handsome Alcibiades in the Epicurean school and was a general favorite. He migrated to Athens along with other members of the school and is known to have made a return trip to Lampsacus as companion of Polyaenus.[36]

Epicurus also recruited Colotes at this time, who exhibited a talent for satire and criticized various philosophers, including Democritus, Socrates, Plato, and Arcesilaus of the New Academy. His most famous work was *On the Point that Conformity to the Doctrines of the Other Philosophers Actually Makes It Impossible to Live.* Plutarch, centuries later, responded to Colotes in his anti-Epicurean tracts *Reply to Colotes in Defense of the Other Philosophers* and *That Epicurus Actually Makes a Pleasant Life Impossible.*

Two early adherents to Epicurus's philosophy, who joined the Epicurean school in Lampsacus, were Timocrates and Herodotus, both of whom were to play the unusual role of renegades from Epicureanism, and who were eventually to join forces. Timocrates was the brother of Metrodorus. After the removal of the main Epicurean school to Athens, Timocrates broke away and returned to Lampsacus. From there he issued various calumnies against the school that were widely rejected as false.[37]

Athens and the Wars of the Diadochi

The wars of the Diadochi (Alexander's Successors) to determine who was to rule Alexander's Hellenistic empire after his death in 323 lasted for forty-three years, extending beyond the first generation of Alexander's generals. In 310–309, Antipater's son Cassander murdered Alexander the Great's son, Alexander IV, who was then thirteen years old, ending any possibility of a direct succession in the Argead dynasty of the Macedonian royal house. The Diadochi were then free to declare themselves kings in their own right, though they hesitated at first to do so. Around 307–306, as Lysimachus was preparing to take the title of king of Thrace and declare war on Antigonus the One-Eyed (Monopthalmus) to the south, he shifted his capital from Lampsacus to the new, more defensible city, Lysimachia, which he had built on the neck of the Thracian Chersonese (the modern Gallipoli peninsula) to the west of the Hellespont. In 307, Demetrius Poliorcetes (Demetrius the Besieger), the son of Antigonus, "liberated" Athens from the hegemony of Cassander, ending the oligarchic rule of Demetrius Phalerum and ostensibly restoring the democracy. In the face of renewed anti-Macedonian sentiment, Theophrastus, still head of the Lyceum, temporarily fled the city. A law was soon passed requiring that all philosophers acting as public teachers first obtain the approval of the Athenian Senate and Assembly, on penalty of death. The law, however, was repealed within a year.[38]

Although the democracy had been formally restored, Demetrius the Besieger effectively ruled the city as a hegemon. Known for his licentious conduct, he located himself in the Parthenon, which he turned into a brothel. He is said to have demanded that the Athenians pay an enormous tax of 250 talents, and he then turned the entire sum over to his favorite courtesan to pay for her luxuries.[39]

In 301, the Antigonids, Antigonus the One-Eyed and his son Demetrius the Besieger, engaged in a major battle against the alliance consisting of all of the other Diadochi, including the combined forces of Cassander, Ptolemy, Lysimachus, and Seleucus, near the small town of Ipsus in Phrygia. The Antigonids were soundly defeated. Antigonus was killed in the battle, while Demetrius managed to retreat to Ephesus, where he was able to reunite with his powerful navy. Much of Antigonus's empire was carved up by the victors. The Athenian Assembly took advantage of Demetrius's weakness to pass a law indicating that it would never again allow a king to enter within its city walls, declaring a policy of neutrality in the wars of the Diadochi. Athens expelled Demetrius's wife from the city and sent a message to him as he was approaching the city that their gates were closed to him.

Not long after, Athens fell under the control of Lachares, an Athenian mercenary commander, who established himself as a tyrant. Lachares was initially backed by Cassander, who, however, died in 297. In order to pay his mercenaries, through which he maintained power, Lachares plundered the city, including the Parthenon, melting down the gold and silver statues of the various temples, and removed the gold plates from the statue of Athena. In 295–94, Demetrius laid siege to Athens, seizing and blockading grain ships headed to the city, generating an extreme famine. The Athenians rose up against Lachares, who fled to Thebes. Facing starvation, the Athenians opened the gates of the city to Demetrius. Once in control of the city, Demetrius installed a garrison on the Hill of the Muses, across from the Acropolis, in order to prevent further rebellions.[40]

After murdering Cassender's son in 294, Demetrius seized the throne of Macedonia. In 288–87, in the midst of what is sometimes called the Fifth War of the Diadochi, this time over who was to rule Macedonia, Athens finally revolted against Demetrius the Besieger, overthrowing the Macedonian garrison on the Hill of the Muses in an assault that largely depended on old men and youth. Demetrius then placed the city under siege, until he was forced to retreat before the forces of Pyrrhus, King of Epirus, part of a coalition with Ptolemy and Lysimachus that succeeded in driving Demetrius out of Europe. Following Demetrius's defeat, Pyrrhus declared himself King of Macedonia. Three years later, in 285–84, Lysimachus drove Pyrrhus from Macedonia, seizing the throne, only to be killed in battle with Seleucus in 282. While in the process of invading Europe that same year, Seleucus, the last of the original Diadochi, was assassinated by his protégé, Ptolemy Ceraunus, the eldest son of Ptolemy I. Ptolemy Ceraunus then became king of Macedonia, only to die in battle at the hands of invading Galatians in 279. In 277–76 Antigonus Gonatas, Demetrius the Besieger's son, established himself as king of Macedonia, as a member of the Antigonid dynasty. With the end of the wars of the Diadochi and the establishment of the Hellenistic dynasties ca. 275, Macedonia and Greece were to fall to the Antigonids.[41]

Faced with the extreme insecurity and irrationality of political life in the Hellenistic Age, Epicurus introduced a philosophy of inner revolt rooted in nature-materialism, a concept of human freedom, and the creation of a self-conscious community aimed at calm certainty, or *ataraxia*. It is no accident that the last of his *Principal Doctrines* stated: "Those who were best able to provide themselves with the means of security against their neighbours . . . passed the most agreeable life in each other's society."[42]

Members of the Epicurean school were bound together by the pursuit of friendship, security, and tranquility. Epicureanism had an ecumenical basis no longer centered simply on Greece, but also reaching out to the larger Hellenistic world to the East. Moreover, unlike the rest of ancient Greek and Roman schools of philosophy, the Epicurean school embraced all sectors of the population, including women and slaves, freeing philosophy from being an exclusively aristocratic pursuit, and reorienting it to the needs of existence itself. "Vain are the words of a philosopher," Epicurus wrote, "by which no malady of mankind is healed."[43]

The Garden

In 306, following Demetrius the Besieger's "liberation" of Athens and his partial restoration of the democracy, together with the weakening of the dominance of Peripatetic philosophy with the departure of Demetrius of Phalerum, Epicurus decided to establish a school in Athens. The school he had founded in Lampsacus was to continue after his departure. Athens was still at this date the center of Greek philosophy and culture, until it was displaced by Alexandria in this respect later in the third century BCE. As an Athenian citizen Epicurus was able to purchase a small house and a non-contiguous garden out of which he would run his school.[44]

It is frequently underscored that Epicurus remained in Athens for the rest of his life, aside from a voyage or two to Lampsacus and one (we now know) to Samos, and that his travels therefore largely ceased at this point, with the result that the geographical scope of his life was narrowed. Recall, however, that the community of his childhood and youth during the cleruchy on Samos no longer existed, since it had been forcibly removed in 322. Nor could he return to Mytilene, from which he had been compelled to flee.

In 302, Colophon, where he had lived for ten years with his family, was conquered by Lysimachus, who forcibly transferred the entire population to Ephesus. This was part of the synoecism, or forced merging of cities in ancient Greece, which had taken on a more brutal form with the rise of Epaminondas in Thebes, whom Epicurus called the "Iron Heart." It was subsequently to become the fashion as a means of consolidating power. Colophon had sided with Antigonus the One-Eyed in the war between him and Lysimachus, leading to its conquest and destruction. If Epicurus's parents were still alive and living in Colophon in 302—we know from Plutarch that Epicurus's mother was alive at the time he established the Garden in Athens in 306—they would have experienced the conquest of the city, no doubt entailing a siege since the population were known to have resisted, and would have been exiled once again. Any genuine community that Epicurus had known in Colophon would have been displaced. Hence, the fact that his only recorded trips back to Ionia were to visit Lampsacus and Samos and the Epicurean schools/friends there should be viewed as the result in part of the wars of the time, which were ravaging whole communities, while various areas were effectively closed off to him.[45]

There were additional dangers such as storms at sea, shipwrecks, and piracy, imperiling those who traveled the Aegean, so voyages were not taken lightly. Epicurus it seems had narrowly escaped (or else narrowly survived) a shipwreck while voyaging to Lampsacus. A cardinal doctrine in Epicurean philosophy, in its general pursuit of equanimity or calmness (*ataraxia*), was ensuring the security of individuals and the Epicurean community, a requisite in times of the dangers and insecurity, seemingly coming from every direction, in the early Hellenistic Age.[46]

The Athens to which Epicurus returned in 306 BCE, following a decade and a half under a Macedonian-imposed oligarchy, was not the same city he had experienced a decade and a half earlier during his cadetship at the close of the age of Demosthenes. Although the democracy had been ostensibly restored, Athens was no longer the fully autonomous city-state of pre-Hellenistic times and no longer had an empire. It retained its role as the intellectual and cultural center of Greece, although its role in that respect within the Greek world as a whole was soon to be displaced by Alexandria in Egypt. But the public sphere was severely eroded and the direct role of politics in the life of the individual citizen sharply declined.[47]

It is significant that the Athenian population had been declining precipitously over the previous century. At the time of the commencement of the Peloponnesian War in 431, citizens together with their families numbered around 172,000. However, by the time of Alexander's death in 323, this had dropped to 112,000. Meanwhile, the number of metics, foreign residents without full citizenship rights, had increased significantly, while the number of slaves had declined, if only slightly. The total population, including metics and slaves in 323 was 258,000, compared to 315,500 a century before.[48]

The enormous sociological transformation in Athens in this period can be seen in the changing nature of Comedy over the course of a century, reflected in the Old Comedy of Aristophanes in the age of Pericles, as opposed to the New Comedy of Epicurus's contemporary Menander. Aristophanes's play *Peace* in 421, which mocked the recently deceased Athenian pro-war leader Cleon in the Peloponnesian War and was written just before the Peace of Nicias that ended the first half of the war, was typical of Aristophanes's plays in general, which savagely lampooned public figures, such as politicians, sophists, and philosophers, and concentrated on the political life of the city, full of low jokes often of a bawdy nature. In contrast, Menander, the best known of the New Comedy playwrights, staged his first play in 321, at around the time that both Menander and Epicurus had completed their two years as cadets. Compared to Aristophanes's style of comedy, Menander's plays, such as the *Old Cantankerous* and *The Girl from Samos*, were more sedate, less full of belly laughs, and were set in the domestic sphere in rural settings, as far from politics as possible, focusing on comic situations of love and money.[49]

If Aristophanes's plays constitute our best sociological source on the complex class relations of the Athenian polis, the plays of Menander give us a view of the patriarchal household, and of the relations of fathers and mothers, husbands and wives, sons and daughters, propertied men and courtesans, love-inspired youths, and domestic slaves, all in a myriad of situations. Here we are given insights into the Greek household. What is most startling is the disappearance of public life and the escapism associated with the change of scene to the country. Many of Menander's plays were written when Demetrius of Phalerum was lord of the city, which was under Macedonian rule. Menander is said to have had the support of Demetrius in these years and to have been a close friend of Theophrastus. His relation to Epicurus was less certain, though he appears to have incorporated aspects of Epicurus's philosophy into his plays. What is clear from the contrast between the Old Comedy and the New Comedy is that the Athenian population in the early Hellenistic Age sought to escape from all thought of public life in the city and to focus on the domestic life in the country.[50]

In establishing his school in Athens, Epicurus departed from other philosophical schools of the time in not presenting his lectures in a public space, as in Plato's Academy (a walled park) and Aristotle's Lyceum (a gymnasium), but in a private space, a garden, which resulted in his school being referred to as the Garden. All three schools had two non-contiguous physical properties, a separate place for lectures and a private space, containing a library and living quarters. (The Stoics, like the Cynics, did not have a physical habitation associated with the school.) In Epicurus's case, the grounds in which lectures took place were private property and heritable. If the Academy and the Lyceum were organized to primarily attract young, aristocratic men, and thus had their physical bases in the surroundings in which they gathered for socializing and exercise, the Garden had an altogether different character, designed to avoid conflict with public authorities.[51]

The house was relatively small given the purposes it served, since it was a lodging not only for some central members of the Epicurean community, but also for slaves, who were undoubtedly mainly copyists, given that the vast literary production of the Epicurean scholars emanated from there. The house had to contain a library and include meeting rooms as well. As Cicero, who visited the Epicurean school in 78 BCE, was to declare, "What huge throngs of friends did not Epicurus manage to house under one roof, and that not a large one, and how closely knit together they were in a conspiracy of love!"[52] As Elizabeth Asmis writes, "Before Metrodorus's death, we may suppose that the house regularly accommodated Epicurus, Metrodorus and Leontion with their two children, a few slaves, and a steady stream of guests."[53] The house was situated in a respectable part of the city, the deme Melite west of the Agora, and the Garden was not far away, outside the walls of the city by way of the Dipylon Gate, on the road that also led to the Academy. Still, on occasions when he was ill, Epicurus had to be conveyed to the Garden in a three-wheeled cart. On the gate to the Garden, it read: "Stranger, here you will do well to tarry; here our highest good is pleasure."[54]

The garden itself is often assumed to be small, given the price paid for it, 80 minae. But a comparison of prices at the time suggests that this would have been more than sufficient to purchase fifteen acres or so of ground (assuming that the purchase price included both house and garden). The garden served a number of purposes since food was grown there and some members of the community, it can be supposed, lived there in hutments of the kind common in the time, surrounded by vegetable crops. The garden was thus not physically a park (*paradeisos*), but rather a kitchen garden (*Kepos*) of the kind used for growing beans, cabbages, turnips, radishes, lettuce, beets, coriander, onions, dill, cress, cucumbers, basil, and savory. It provided food for communal meals and a modicum of self-sufficiency. In Epicurus's will, the house was assigned to the head of the school, while the garden was to provide a residence for future members of the community.[55]

During the famine resulting from the siege of Athens by Demetrius the Besieger in 295–94 at the time of the despotic rule of Lachares, the hunger in Athens was so intense that a father and son were said to have fought each other over a starved mouse that dropped from the ceiling. Nevertheless, Epicurus "sustained the lives of his associates," as Plutarch wrote, "with beans, which he counted out and distributed among them."[56] Epicurus was known to send bushels of food to friends in need.[57]

Philosophical studies in the Garden were led by Epicurus along with three of his associates from Mytilene and Lampsacus: Metrodorus, Hermarchus, and Polyaenus, who were known as leaders or guides. The term schoolteacher was banned, no doubt in part because of Epicurus's negative experience, but it was also associated with a purely top-down mode of instruction. In contrast, Epicurus insisted that, in all things, "one must not force nature but persuade her." This reflected a new form of pedagogy that respected the students and encouraged frank criticism, Nevertheless, the hegemony exercised by Epicurus's ideas was understood as the consensual basis of the community; those who chose to live in the Garden were expected to pledge their faithfulness to him, adopting him as their guide. Aside from Metrodorus, Hermarchus, and Polynaeus as associate leaders, there were also assistant leaders. While the former primarily taught individuals, the latter were assigned to groups.[58]

The major Epicurean works took a variety of forms, consisting of (1) doctrinal treatises, such as his 37-volume work *On Nature*, laying out the fundamental concepts of the Epicurean system, consisting largely of works by Epicurus himself; (2) works of critique and refutation directed at rival schools, especially Plato's Academy, Aristotle's Lyceum, and Arcesilaus's New Academy; (3) memorial works, largely consisting of eulogies to departed members of the school, such as Epicurus's memoir of his brother Neocles; and (4) epitomes or abstracts, again mainly by Epicurus, summarizing wide aspects of Epicurean doctrine. His four works that have survived intact—three in the form of letters, plus his list of *Principal Doctrines*—were all epitomes. (The collection the *Vatican Sayings*, which may have been compiled much later, consists of maxims, drawn from his works.) It was also common for Epicurus and thinkers in the Epicurean community to circulate didactic letters written to friends, epistles aimed at instruction, and then collected together. Epicurus himself wrote some three hundred books, embracing all of these categories, of which we have the titles of a few dozen, and fragments from seven of the thirty-seven books of *On Nature*. Some of these titles include: *On the Criterion, or the Canon*; *Epitome of Objections to the Physicists*; *Problems*; *Key Doctrines*; *On Atoms and Void*; *On Love*; *On Lives* (four books); *On Fate*; *On Choice and Avoidance*; *Theories of the Feelings*; *On Images*; *On Vision*; *On Perception*; *On Piety*; *Theories of Disease and Death*; *On Just Dealing*; *On Justice and the Other Virtues*; *Of Kingship*; and *Discovery of the Future*.[59]

The class basis of the Garden was widely divergent from that of other ancient philosophical schools, particularly those of the Academy and the Lyceum, both of which were based in the aristocracy. Thus, Cicero referred to the Epicureans as "plebeians" (or lower order), contrasting them to the aristocratic basis of the philosophical schools of Plato and Aristotle. In contrast to the

Academy and Lyceum, the Garden did not require that its students, prior to entering the school, have the cultivated training of the leisure class, merely that they should have a basic literacy. According to Seneca and Lactantius, Epicurus's followers included the uneducated as well as the educated, embracing slaves, paupers, craftsmen, country folk, and women. Epicurus's entire philosophy required as its basis only the satisfaction of basic needs, and thus was open to the less privileged classes of all ages.[60]

As Bernard Frischer argues in *The Sculpted World*, "The sociological basis of Epicureanism's appeal" was that it attracted "the deracinated [uprooted in terms of class and/or geography] and alienated intellectual," providing "a genuinely positive and legitimate alternative to the dominant culture of Greece."[61]

Unique among the philosophical schools of antiquity, the Epicurean community embraced both slaves and women. Slavery was a foundational institution in Ancient Greece. Epicurus's household incorporated a number of literate slaves as copyists. In a major departure, slaves were admitted to the Epicurean community of friends. The very talented slave Mys, who had studied alongside Epicurus from the beginning, likely exercised oversight over the work of the copyists, and was himself known as an Epicurean philosopher in his own right. In his will, Epicurus freed Mys along with three other slaves. According to Diogenes Laertius, Epicurus was known as having an unusually humane attitude toward servants/slaves.[62]

Most disturbing to Epicurus's critics in antiquity was the inclusion of women as full members of Epicurus's philosophical community. The status of women in ancient Greece, particularly Athens, as opposed to Sparta or Lesbos, where women were held in somewhat higher regard, was very low. Married women were generally not to be seen and were viewed largely in terms of their reproductive role, and managing the household. This extreme patriarchal rule struck a discordant note with the traditional goddesses inherited from the archaic age, notably Athena, who was a goddess of wisdom, warfare, and craftsmanship, and the patron and protector of Athens. Epicurus's inclusion of women in the inner circle of his school was thus a direct challenge to the norms of the time.[63] Plutarch chastised Epicurus for allowing "young and attractive women" to be full members of his Garden, where they "ranged at will."[64]

The gifted Themista, Leonteus's wife, was listed by Diogenes Laertius as one of the important Epicureans. She was greatly admired for her wisdom and for the style of her writings, which were referred to by Cicero and others, and which included extensive published correspondence with Epicurus. It is significant that Epicurus's memoir to his elder brother was titled *Neocles: Dedicated to Themista.* The only other persons that Epicurus dedicated books to, that we know of, were Metrodorus and Mithres. Cicero goes so far as to protest that the Epicureans chose to "devote . . . bulky volumes to Themista," a mere woman, however talented, instead of to Greek political and military leaders such as "Lycurgus, Solon, Miltiades, Themistocles, and Epaminondas." Yet, the fact that Cicero referred to Themista at all, and in one of his major philosophical works, attests to her importance. He presented her as symbolizing wisdom, indicating that her reputation for sagacity had become proverbial. Much later, Clement of Alexandria (ca. 150–215 CE) was to refer to Themista as proof that women were capable of acquiring philosophical wisdom. Lactantius saw her as unique, a woman taught by a major philosopher.[65]

In Lampsacus, Metrodorus's sister Batis married Idomeneus, Epicurus's high-placed supporter. It has been suggested that one of the Herculaneum papyri included a biography of Batis, as well as five of her letters, but the damaged state of the papyrus has made it impossible to be certain, with her actual name not appearing in the surviving copies of the book. Nevertheless, her role as an Epicurean thinker is a plausible one.[66]

The rest of the women associated with the Garden, particularly in Athens as opposed to Lampsacus, were all characterized, usually by opponents of the Epicureans, as *hetaerae*. The names that have come down to us in this regard are: Leontion, Hedia, Erotion, Nicidion, Mammarion, Boïdon, Demetria, and Philainis. A *hetaera* (literally, female companion) is usually thought of as a highly cultured courtesan. But the assignment of women to this status, as Pamela Gordon has pointed out, could mean many different things, often perhaps simply indicating a woman who is not a respectable wife or marriageable daughter. Most of the Epicurean women in the Garden that we know of were referred to as attractive young women and hetaerae by critics who wanted to suggest licentious conduct. This, however, was conduct of a kind that if carried to excess was proscribed by Epicurus's philosophy, which emphasized avoiding overindulgence in pleasure, such as food and sex, if happiness were to be secured. All the women listed as belonging to the Garden had Greek names, while courtesans were more often non-Greeks. What is clear is the openness of Epicurus's Garden to the participation of women, some of whom were no doubt seeking to escape from the extreme limitations placed on women in Greek society.[67]

Leontion, who appears to have been a friend of Themista (Epicurus wrote of meeting with them together) is the one woman among those referred to as hetaerae in Epicurus's Garden of whom we have some definite knowledge. She was a member of the inner circle of the Garden and herself a major Epicurean philosopher. Cicero, while complaining of her effrontery, commended her work *Against Theophrastus* for the elegance of its style. In writing a critique of Theophrastus, Plato's and Aristotle's pupil, and Aristotle's successor as head of the Lyceum, Leontion clearly stood out in her sheer audacity. Epicurus, who had the highest opinion of her, wrote to her on one occasion: "With what tumultuous applause we were inspired as we read your letter."[68]

Metrodorus was completely enamored of Leontion, who became his wife. In his will, Epicurus provides for the children of Metrodorus, who would, we presume, have been children of Leontion as well. According to Pliny the Elder, two Theban artists painted Leontion's portrait. One of these was the celebrated Aristides of Thebes and a lesser-known painter Theorus. Aristides, according to Pliny, "was the first of all the painters to give full expression to the mind and passions of man." His choice of Leontion for the painting called *Epicurus's Leontion*, is thus intriguing. No doubt he was attracted by the desire to paint a beautiful hetaera, but also one who was also an Epicurean philosopher, and so capturing the mind and body. Theorus's painting was clearly based on a similar conception as it was titled *Leontion of Epicurus Thinking*.[69]

What brought the Epicurean community together was a reflexive materialist philosophy that found freedom, security, and meaning in friendship itself. For Epicurus, friendship was the highest value, beginning with the love of humanity *(philia)*: "Love goes dancing round and round the inhabited earth, veritably shouting to us all to awake to the blessedness of the happy life." Starting from a materialist basis, Epicurus contended that friendship typically arises out of some mutual need, but evolves into love, loyalty, and even the willingness to die for one's friend. Genuine friendship is nurtured in a community. As DeWitt remarks in *Epicurus and His Philosophy*, "The Greek language lacked a specific term for fellowship," but the word "'intimacy,' *oikeiotes*, which etymologically means 'membership in the family,'" as utilized in the last of Epicurus's *Principal Doctrines*, can be interpreted in that way. Such deep friendship was described by Epicurus as providing a sense of fullness acquired by those consciously living in accord with material nature and concerned with the lives of others as well as their own.[70] For Epicurus, "True fellowship can be enjoyed only among those who live within the 'the limits of Nature,' for whom alone 'the fullness of pleasure' is logically possible."[71]

Friendship was impossible without mutual accord. Justice was viewed as naturally reciprocal and changing with changing conditions. "The justice of nature," Epicurus wrote, "is a pledge of reciprocal usefulness, [i.e.] neither to harm one another nor be harmed." Moreover, "If objective conditions . . . change, and the same things which had been just turn out to be no longer useful, then those things were just as long as they were useful for the mutual associations of fellow citizens; but later, when they were not useful, they were no longer just." Beyond this love for humanity, there is community, fellowship, and individual friendship. Human community is based on a social contract, or compact, establishing mutual association.[72]

Pleasure and Pain

In the face of a cosmos of whirling atoms and ceaseless change, and a social order dominated by wars and injustice, individuals, Epicurus argued, must rely on themselves, their friends, and their community to find happiness. Everything material perishes except the atoms and the void, which leads eventually to regeneration, but not in any sense that can be said to have meaning to the individual human being. To all of this he famously offered the "fourfold remedy" or *tetrapharmakon*: "God presents no fears; death no cause for alarm; it is easy to procure what is good; it is also easy to endure what is evil." Through its strict materialism accompanied by a sense of human freedom and self-determination Epicureanism drew its persuasive power.[73]

Although emphasizing the pursuit of pleasure and the avoidance of pain, Epicurus was not strictly hedonistic in that he strongly warned against indulgence and emphasized that the path to happiness lay in satisfying basic needs, symbolized by bread, cheese, olives, weak wine, and water, while avoiding a life of acquisition and the pursuit of wealth. The goal rather should be one of "self-sufficiency." Yet, despite Epicurus's emphasis on frugality, philosophical symposiums, or banquets of reason, were held in the Garden on special occasions, during which customary limits on diet and abstinence were set aside. These occasions were all the more significant because they were restricted to certain points in the calendar, usually the twentieth of each month.[74] Property was not held in common, but rather privately, in order to avoid conflict, in the context of a non-acquisitive community where most property was personal property, unconnected to production or accumulation. "A free life," Epicurus wrote, "cannot acquire great wealth."[75]

As a materialist, Epicurus strongly rejected Plato's astral gods as depicted in *The Laws*. However, acceptance of the traditional anthropomorphic gods of Homer and Hesiod, viewed as guides and exemplars of virtues, was encouraged in the Garden, along with a kind of civic piety. Knowledge of the gods was seen as being obtained through preconception (*prolepsis*), often in dreams. Nevertheless, the gods were viewed as having no relation to the material earth itself and did not interfere with human lives. Rather, they lived in the *intermundia* or pores between the worlds. They were in effect, as Marx tersely stated, "the plastic gods of Greek art."[76]

Epicurus was strongly opposed to all teleological views based on final causes. He developed a proto-evolutionary analysis, with all life including human life having originated from the earth while changing over time, particularly through the natural elimination of monstrous forms. His analysis pointed to a kind of normalizing selection. This was clearly conveyed by Lucretius, his Roman follower in the first century BCE, author of the great poem *De rerum natura (On the Nature of Things)*, who wrote that those species that were able to continue and perpetuate themselves through "the chain of offspring," forging "the chain of a species in procreation," were those that had special organs that served to protect them from the environment. "But those that were gifted with none of these natural assets . . . were fair game and an easy prey for others, till nature brought their race to extinction."

Epicurus was the strongest critic in antiquity of the creationism associated with the philosophies of Socrates and Plato. "Nothing," he wrote, "ever comes to be from nothing by divine intervention."[77]

This materially grounded outlook left considerable room for human freedom based on the development of a philosophy of self-consciousness. Human beings were seen by Epicurus as belonging to a world rooted fundamentally in material nature, out of which emerged the mind and reason. Human beings were free, within limits, to exercise their reason and self-determination in their own lives and communities. Epicurus carefully distinguished between the needs that were natural and those that were not, and among those that were natural, those that were necessary and those that were not. "We must remember," he wrote, "that the future is neither wholly ours nor wholly not ours."[78]

At the center of Epicurus's philosophy was the notion of mortality. "Death," he wrote, "is nothing to us." This meant quite literally that upon death our atoms are disassociated, and the soul perishes with the body, bringing on a state of nothing for us, since life does not exist apart from the sense organs and the senses. He therefore rejected the fear of the afterlife that played such a dominant role in ancient Greek religion. He died in 270. Suffering from kidney stones, he entered "a bronze bathtub filled with warm water, asked for unmixed wine, and tossed it back. He then bade his friends to remember his teachings and died thus."[79]

Epicurus's revolt against the dominant class views of his time was all-encompassing. In an age of social collapse, he sought to provide guidance to individuals and to encourage a new form of social compact. Although rejecting the politics of his time, he sought to generate an alternative *praxis*—reuniting theory and practice at the level of the community rather than the polis—in a way that circumvented the dominant struggle for wealth and power.

Judged by its numbers of adherents, Epicureanism was the most successful philosophy in Greek, Hellenistic, and Roman antiquity. It spread to the east throughout the Hellenistic world and then west to Rome. According to Diogenes Laertius, Epicurus's Athens "honored him with bronze statues." The Garden in Athens survived until late in the first century BCE, while as a school of philosophy Epicureanism survived for seven centuries, three centuries BCE and as much as four centuries CE. Important extant traces of Epicurean philosophy and its adherents can be found up to the second century CE, after which, it is believed, given the continuing responses to it by opponents, to have persisted into the fourth century, though peaking in the second century. Unlike other ancient philosophies its adherents were not primarily drawn from the aristocracy, but rather emanated from a much larger, poorer populace, who were attracted to its materialism and its doctrine of human freedom.[80]

CHAPTER TWO

Epicurus's Materialist Philosophy

Epicurus's philosophical system was admired from antiquity for the tightness of its construction, which was built around three main divisions: the Canonic (epistemology), Physics, and Ethics. The object of his philosophy was ethics, governing human action in the world. But since human beings were physical beings, this found its determinant basis in nature or physics, and in those contingent conditions that allowed for free will and voluntary action, swerving away from any fixed determinism or fatalism. His philosophical investigations, moreover, commenced logically not with nature or ethics but with a materialist epistemology, directed at how knowledge of the world is obtained through the senses, preconceptions, and feelings, when coupled with reason and methods of scientific inference. Studies of Book 25 from Epicurus's *On Nature*, recovered from the Herculaneum papyri, have shown that Epicurus's philosophical system was to culminate in a complex philosophy of mind rooted in his overall emergent materialism.

Epicurus's chief epistemological treatise was called *The Criterion*, or *The Canon*. Although the work itself did not survive, Diogenes Laertius provided a short summary of it in Book 10 of his *Lives of the Eminent Philosophers*, characterizing it as "the introduction to the [Epicurean] system."[1] There are also brief demarcations of Epicurus's epistemological approach in his Letter to Herodotus and in the *Principal Doctrines*. Lucretius's *De rerum natura* and works by Philodemus recovered from the Herculaneum papyri provide additional background on the relation between Epicurus's epistemology and methods of scientific inference.[2]

Greek philosophy commenced in its earliest Ionian stages in the sixth century BCE. Initially, it took the form of a monistic materialism aimed at drawing universal conclusions about the stuff of the world.[3] It would adopt a more explicitly dialectical form focusing on constant change and movement with Heraclitus (ca. 540–480 BCE). However, the ideas of the original Ionian philosophers, who had employed a common-sense view of the senses as a guide to knowledge, were to be strongly rejected with the rise to prominence, primarily in Sicily, of the philosophy of Parmenides and the Eleatic school of Presocratic philosophers in the early fifth century BCE. Likewise, Plato's fourth-century idealist philosophy, influenced in this respect by the Eleatics, rejected the authority of the senses in favor of ideal Forms. Even the great atomist Democritus (ca. 460–356 BCE), part of the Ionian or neo-Ionian revival responding to the challenges of the Eleatics, which also included Anaxagoras and Empedocles, evinced strong skeptical views, throwing doubt on the senses as a basis of knowledge.

As Jonathan Barnes observed in *The Presocratic Philosophers*, the Eleatic philosophers, overthrowing all common-sense notions, moved philosophy forward while creating a series of paradoxes by arguing in terms of pure logic or ratiocination that "nothing can ever be generated or destroyed, that nothing can ever alter, that nothing can ever move—and that, were change possible, there would be no reason why it should ever occur."[4] The neo-Ionians of the fifth century responded to this challenge most fundamentally by accepting that nothing could originate out of nothing and nothing being destroyed could be reduced to nothing—propositions that were to be a key Greek philosophy, and were to be deeply embedded in Epicurus's later perspective—while seeking to reaffirm the senses as a basis of knowledge and data of perception, and to reconstruct a conception of matter and motion. In doing so, the neo-Ionian revival by figures such as Anaxagoras and Democritus "pursued the old Ionian ideal of *historia* [meaning inquiry] despite the pressure of the Eleatic *logos*" or "*a priori* ratiocination."[5]

But it was the revolt of Epicurus that constituted the most cogent and consistent answer in antiquity to Skepticism, Platonic idealism, and the paradoxes of the Eleatics. He argued that knowledge of the world was based on the senses as mediated by reason. He thus represented, as George Thomson stated in *Aeschylus and Athens*, "the heir to Ionian materialism."[6] This led Epicurus to be characterized in modern times by Immanuel Kant, George Wilhelm Friedrich Hegel, and others as the principal proponent of empirical natural science in antiquity.[7]

There can be no doubt about what drew Epicurus into the epistemological realm, leading him to provide his foundational work *The Canon*, as a necessary first step in the development of his philosophical system. His entire materialist philosophy and ethics aimed at *ataraxia* (ἀταραξία), or freedom from worry and a sustainable existence promoting human happiness, was rooted in naturalism. It depended entirely on the defense, although at a higher level, of a common-sense realism. As Cyril Bailey remarked in *The Greek Atomists and Epicurus*, "The whole of Epicurean philosophy is based, as its founder intended it to be, on the common-sense point of view that 'sensation is true.'"[8] Further, rather than succumbing to mechanism, Epicurus insisted on the reality of human freedom and voluntary action. In this way, he provided a basis for a human-centered materialist analysis that responded, in equal measure, to Plato's idealist philosophy and to the skepticism of Democritus, as well as replying to the entire Eleatic tradition. He did so in an age when social disruption and collapse required a philosophy that could speak to the plebeian majority, placing its emphasis on freedom, friendship, and living well.

The Revolt of Epicurus

As opposed to the neo-Ionian revival, Epicurus's philosophy was not directed as much against the Eleatics as it was against Plato's idealist philosophy and the Skepticism that was often associated with thinkers as varied as Socrates and Democritus. In his dialogue *Meno*, Plato had raised the question of how something can be investigated if one has no words for or knowledge of what one is seeking. His answer was that such knowledge could be traced to the immortal soul, even in its prenatal phase, giving it access to the transcendent form, in line with his idealistic philosophy.[9]

In many ways more directly challenging to Epicurus, however, was the position of Democritus, who, while an atomist, evidenced a skeptical view of sense perception as a basis of truth. Thus, he famously depicted the senses as declaring to the mind: "Wretched mind! Do you take your evidence from us and then overthrow us? Our overthrow is your downfall." Although insisting on atoms and the void as the ultimate reality, Democritus continually questioned the validity of sensual perception, and evinced a strong skeptical attitude with regard to the truth value of the world of phenomena (although his views should not be confused with those of the ancient schools of skepticism as in Pyrrhonism or the Middle/New Academies). Thus, he wrote: "In reality we know nothing—for truth is in the depths."[10]

In developing an epistemology (which Hegel said, in Epicurus's case, was "really a system of logic") consonant with his materialism, Epicurus was bold to an extreme, introducing entirely new concepts to explain how sense perception was the basis of knowledge when mediated by human reason.[11] The term *criterion* (κριτήριον), the literal translation of which was instrument of judgment, had been used by both Plato and Aristotle to refer to thought processes and cognitive faculties. However, Epicurus gave it a new, more specific meaning, in which it referred to the fundamental epistemological bases through which we ascertain truth with regard to the material world. The word *canon* (κανών), employed as a technical term, may have been taken from Democritus's work *Canons* of which we have no concrete knowledge beyond the title. Nevertheless, Epicurus characteristically took the notion of a "canon," a mason's rule or straightedge, and turned it into a category of truth determination. A "canon" was used to judge straightness of a wall or beam and thus had to be straight in itself in order to serve as a standard for other things. Epicurus's epistemological Canonic was thus meant to provide an instrument or criterion for discovering truth in relation to the material world.[12]

Epicurus's Canonic included three standards of truth underlying perceptions of the material world: the senses, preconceptions, and feelings. The senses were viewed as passive receptors devoid of reason or memory. As such, the various senses cannot refute each other but are all of equal value and complementary. According to Diogenes Laertius's account of *The Canon*, it is only by virtue of "plain facts" provided by sense data that we are able to draw meaningful inferences about the world. "For all our notions are derived from perceptions, either by actual contact or analogy, or resemblance, or composition, with some slight aid from reasoning."[13] The reliability of the senses is thus the underlying principle on which all our knowledge claims with respect to the material world ultimately depend. "If you fight against all your sensations," Epicurus states, in *Principle Doctrine* number 23, "you will have no standard to which to refer, and thus no means of judging even those judgments which you pronounce false."[14]

"Clear evidence of sense" is for Epicurus the ultimate basis on which our perceptions of the world rest.[15] While the evidence of the senses is not to be denied, and any attempt by reason to overthrow the senses is to be decried as irrational and self-defeating, sensual perception is insufficient in getting at the reality of things. The sense impressions we receive are supplemented by memory (a thought process), experience, and accumulated knowledge allowing us to make valid inferences. Epicurus thus separates the content of sensation from the perceptual judgments based on this content, making possible the rational evaluation of sense data against what the mind has already perceived—or else is in accord with what still needs to be ascertained from the senses themselves, since what we at first perceive in a limited way always must "'await' confirmation." A tower that appears round from the distance may turn out to be square when approached up close. This leads to the principle that preliminary judgments based on the senses have to be confirmed by further sense impressions, which, because of factors such as greater proximity, allow for increased accuracy.[16]

Epicurus's whole approach to the senses, as Bailey emphasized in *Greek Atomists and Epicurus*, was directed at advancing a more sophisticated common-sense realism, consonant with the views of the plebeian classes, as a polemical response to the dominant idealist and skeptical philosophies of the day, which were all aristocratic in nature.[17] If not quite following the Sophist Protagoras in declaring "Man is the measure of all things," Epicurus's materialist approach to the senses was a radical extension of the neo-Ionian revival, in defiance of the philosophies of the Eleatics and the Academy and Lyceum. It thus constituted a reassertion of a materialist outlook on a much firmer basis than before.[18] This is evident as well in the remainder of *The Canon*, in which he focused on preconceptions and feelings as criteria in making affirmations of truth with respect to the material world.

Epicurus seems to have introduced his concept of *preconception* or *prolepsis* (πρόληψις) as a direct response to the argument in Plato's *Meno*. There Meno asks Socrates, with respect to his search for virtue or truth, "How will you look for it, Socrates, when you do not know at all what it is? How will you aim to search for something you do not know at all? If you should meet with it, how will you know that this is the thing that you did not know?" Socrates's answer in the dialogue was to refer to the immortal soul, which could recollect its half-forgotten memories before, including prenatal ones.[19]

Not having recourse to the concept of an immortal soul as a fundamental criterion of truth, which would have gone against his materialism, Epicurus employed the category *preconception*, or prolepsis, as crucial to his *criterion*, and as a way of addressing Meno's paradox. As described by A. A. Long and David Sedley in *The Hellenistic Philosophers*, "A preconception is a generic notion of any type of object or experience, the concept naturally evoked by the name of the thing," representing a basic grasp. It is "synthesized out of repeated experiences of something external." Thus, when the word "horse" is evoked, a basic grasp or preconception arises from the cumulative experience of the senses, upon which cognition acts. Preconceptions, Long and Sedley observe, can extend beyond physical objects to include "data of introspection" such as one's "own responsibility or agency."[20] Although preconceptions for Epicurus mainly derived from what would today be considered sensory data, they could in his philosophy also enter into the mind through dreams, as in the case of the gods.

The significance of the concept of preconception is that it allowed a way out of the infinite regress of proofs regarding the starting points in philosophy, a problem raised in Aristotle's *Posterior Analytics*.[21] The notion of preconception in this sense came to be fundamental to philosophy as a whole. "It is as a matter of fact, from Epicurus on, a philosophical commonplace," Long and Sedley write, "that preconceptions are what make inquiry possible."[22] It is now understood that the first considerations raised in Epicurus's *Letter to Herodotus* in which a thinker is encouraged to "grasp the things which underlie words" is related to preconception and that preconception is at the basis of language, establishing a generic function crucial to thought and the analysis of the nature of things.[23] In preconception, moreover, Epicurus was able to defend a common-sense materialist view of the world in which the senses, experience, and memory contributed to strong preconceptions.[24]

Feelings constitute the third arbiter of truth in Epicurus's criterion.[25] The primary feelings are depicted as pleasure and pain used as generic terms, referring not only to physical responses but also to positive and negative emotions. Feelings as such are related to the senses, and thus can be subsumed under perception, but are less windows to the external world than indications of the impact of the world on the body and mind, or "the internal aspect of our perceptions."[26] For Epicurus, feelings also connect truth to action and thus to ethical considerations, as pleasure and pain provide standards for choice and avoidance. A major consequence of the Epicurean emphasis on the senses, preconceptions, and feelings as criteria of truth/experience, coupled with a materialist approach to the mind, was to link human beings with non-human animals. Non-human and human animals were seen as representing differences in degree rather than kind in all of these respects.[27]

For Epicurus, the threefold criteria of the senses, preconceptions, and feelings formed the basis for "sign-inferences about evidence [that] yet awaited and about the non-evident."[28] The emphasis placed on the senses was complemented by a method of scientific inference that was clearly articulated in his work, and in that of subsequent Epicureans. The object was to demonstrate how evidence could be employed by cognitive faculties, building on the criteria. In this respect, Epicurus argued that falsehood was apparent where evidence was not attested, or where it was contested, while truth was apparent where the evidence was attested or where it was not contested. In terms of direct evidence, truth and falsehood were fairly clear, either attested or not attested, though this often meant awaiting confirmation based on close observation. For example, the existence of human locomotion, though denied by the Eleatics in Zeno's famous paradox, could be attested, in Epicurus's philosophy, by the mere fact of its presence in our experience.[29]

In those areas that were non-observable, "sign-inferences" were often required based on analogous experiences, making it possible for particular hypotheses to be either contested or not contested through known principles as a means of ascertaining the truth.[30] Contestation of particular hypotheses often took the form of a logic of elimination. Thus, proof of the existence of the void, for Epicurus, was that without it there could be no motion, which was firmly rooted in experience. This reflected a logic that the Epicureans called "counter-witnessing." Non-observable phenomena, as in the case of the void, sometimes allowed for a singular causal explanation. Motion exists, but without the void there could be no motion, so the void exists. Yet, in other cases, where non-observable phenomena were at issue, and where the analogues from experience were numerous, multiple causal relations were equally conceivable, which meant that it was necessary to remain open to different possibilities, which were treated as equally valid, according to the principle of non-contestation, essential for scientific inference in such cases.[31]

Epicurus provided a sophisticated theory of sign-inferences in which observations of the phenomenal world were "signs" of what was unobserved.[32] He explicitly questioned disjunctive, either-or propositions and the principle of bivalence according to which a declarative statement is either true or false even in relation to future contingencies. Instead, he emphasized complexity, change, contingency, and immanently dialectical contradictions.[33]

Epicurus is usually regarded as the great empirical thinker of antiquity, contrasted especially to Plato in this respect. Knowledge in his analysis is fundamentally dependent on the senses. As Sedley states, "The Epicureans" were "the ancient philosophical world's most ardent empiricists," representing "the opposite extreme from Plato. Not only the preconceptions of biological genera and species but *all* our preconceptions, they assume, have an empirical origin."[34] However, it would be wrong to exaggerate this and to characterize Epicurus's views as radically empiricist in the sense that knowledge is derived entirely from the senses, a view that did not exist in antiquity.[35] His notion of preconception and the role attributed to reason meant that knowledge, while dependent on experience, had both an *a posteriori* basis and a critical *a priori* element, else reason could not adjudicate with respect to sense perception.

Materiality and the Atom

Democritus (ca. 460–356 BCE) is often regarded as the primary originator of the atomistic theory, although he, in fact, built his philosophy on the basis of the work of Leucippus (ca. 480–420 BCE) before him, of whom we know little. Epicurus was to draw directly on Democritus's atomism to develop his own materialist philosophy, amending the analysis at critical points to eliminate rigid determinism and skepticism, and to create a more defensible materialism with room for human agency. As the noted Irish scholar of the Greek classics, Benjamin Farrington, summarized the relation between these thinkers in his book *The Faith of Epicurus*:

> Democritus, coming at the end of the fifth century, summed up in his atomic theory two hundred fruitful years of Greek physical speculation. His doctrine of the atom and the void was a generalization of the physical knowledge of his day. In accordance with his scientific purpose he granted to his atoms only such qualities as would enable them, by entering into combination with one another, to produce the familiar world of sense phenomena. His atomic theory was an hypothesis to serve as a base for the natural sciences. As such it carried with it a belief in the universality of the law of cause and effect. Philosophically Democritus was a determinist; he made the law of cause and effect apply to the world of man as well as the world of nature.
>
> Epicurus, more than a century later, constructed his system under different conditions and for a different purpose. His age demanded of philosophy that it should provide a guide for the individual in the conduct of life in a period of social collapse. . . . Epicurus . . . was primarily concerned to assert the autonomy of the individual will. He accepted from Democritus the atomic theory as in the main a correct account of the constitution and behaviour of matter, but he repudiated the philosophical doctrine of determinism. . . . He therefore made such changes in the

> description of the atom as he conceived necessary to preserve the observed fact of the freedom of the individual to follow a preferred course of action. This meant including in the atom an element of spontaneity. His conception of the atom allowed both for the development of a world of inanimate nature under the rule of mechanical law and a world of animate nature distinguished from it by being in various degrees the theatre of will.[36]

For a long time, it was believed that Democritus had provided the more profound philosophy. But "Marx," Farrington explains, "reversed their roles, making Epicurus appear as the deeper of the two inasmuch as he had labored to find room in his system for both animate and inanimate being, both for nature and society, both for the phenomena of the external world and the demands of the moral consciousness."[37] This has been borne out in the research into Epicurean philosophy over the last century.

In much of its initial propositions Epicurus's materialism thus appears very similar to that of Democritus. The atomists adhered to the Eleatic proposition that nothing is created out of nothing, and nothing being destroyed is reduced to nothing. The underlying material world consisted simply of atoms (from the Greek for "unsplittables") and void.[38] "The sum of things" (atoms and void), constituting the universe, was infinite.[39] For Democritus, dimension and shape were the two primary characteristics of atoms.[40] Atoms, in his conception, were continually in motion. The phenomenal world arose through the conglomeration of atoms, creating new compounds or "assemblages."[41] Perception at a distance depended on *eidola* or images, atoms that emanate from the surfaces of compound objects. Atoms were strictly limited in their properties, lacking qualities such as color, heat, taste, etc., which were accidental and existed by "convention." All of this was also found in Epicurus.[42]

Yet what stands out is not so much the way in which Democritus influenced Epicurus's thought, as the deviations of the latter from the former. Democritus, according to Aëtius, saw atoms as potentially any size, conceivably "as big as the cosmos," although generally of a size that was imperceptible.[43] They were of infinite variety and moved in all directions.[44] Necessity of a purely mechanical nature governed everything. In Diogenes Laertius's account of Democritus's philosophy, "All things happen by virtue of necessity."[45] Likewise, according to Eusebius, "Democritus of Abdera [assumed] . . . that all the past as well as the present and the future, has been determined always, since time immemorial, by necessity."[46] As Cicero wrote in *On Fate*, "Democritus preferred to accept the view that all events are caused by necessity."[47]

Against all of these propositions of Democritus, Epicurus was to rebel, constructing a philosophy that gave a larger role to freedom and agency, and that limited the absolute determinism or fatalism of the atomistic view. Although rejecting the teleological views of Greek religion and the fatalist notion of some, like Theognis, that birth and life constituted no more than a preparation for passing through "the gates of Hades," Epicurus was no less critical of the rigid mechanism of natural philosophers such as Democritus, who removed all human agency and free will from the causal determination of things. "It was better, indeed," he held, "to accept the legends of the gods than to bow beneath that yoke of destiny which natural philosophers have imposed. The one holds out some hope that we may escape if we honour the gods, while the necessity of the naturalists is deaf to all entreaties."[48]

Rather than moving in every direction, as in Democritus, Epicurus's atoms fall to the earth in parallel lines. Although the atoms are of different sizes and weights—Epicurus added weight to the primary properties of atoms—they all fall at the same speed, since the void lacks all resistance.[49] In this respect Epicurus was at odds with Aristotle, who thought objects fell at a speed determined by their mass. Here Epicurus anticipated *a priori* a fundamental principle of modern physics first demonstrated by Galileo in his famous late sixteenth-century Leaning Tower of Pisa experiment.[50]

A major innovation of Epicurus's atomism was to specify that atoms contained minimal parts, or *minima*, even though the atom itself was by definition unsplittable. The minima meant that it was possible to explain why atoms had different shapes, and also account for parts such as hooks that allowed atoms to interlock. Atoms, since they varied in size as well as shape, could thus be seen as consisting of minima. The outermost edges to the atoms could themselves be conceived as minima. Epicurus hypothesized that the minima were "infinitesimal" in size. Atoms thus could embody a *not strictly infinite* number of variations resulting from an *inconceivably large* number of minima.

Yet the minima were themselves so infinitesimal in size that this was consistent with atoms that remained below the level of perception. Hence, contrary to Democritus's postulate of an infinite variation in the size of atoms, Epicurus insisted that variations in the atoms were incomprehensibly large, but not infinite, since atoms could never be so large as to cross the threshold into the realm of perception.[51]

Epicurus, like Democritus, viewed sense perception, particularly at a distance, as resulting from *eidola*, or images/effluences, consisting of fine atomic films, which detach themselves like skins or membranes, flowing from objects and activating the senses and therefore the soul/mind. Lucretius translated *eidola* in Latin as *simulacra*. The mind through a process of *focusing* was able to concentrate on some among many *eidola*/simulacra which then take sharper form. This then led to the development of memory, preconceptions, and reason.[52]

The most important distinguishing feature of Epicurus's Atomism, through which he broke with Democritus's mechanism, was his concept of the swerve, or declination (Greek: παϱέγκλισις, *parénklisis*, Latin: *clinamen*). The swerve introduced a departure from the linear movement of atoms by exactly one minimum, occurring at random times and places, constituting an oblique movement going in any direction, or a declination of the straight line. The swerve is a primary property of the atom and so like the atom itself needs no causal explanation.[53] Lucretius's account of atoms falling in a straight line attributed this to weight and motion that could be impacted by force or blows. But the third determinant of motion was the swerve from the straight line, which was integral to the very concept of the atom.[54]

No direct reference to the swerve/declination is found in Epicurus's extant writings, but its presence as a crucial postulate of his theory is clearly attested in numerous ancient sources including Carneades (as attested in Cicero), Lucretius, Cicero, Philodemus, Aetius, Diogenes of Oenoanda, Galen, Plutarch, Plotinus, and Augustine.[55] In terms of Epicurean physics, the swerve meant that atoms could collide with one another, or, more precisely, were subject to repulsion and attraction, leading to conglomerations or assemblages of atoms and thus the phenomenal world. In terms of human agency, the swerve went against mechanism and fatalism, signifying that non-human and human animals could initiate their own actions. Indeed, Lucretius provided two explanations as to why the concept of the swerve was necessary: (1) without the swerve atoms could never meet; and (2) the swerve was necessary to explain human volition.[56] The swerve thus "breaks 'the bonds of fate.'"[57]

Contemporary scholarship on Atomism emphasizes the role of repulsion and attraction in the overall atomistics perspective. A concise explanation is provided by C. C. W. Taylor, who writes of "The Atomists":

> We have, however, to recall the evidence from Philoponus that atoms never actually collide or come into contact, with its implication that the basic physical forces are attraction and repulsion. On that view, most atomic motion is explained by the analogue of impact, namely repulsion, while the immobility of atoms relative to one another is explained by attraction, since the relative stability of atoms in an aggregate has to be explained, not by their literal interlocking but by their being held together *as if* interlocked by an attractive force operating over the tiny gaps between the atoms in the aggregate.[58]

Thus, the references to interlocked atoms and to collisions (and rebounds) in Epicurus and Lucretius in this interpretation were essentially analogues for a more sophisticated understanding of attraction and repulsion, first conceived in terms of magnetism.

Marx in his 1841 doctoral thesis (not published until 1902) compared the natural philosophies of Democritus and Epicurus, explaining the role of repulsion in ancient atomism. Epicurus's philosophy, according to Marx, was linked to "*lex atomi*," or the law of the atom.[59] Most ancient and modern criticisms of Epicurus's swerve have seen the motion of the atom in a straight line and the oblique movement of the swerve as operating sequentially, entirely separate from each other, and thus each formally negating the other. The role of repulsion was most often ignored or downplayed.

In contrast to such accounts, emphasizing the contradictory nature of Epicurus's analysis, Marx argued that these partial movements in Epicurus's physics made up a dialectical unity, with repulsion constituting the "realization" of the declination or swerve. Thus, as he put it, "Epicurus assumes a *threefold* motion of the atoms in the void. One motion is the *fall in a straight line*, the second originates in the deviation of the atom *from the straight line*, and the third is established through the *repulsion of the many atoms*. Both Democritus and Epicurus accept the first and third motion. The *declination of the atom* from the straight line differentiates the one from the other."[60] Epicurus, in contrast to Democritus, was "the first to grasp the essence of the repulsion . . . in sensuous form." Thus, "it is from repulsion and the ensuing conglomerations of the qualified atoms that the world of appearance now emerges. . . . The atoms are . . . the substance of nature out of which everything emerges, into which everything dissolves."[61]

Book 25 of On Nature: Freedom and Determinism

Epicurus is widely acknowledged today as the first thinker in the Greco-Roman tradition to pose the question of determinism and free will.[62] The recovery over the last century and a half of significant portions of Book 25 of Epicurus's *On Nature* led to a wide-ranging debate over Epicurus's notion of free volition centering on his philosophy of mind, or psychology. This also raises issues of moral responsibility. In the last half-century, these issues have colored all discussions of Epicureanism, though the analysis of Book 25 in this respect actually goes back much further to Theodor Gomperz's research into the Herculaneum papyri in the 1860s and 1870s. As we shall see in the next chapter, these questions were also addressed by Marx, but without the benefit of Book 25 of *On Nature*.

The eruption of Mt. Vesuvius in 79 CE buried the towns of

Pompei and Herculaneum in ash. Excavations carried out in 1752 into a buried house in Herculaneum, once a seaside retreat for wealthy Romans, found in a small room attached to what was clearly a study a considerable number of what appeared to be "cylindrical briquettes of charcoal," stacked on shelves. Many were destroyed before it was discovered that they were carbonized papyri. Recognizing that what had been discovered was a classical library, consisting of what turned out to be 1,787 papyrus scrolls, persistent attempts were made, mostly unsuccessful at first, to unroll them, during which many of the papyri were destroyed, but which eventually led to the construction of crude mechanisms for opening them. It was soon determined that the library in Herculaneum consisted primarily of books associated with the Epicurean philosopher Philodemus of Gadara (ca. 110–37 BCE), along with various classical Epicurean works, including Epicurus's *On Nature*. It is widely believed that Philodemus's patron and the owner of the villa was Lucius Calpernius Piso Caesoninus, Julius Caesar's father-in-law, although much of this is conjecture. In fact, more than a century lay between Philodemus's death (ca. 37 BCE) and the eruption of Mt. Vesuvius that buried Herculaneum.[63]

In 1800, the Prince of Wales (later George IV) undertook at his own expense, with the cooperation of the Neapolitan government, a project of unrolling and copying the papyri under the supervision of his representative, the Reverend John Hayter. During the years 1802 to 1806, hundreds of papyri were unrolled and almost a hundred copied in the form of lead-pencil facsimiles under Hayter's supervision. When a French army under Marshal Masséna entered Naples in 1806, Hayter returned to England and brought with him all the lead-pencil facsimiles existing at the time. A number of unopened rolls were also sent to the Prince of Wales in England as a present from the Neapolitan government, then exiled in Sicily. In 1810, the Prince of Wales presented the facsimiles and engraved plates of the papyri, along with some of the unopened papyri rolls, to the University of Oxford where they were deposited in the Bodleian Library. Other Herculaneum materials that Hayter had retained were also later recovered by the Bodleian. In 1824, a book, *Voluminum Pars Prima Oxonii, Sumptibus Typ. Clarend. lithographice exudebat N. Whittock*, was published by Oxford, "containing a meagre and not very accurate catalogue of the Oxford facsimiles, and lithographed reproductions of four of the best preserved."[64]

However, the unpublished facsimiles were to be almost completely forgotten for nearly four decades, until 1863. In that year Gomperz, then a young scholar and later the leading philologist, papyrologist, and specialist in ancient philosophy at the University of Vienna, traveled to the Bodleian Library in search of the facsimiles of the Herculaneum papyri. As he explained:

> I made my way to Oxford to exploit this important aid for my studies in the spring of 1863, with [George] Grote's recommendation. There they had curiously lost all track of that object [the facsimiles of the Herculanean papyri]. They did not know where Hayter's copies were. Only after a long search, when I had already rashly wanted to depart, the chair of the library found a small key, upon which hung a small note that read "Oxonii Herculanean papyri." Then followed another search of the attics and storage rooms. Finally, we came across a crate that this small key opened, and thus we came into possession of these copies that are so exceptionally valuable to the study of the papyri.[65]

Gomperz was able to use copies of the original facsimiles that Reverend J. J. Cohen made for him. The *Apographa Oxoniensa*, as the facsimiles from the Bodleian were called, were to be critically important, since, as Gomperz noted, "Much of what was still clearly legible" in the original papyri when Hayter made his facsimiles "was already unreadable by the time the originals . . . were finally copied again. This didn't just apply to individual syllables, words, or lines, but to half and whole columns."[66] The ink in the papyri began to fade the moment they were opened.[67]

Using the *Apographa Oxoniensa*, along with later Neapolitan facsimiles and the original papyri, Gomperz was able to translate and publish some of Philodemus's works, beginning with *On Anger* in 1864. More importantly, he made significant progress in the decipherment of Book 25 of Epicurus's *On Nature* (although the number of the book was for many years misconstrued) based on PHerc (Herculanean papyri) fragments 697, 1056, and 1191, recognizing that all three of these fragments came from the same book of *On Nature*. "From 1867, when he became a Privadozent at the University of Vienna until at least the end of the century, Gomperz worked continually on the Herculanean papyri." In the 1870s, he published most of the key extant passages of Book 25.[68]

In 1876, Gomperz wrote "New Fragments by Epicurus, in Particular on the Question of the Will," a major assessment of Book 25 of Epicurus's *On Nature*, including extensive passages in Greek from PHerc 1056 and 697. He concluded:

> In Epicurus's doctrine of the human will we receive, for the first time, an insight that is more exact and clearer than we could have wished for, while being fully sufficient to get rid of the errors and misunderstandings that hitherto have held the place of knowledge in the field. . . . From these fragments . . . results a series, it seems to me of irrefutable conclusions: Epicurus was not, as one had hitherto assumed, an *indeterminist*; he was an *opponent of fatalism*, not of *determinism*; he did not believe in the

> non-causality of human will; for him (as for Voltaire and others) those who were ethically [*sittlich*] free, were those whose actions were determined by their convictions; like the best thinkers of our times (the likes of a Mill, Grote, or Bain) he avoided the use of the word "*necessity*" in the representation of the process of the will, since it is a misleading expression that obscures the clear understanding of the true state of affairs; like these philosophers he held it to be inappropriate to signify the effectivity of *irresistible* causes and the effectivity of all causes in general with one and the same expression. Finally, the theory of the will receives a particular color through its connection with the theory of knowledge particular to him and Democritus. The problem of the will evidently comes to a head in the question: How can an act of the will be aroused by an *image* [*Abbild*, εἴδολον] that enters us from without, lacking the antecedents of any perception and mental image [*Vorstellung*] whatsoever, and simultaneously be determined by the totality of our convictions, i.e., (in his sense) by our whole personality [*Gessampersönlichkeit*]?[69]

In "The Remains of a Book by Epicurus," addressing Book 25, Gomperz reasserted his conclusion that Epicurus "was not an opponent of determinism—as one had hitherto believed almost without exception—but rather only of fatalism."[70]

Gomperz's argument here is complex and derives from the close conformity to Epicurus's analysis. In the first place, Gomperz argues that Epicurus's acceptance of causal determinism together with free volition and the rejection of fatalism conforms to the compatibilist arguments of thinkers like John Stuart Mill, emphasizing that causal determinism does not take away our ability to act, the efficacy of our actions, and our moral responsibility.[71] Thus, in Book 25 of *On Nature* in his rejection of fatalistic views, Epicurus, although clearly adhering to causal determinism in his underlying physics, insists that we act through "our own agency" of which we have a clear preconception and attached to this is moral responsibility.[72] This is in line with other known views of Epicurus, as reflected in the collection *The Vatican Sayings*, where he declares, consistently with the argument in Book 25: "The man who says that all events are necessitated has no ground for criticizing the man who says that not all events are necessitated. For according to him this is itself a necessitated event."[73] As Epicurus wrote in his *Letter to Menoeceus*: "Destiny, which some introduce as sovereign over all things, he [the wise man] laughs to scorn, affirming rather that some things happen of necessity, others by chance, others through our own agency. For he sees that necessity destroys responsibility and that chance or fortune is inconstant; whereas our own actions are free, and it is to them that praise and blame naturally attach." In Epicureanism, it is crucial that the realm of human agency is reflected in those events which "depend on us."[74]

The implications of Gomperz's analysis of Epicurus on free will and determinism, however, goes beyond pointing out that the argument in Book 25 of *On Nature* was consistent with compatibilism. He also highlighted the way in which a concept of human freedom evolved out of Epicurus's materialist philosophy of mind. In Book 25, Epicurus is clear that human beings over their lifetimes undergo the "development" (sometimes translated as "product" or "production," or "the way we develop") of "character," transcending their "original constitutions." The implication is that individuals in their development acquire new mental powers of discernment and volition that allow them to act in relation to the images (*eidola*), the product of atomic motion and sensory perceptions, no longer on the basis of their "original constitutions," but now as a "product" of the whole "developed" personality.[75] Such a view was perfectly consistent with the notion of a movement or reorganization of the soul atoms affecting the mind. It is precisely such issues that lie at the center of the contemporary debate on freedom and determinism in Epicurus's philosophy.

A central part of Epicurus's argument in Book 25 of *On Nature* was the criticism of those who insist on absolute necessity (fatalism), which did not allow for human freedom or moral responsibility. Such views always ran into contradictions, he argued, since they could not help but refer to undetermined human actions as part of their own argument, or else both their ideas and those of their opponents were determined, and there was no moral responsibility. The word "necessity" was erroneously used to encompass human actions that were freely chosen and where choice was possible, thus negating the meaning of the word "necessity" itself.[76] It followed, as he had said in his *Letter to Menoeceus*, that some external and internal influences affecting individuals were necessary, some were contingent, and there remained free actions that broke the bonds of fate. For Epicurus, it is always important to recognize that in a world of necessity and chance, there is also a realm of free will and voluntary human agency.[77] Diogenes of Oenoanda in his great inscription provided an additional glimpse into this argument, writing:

> Once prophecy is eliminated, how can there be any other evidence for fate? For if someone uses Democritus's account, saying that because of their collisions with each other atoms have no free movement, and that as a result it appears that all motions are necessitated, we will reply to him: "Don't you know, whoever you are, that there is also a free movement in atoms, which Democritus failed to discover but Epicurus brought to the light, a swerving movement, as he demonstrates from evident facts? But the chief

point is this: if fate is believed in, that is the end of all censure and admonition, and even the wicked will not be open to blame.[78]

Gomperz's work on Book 25 was the definitive edition for sixty-seven years but has been supplanted in the last half-century by further reconstructions and translations.[79] The contemporary raging debate in classical scholarship on the meaning of freedom and determinism in Epicurus is a product not simply of Epicurus's Book 25 discussion, but also of Lucretius's treatment of the swerve in Book 2 of *De rerum natura*.[80] A central issue is thus the role that the swerve plays in Epicurus's conception of freedom and moral responsibility in the context of his overall materialism and causal determinism. The present debate is principally between those who see Epicurus as a "radical emergentist," and those who insist on characterizing him as a weak "reductionist." The emergentist view was pioneered by David Sedley, one of the principal translators of the fragments of Book 25 of *On Nature*, and the rival contemporary interpretation of Epicurus as a reductionist is associated most notably with Tim O'Keefe, author of *Epicurus on Freedom*.[81]

Sedley starts out in his 1983 article "Epicurus's Refutation of Determinism" by arguing, as Marx had almost a century and a half before, that Epicurus had radically transformed Atomism from the form advanced by Democritus with its "rigidly deterministic laws" through the introduction of the swerve that allowed for minimal indeterminate movements at "no fixed place or time." The swerve, as Lucretius emphasized, allowed for collision (repulsion) of atoms and somehow generated the "autonomy of animate beings—a power often identified with free will. . . . The swerve is a minimal degree of indeterminism, and indeterminism is the negation of determinism."[82] For Philodemus, it is the existence of "chance and free will" that itself points to the swerve.[83]

Yet it remains unclear in Epicurean writing exactly how such indeterminism establishes free will. In Sedley's view, the swerve is not a sufficient condition for a theory of autonomy, even if a necessary one within Epicurus's materialist philosophy.

Sedley approaches the issue by focusing on Book 25 of *On Nature* (PHerc. 697, 1056, and 1191), of which he is one of the leading decoders and translators since the days of Gomperz. Key to the analysis is that in these passages Epicurus provides a conception of psychological development, in which he refers to "developments," or "productions," in the human character, and thus a degree of self-determination, constituting a "refutation of determinism." This is to be understood not in the sense of a rejection of causal determinism but rather, as Gomperz pointed out, of fatalism, thus leaving room for human agency.[84] Epicurus wrote in Book 25: "That which we develop—characteristics of this or that kind—is at first absolutely up to us; and the things which of necessity flow in through our passages from that which surrounds us are at one stage up to us and dependent on beliefs of our own making." From this arises "the preconception of our responsibility." Those who say necessity determines everything are simply "changing a name," applying rigidly deterministic notions to "our own agency" of which "we have a preconception."[85]

According to Sedley, "Epicurus is arguing for our ability to shape our lives." Human beings, like other animate beings, start out with what Epicurus in Book 25 called an "original constitution," which, in the case of human beings, is the basis for development and self-determination, in response to our surroundings.[86] Determinism in the sense of fatalism, Epicurus argues, refutes itself because it cannot eliminate human agency from its own argument. As Lucretius said of the skeptic (and the idealist), he is an individual who "has stood with his own head where his feet belong."[87]

The main target of Epicurus's criticism of rigid determinism or fatalism was Democritean mechanism (accompanied by skepticism), most likely in the cruder, more entirely fatalistic form advanced by Epicurus's teacher, Nausiphanes.[88] Sedley stated:

> Epicurus' response to this is perhaps the least appreciated aspect of his thought. It was to reject reductionist Atomism. Almost uniquely among Greek philosophers he arrived at what is nowadays the unreflective assumption of almost anyone with a smattering of science, that there are truths at the microscopic level of elementary particles, and further very different truths at the phenomenal level; that the former must be capable of explaining the latter; but that neither level of description has a monopoly on truth. . . . The metaphysical status of phenomenal properties, states of mind, etc. is that of accidental properties of groups of atoms. That is, they cannot exist independently of the atoms. But the common assumption that they *are* just patterns of atomic motion does not follow from this, and is ruled out by Epicurus' epistemology. . . . Epicurus' primary motivation was . . . to rescue the atomistic tradition with which he had aligned himself from the internal rot of reductionism.[89]

Sedley argues that Epicurus saw the mind as operating on principles that could not be explained simply by the movements of atoms. Rather, he viewed the mind as taking an active role in the disposition of soul atoms transcending atomic movements. Here, he suggests that Epicurus had drawn on Anaxagoras's concept of Mind as an active power.[90] "What is envisaged" in Epicurus, Sedley writes, "has much in common with the modern notion of 'emergence.' "[91] And further: "In Epicurus' view matter in certain complex states can take on non-physical properties which in turn bring genuinely new behavioural laws into operation." Sedley's account here would, however, be more cogent if instead of "non-physical properties" he emphasized, as in the modern conception of emergence, *organizational properties* that do not actually transcend the physical realm. This can be seen in Lucretius's own use of the analogy of the alphabet to indicate how a common set of elements can be organized or assembled in different ways, leading to qualitatively different results that transcend the elements themselves.[92] It is through organization that differences in the realm of appearance arise. Thus, as "movements, order, positions, and configurations of their matter/are completely changed, the things also ought to be changed . . . and a new appearance of things reveals itself."[93]

In order to understand the full import of Book 25 of *On Nature*, it is necessary, in the view of all participants in the debate on freedom and determinism in Epicurus's philosophy, to draw on the treatment of the swerve in Book 2 of Lucretius's *De rerum natura*. Although the swerve is not mentioned in surviving fragments of Book 25, it is generally agreed that the proper interpretation of Epicurus's argument on freedom and determinism must account in some way for the role of the swerve. In Sedley's account, the swerve establishes the possibility that mere physical laws at the level of atomic movements are not sufficient to determine outcomes, leaving room for human volition. Thus, the swerve enlarges the realm of possibility. Sedley argues that volitions are implicitly non-physical causes, insofar as they are mental causes made possible by the modicum of indeterminism provided by the swerve.[94]

It is an explicit part of Sedley's theory that swerves "are not involved in volition itself but are the element of indeterminacy in atomic motion that enables volition." He argues, along with others such as David Furley (who first raised the issue) and Suzanne Bobzien that "swerves are not involved in volition itself," as some have contended, "but are the element of indeterminacy in atomic motion which enables volition."[95] Cicero in his *On Fate* had presented an argument by Carneades (214–129 BCE, founder of the Third or New Academy) that because Epicurus had recognized that human volition was autonomous from mere atomic movements the introduction of the swerve to explain human volition offered nothing substantial to the argument and was superfluous.[96] The swerve thus points to the possibility of free will, but the heavy lifting lies in Epicurus's concept of the mind as an autonomous, emergent basis of the freedom to act on one's own volition.

In 1988, Sedley extended his argument on Epicurus's concept of determinism and freedom into one of radical emergentism. Here he went so far as to question the almost universal notion that Epicurus was "some sort of materialist" (confusing this with reductionism) in the sense that all states were physical states. Hence, emergence was seen as a departure from physicalism, constituting a theory of "emergent vitalism," in which something "vitalistic" and non-physical was added, which could not be accounted for in physical terms.[97]

In Sedley's view, this non-physical, vitalistic element, accounting for the mind, was, then, for Epicurus, responsible for a downward causality, opposed to both materialist and reductionist explanations. This vitalistic view, however, has no discernible basis in Epicurus's philosophy. Moreover, it conflicts with modern materialist and scientific notions of emergence, which sees it not as the result of some inexplicable vitalistic force, but rather based on the role of organization.[98] Ironically, the significance of organization in differentiating emergent levels has often been seen, in the work of scientists and materialists developing the concept in the early twentieth century, as having its origins in Epicurus and Lucretius.[99]

Nevertheless, in his radical emergentist extension of his original argument, Sedley moved in the direction of an interpretation of Epicurus as an indeterminist and anti-materialist, pushing his analysis in a vitalistic, if not idealist, direction. This served to weaken his analysis in the eyes of many scholars engaged with Epicurean philosophy.

The diametrical opposite of Sedley's position has been advanced by O'Keefe. His central proposition is that Epicurus is a "reductionist" in the sense that all properties are determined from the "bottom up" and that "macroscopic bodies are not 'irreducibly different'" from microscopic bodies. "Epicurus," he states, "believes that freedom and determinism are incompatible." All phenomenal forms can be reduced to the motions of atoms and their spatial relations.[100] O'Keefe does not deny "emergent properties" in Epicurus's conception of things, or that these arise out of the mechanical organization of the atoms (the example of a spark plug and a car is used).[101] He thus gives this a restrictive frame and suggests, since he divorces emergence from any notion of integrative levels and perceives it in merely mechanical terms, that it is consistent with seeing Epicurus as a reductionist.[102]

In this way, Epicurus is said to adhere to emergence only in the very weak and mechanical sense in which this is consistent with reductionism. O'Keefe goes so far as to say: "Somebody can hold that the mind is real and that it has powers and properties that none of its constituent atoms do, while identifying the mind with a bodily organ that is nothing more than an atomic aggregate and mental events with bodily events that are explained from the 'bottom up' in terms of the motions of the atoms that compose the mind. In fact, I think that this *is* the Epicurean view."[103]

Yet, *emergentist materialism*, as distinct from Sedley's emergentist vitalism. does not deny the physicalist basis of reality.

Rather it postulates that integrative levels—from atoms all the way to mind—result from the *organization* of that physical basis, such that new emergent powers arise that are irreducible to the levels below them.[104] It is the irreducibility of the powers of the mind to mere matter independent of its organization, not the material dependence of the former on the latter, that constitutes the core of an emergentist materialism, with its opposition to reductionism.[105] And it is to this that Epicurus's analysis, as even O'Keefe is forced to concede in part, is ultimately directed.

Like Gomperz in the nineteenth century, O'Keefe insists that Epicurus is both a causal determinist and an "anti-fatalist." However, Epicurus's causal determinism, in O'Keefe's view, is inherently in conflict with any notion of free will—a view he associates with Lucretius.[106] Hence any compatibilism of free will and determinism in Epicurus is ruled out of court. Epicurus's theory, since it is materialist, which O'Keefe associates with reductionism, is assumed to be a form of incompatibilism: free will and determinism can never be reconciled.[107] Although the phenomenon of emergence, he argues, plays a weak role in Epicurus's theory, the mind has no new powers that are not entirely reducible to atomic motion. Much of O'Keefe's position involves an extended argument aimed at rejecting the notion, clearly advanced in Book 25 of *On Nature*, that the development (production) of the character beyond the original constitution endows the human mind with emergent powers. For O'Keefe it is wrong to place too much emphasis, as Sedley does, on the notion that the self acquires a degree of "causal independence from the atoms," since this would contradict Epicurus's purported reductionism.[108] O'Keefe has a stronger case when he criticizes Sedley for Epicurus's philosophy of mind as pointing to non-physical, non-reductive powers in line with an emergent vitalism.[109] Here the problem is vitalism itself, which always consists in adding some undefined vital power/entity to the material realm, rather than recognizing, as Epicurus clearly did, that the physical realm plus processes of organization create our world.[110] Yet, with all of this, O'Keefe oddly sticks with his interpretation of Epicurus as a reductionist.

Adopting in the end a view that is the opposite of Sedley, O'Keefe counters the former's notion of Epicurus as an advocate of "emergentist vitalism," by providing a view characterizing Epicurus's philosophy instead as a "reductive materialism." Epicurus is said to have believed that "causal determinism . . . threatens our ability to use our reason and to shape our character and to control our actions," and thus introduced the swerve and indeterminism (as well as rejecting the principle of bivalence and fatalism about the future).[111]

In truth, Epicurus's arguments with respect to freedom and determinism are all aimed at showing that they are not absolutely opposed, and that in the end it is in many ways "up to us."[112] Moreover, the Epicurean argument is not a reductionist but an emergentist one. Hence, Lucretius argues that it is the reality of organization of their elements that explains how "the same things, a little changed among themselves, create firs and fires."[113] Qualitative transformations resulting from organizational changes in the combination of elements define the material world beyond the mere motions of atoms.

Closely related to this debate on reductionism versus antireductionism in Epicurus is the frequent assumption that all individual acts of human volition are accompanied by a swerve, thus consigning all such volition to atomic motions in a kind of one-to-one correspondence, even if this entails an oblique motion or declination, that is, a minimal swerve. This view, held by such leading Epicurean scholars as Bailey, Walter Englert, and Elizabeth Asmis, is traced to Lucretius's discussion of the swerve and free will.[114] Lucretius, in explaining the relation of the swerve to mind or volition, referred to two examples: the racehorse at the starting gate whose momentary apparent hesitation before bursting forth suggests an act of will, and the individual who is able to parry a blow and recover stability through an act of volition.[115] In each case it is assumed that Lucretius is saying that a swerve is directly involved in the action that follows.

However, such a one-to-one-correspondence between the swerve and free volition is never explicitly stated by Lucretius, and the whole premise of such a correspondence was challenged by David J. Furley in his 1967 *Two Studies in the Greek Atomists*. In Furley's words, "The swerve, then, plays a purely negative role in Epicurean psychology. It saves *voluntas* from necessity, as Lucretius says it does, but it does not feature in every act of *voluntas*. . . . The peculiar vulnerability of Epicurean freedom—that it seemed to serve random actions rather than deliberate purposive ones—is a myth."[116] For Furley, and other noted scholars of Epicureanism such as Sedley, Julia Annas, and Suzanne Bobzien—with O'Keefe, despite his emphasis on Epicurus's reductionism, also concurring with this view—the import of Lucretius's discussion of the swerve was to establish an argument for the *possibility of human autonomy*, and not, as in the traditionalist interpretation, depicting an absolute identity between the swerve and human volition.[117] As Epicurus wrote in his *Letter to Menoeceus*, "What occurs by our own agency is autonomous" from necessity and chance.[118]

O'Keefe emphasizes that "no standard interpretation" of "Epicurus's position on freedom and the role of the swerve within it . . . exists. The texts on this topic are suggestive and philosophically rich enough to fuel a huge range of views, but sketchy and obscure enough that no consensus has emerged."[119] Nevertheless, it is possible at this point to suggest a synthesis based on the significant areas of overlap, while avoiding those differences that, as Epicurus noted in *On Nature*, are due to mere words that involve "changing a name," that is, using a term in such a way that it embraces its opposite.[120] This synthesis involves recognizing that Epicurus was a non-reductive materialist, who relied on emergentist arguments and notions of human development (or the production of the human character) in which individuals in a social context evolved beyond their original constitutions into whole personalities with moral responsibility, through the action of the mind and its effect on the organization of images/soul atoms. Bobzien calls Epicurus's view here "the whole-person model of agency," while Gomperz in the 1870s referred to it as a view in which eidola/images entering us from without coalesce with our mental faculties and are finally "determined by the totality of our convictions," that is, in Epicurus's sense, "by our whole personality."[121]

What is abundantly clear is that, in Epicurus's view, human beings are faced with necessity and chance, but there also remains a sense in which our relations to the world can be said to be "up to us" and occur *through us*. The swerve establishes the *possibility* of human autonomy. Epicurus's rejection of the logical principle of bivalence with respect to the future—plus his preference for a multivalent logic that included a level of indeterminacy or randomness—meant that the future was contingent and open.[122]

Such an overall synthesis requires avoiding any confusion resulting from the logical but non-dialectical identification of materialism and causal determinism with reductionism. Likewise, it is necessary to avoid the identification of emergence with non-physicalism and vitalism.[123] It is significant that most elements of this synthesis in the understanding of Epicurus on freedom and determinism were already captured succinctly by Gomperz in the nineteenth century as a result of his intensive studies of Book 25 of *On Nature*.

In his 2021 book *Epicurus on Self*, Attila Németh resists characterizing Epicurus's philosophy as "emergentist," and classifies it instead as simply a form of "non-reductive physicalism."[124] Such a guarded stance appears to be due to a tendency to identify emergence with a defunct vitalism, along with a lack of familiarity with emergentist materialism and its fundamental role in modern science, together with the long tradition within the history of science of viewing Epicurus's philosophy as fundamental in these terms.

The great biologist and historian of science and theorist of integrative levels Joseph Needham wrote in *Time: The Refreshing River* in 1943, with respect to emergence:

> We cannot consider nature otherwise than as a series of levels of organization, a series of dialectical syntheses. From the ultimate particle to atom, from atom to molecule, from molecule to colloidal aggregate, from aggregate to living cell, from cell to organ, from organ to body, from animal body to social association, the series of organisational levels is complete. Nothing but energy (as we now call matter and motion) and levels of organization (or the stabilised dialectical syntheses) at different levels have been required for the building of our world.[125]

Emergence in this sense, constituting levels of organization of matter and motion, is crucial to the entire modern materialist and dialectical view of the world. Moreover, the origin of this emergentist materialist perspective has often been traced to Epicurus.[126]As A. A. Long has written, for Epicurus, "Life and mind are not basic to the world, but [are] emergent properties of particular types of atomic conglomerates."[127]

The swerve manifested Epicurus's breaking the bonds of fate, and his insistence that "we always hold fast to what is possible."[128] It allowed for a minimal level of indeterminism or randomness that symbolized the free volition of human beings (and to a lesser extent that of non-human animals). It thus established the basis for Epicurus's ethics, which was to constitute the culmination of his entire system.

The Ethics of Freedom and Ataraxia

Epicurus's ethics were a dialectical product of both his materialist philosophy and the social context of his time, governed by the collapse of the Greek polis, and the wider dangers and uncertainties of the Hellenistic Age. Epicureanism thus sought to promote a conception of innate human freedom, the overcoming of fear, and a spirit of ataraxia, or calmness. This philosophy was the basis of the community in the Garden and for the enormous spread and influence of Epicureanism in plebeian circles in the Hellenistic and Roman worlds that followed. Although Epicurus's great ethical treatise *Human Life* is lost, his main ethical views are preserved in abbreviated form in his *Letter to Menoeceus*, the *Principal Doctrines*, and the *Vatican Sayings*.

Epicurus's ethics begin by countering the fear of death, the terror of Hades and everlasting punishment, and of the exercise of heavenly power over humanity, along with fears of pain and insecurity.[129] In this regard, the key proposition was the corporeal existence of human beings, that is, the materiality of both body and soul. There is no existence apart from the material senses, and when the sense organs depart so does the soul. "The mortality of life [becomes] enjoyable," Epicurus wrote, by removing the desire of immortality. "Death . . . is nothing to us, seeing that, when we are, death is not come, and, when death is come, we are not. It is nothing, then, either to the living or the dead."[130] Material existence is thus characterized by *mors immortalis*, death the immortal.[131]

For Epicurus, time is the "accident of accidents." It marks the coming into being and the passing of the accidental, including "accidents of bodies."[132] It is in this world of time, of impermanence, of contingency, and change that the individual necessarily lives, and in which human agency becomes possible. As Lucretius wrote, conveying Epicurus's views:

> Time . . . does not exist independently, but from things themselves
> comes a sense of what has happened in ages past, then what
> thing looms before us, and then further what will follow.
> No one, it must be confessed, senses time through itself,
> separated off from the motion and the quiet immobility of things.[133]

All of the things that were done, occurring in what we call history, were accidents, with time as the accident of accidents. Such contingency leaves room for human volition. Human actions are not simply fated to occur in a particular way. With regard to human life, "we must remember," Epicurus wrote in his *Letter to Menoeceus*, "that the future is neither wholly ours nor wholly not ours, so that neither must we count upon it as quite certain to come nor despair of it as quite certain not to come." What is left to us is "to live well and to die well."[134]

The wise person therefore sees in corporeal existence no reason for fatalistic fears either in the present or in a false afterlife. Instead, one must focus on one's own agency through the pursuit of pleasure and the avoidance of pain, clear reasoning, and a secure and calm existence, or ataraxia. This was best achieved, Epicurus argued, through the establishment of a community of friends and a climate of justice based on reciprocity and the social compact.

Epicurean ethics is often described as hedonistic because of the emphasis that it places on the avoidance of pain, and the pursuit of pleasure. However, it was removed from hedonism as usually conceived, since it saw the unrestrained pursuit of desires as antithetical to free development of the individual and to ataraxia. Emphasis was placed rather on individual self-development and self-awareness, within a context of human community.[135]

"Pleasure," Epicurus wrote, "is . . . the starting-point of every choice and of every aversion, and to it we come back, inasmuch as we make feeling the rule by which we judge every good thing." Nevertheless,

> when we say . . . that pleasure is the end and aim we do not mean . . . the pleasures of sensuality, as we are understood to do by some through ignorance, prejudice, or willful misrepresentation. By pleasure we mean the absence of pain in the body and trouble in the soul. It is not an unbroken succession of drinking-bouts and of revelry, not sexual love, not the enjoyment . . . of a luxurious table . . . it is sober reasoning, searching out the grounds of every choice and avoidance, and banishing those beliefs through which the greatest tumults take possession of the soul.[136]

Sexual love is empty, if limited to itself: "If you take away the chance to see and talk and spend time with [the beloved], then the passion of sexual love is dissolved."[137]

Rebelling against the avariciousness displayed in Hellenistic society, Epicurus taught that physical needs were limited and generally easy to satisfy, while the pursuit of wealth as the aim of life was self-defeating. The "goal of nature" thus entailed limiting material desires, practicing self-sufficiency, and forswearing the pursuit of unlimited wealth. "Poverty," according to the Epicurean maxims preserved in the collection known as *The Vatican Sayings*, "if measured by the goal of nature, is great wealth; and wealth, if limits are not set for it, is great poverty."

Indeed, "Nothing is enough for someone for whom enough is little." Nor can "a free life . . . acquire great wealth, because the task is not easy without slavery to the mob or to those in power." Wealth if by chance acquired should be shared.[138] As he declared in his *Principal Doctrines*, "Natural wealth is both limited and easy to obtain. But wealth [as defined by] groundless opinions extend without limits."[139]

Richard Seaford explains that the critique of wealth acquisition in ancient Greece was a revulsion against the greed and the accumulation of monetary wealth that had arisen with the introduction of the coinage economy beginning in the seventh century BCE. It had reached new stages of corruption and avariciousness at the time that Demetrius the Besieger occupied Athens.[140]

Epicurus's ethical doctrine, which was intended as a guide to living in an era of social collapse, emphasized individual security, which was to be obtained through friendship and a quiet life. In Epicurus's day, politicians and orators often had to flee for their lives with the advent of a new regime. Demosthenes committed suicide to avoid capture and torture by the Macedonians under Antipater's rule following Athens's defeat in the Lamian War. Direct engagement in political life and the pursuit of fame often decreased rather than increased one's security.[141] The greatest source of security and ataraxia was friendship, which for Epicurus was itself a supreme value. "Every friendship," he wrote, "is worth choosing for its own sake, though it takes its origin from the benefits [it confers on us]."[142] In the *Vatican Sayings* we find: "Friendship goes dancing around the world announcing to all of us that we must wake up to blessedness."[143] Farrington noted that almost the entirety of Epicurus's notion of friendship was already present in Aristotle except for one thing: "the priority given by Epicurus to friendship in the practical activity of his life," where it became a basis for praxis.[144]

Epicurus wrote two books on justice. Eight of the last ten of Epicurus's *Principal Doctrines* (nearly a quarter of the total) were devoted to the issue of justice. Epicurus started out by declaring that "the justice of nature is a pledge of reciprocal usefulness [that is,] neither to harm one another nor be harmed."[145] Justice was established practically by a "social compact" due to "mutual intercourse" and the principle of reciprocity, such that "justice is the same for all."[146] Epicurus here famously introduced the notion of the social contract. Significantly, justice, as represented by the law, resulting from mutual association, is subject to change in response to changing historical circumstances. Thus, "If objective circumstances . . . change and the same things which had been just turn out to be no longer useful, then those things were just as long as they were useful for the mutual associations of fellow citizens; but later, when they were not useful, they were no longer just." Justice, then, is related to the social compact and historical circumstances.[147] The system of laws, if it expresses natural justice, arises historically out of reciprocal agreements.[148]

Epicurus's materialist anthropology was conveyed by Lucretius in *De rerum natura*. In his proto-evolutionary view all of life, including human beings, arose from the earth. Life evolved through a process of "normalizing selection," first enunciated by Empedocles, in which monstrous forms are unable to exist within the environment and perish.[149] Those species that were able to continue and perpetuate themselves through the "chain of the generations" had special organs that allowed them to adapt to the environment.[150]

Humanity evolved from a non-reasoning, feral species to one that acquired language through attaching names to things and agreeing to these by social convention (a nominalist-materialist view). Lightning first provided fire, and people learned how to make it themselves. (Thus, Epicurus specifically rejected the Greek myth that fire had been given to humanity by Prometheus, a Titan, and a rebel against the gods.) Technology gradually evolved from the age of stone to that of bronze, and then to iron. It was discovered in the process of human struggle that in friendship lay security, bringing about the original social contract. The rule of law arose at a later stage through mutual association, following social revolt and the death of kings.[151] However, the growth of material wealth and acquisition made people forget the social contract. In addition, there arose the idea that the pursuit of wealth was the path to pleasure and a full life. Such folly, Lucretius wrote, does not "work better now or in the future than it did in the past."[152]

Epicurus's materialism did not kill the gods. They played an important part in his philosophy. He encouraged piety toward the traditional anthropomorphic gods of Greek civilization, though shorn of their irrational characteristics and the notion of their constant interference in human life. Rather, the gods were conceived as dwelling in the *intermundia*, the spaces between the worlds, and as having no material relation to humanity and the earth. The gods then were models of perfection, of calm/ataraxia, for human beings.[153] As Marx was to say, they had an earthly existence only in the sense that Epicurus's gods were "the plastic gods of Greek art," which embodied perfection. For Epicurus, they came as preconceptions via dreams.

But though emphasizing the need for piety with respect to the traditional Greek gods, Epicurus was the leading ancient critic of both creationism and the state religion of the astral gods, both having their fullest philosophical development in Greek antiquity under Plato. He was thus the foremost opponent of all religious views that broke with materialism and with the centrality of humanity and the earth. Notions of teleology, providence, and the immortality of the soul were all rejected in Epicurean philosophy. As a result, Epicureanism was to be anathema to the Platonist Plutarch in the second century CE and to all the Christian Church Fathers, and was considered to be the leading current of atheism and a direct threat to Christianity as late as the time of St. Augustine in the fourth century CE.

In Xenophon's *Memorabilia*, Socrates was presented as an early exponent of the intelligent design defense of creationism.[154] As Sedley remarks, "Xenophon's Socrates" was "a fundamentally anti-scientific creationist," who argued that human beings were uniquely favored by the gods, and exhibited the creator's design in their very being.[155] In this view craftsmanship, as displayed, for example, in sculpture, provided an analogy for the supreme craftsmanship of a divine creator, who could not only produce forms of things but also give them life. Human beings, for Socrates, were "products of design and not of chance" and demonstrated in their basic attributes the "intelligence" of the divine craftsman. The human eye was singled out as an example of this. As Socrates put it in the dialogue:

> Then don't you think that it was for their use that he who originally created men provided them with the various means of perception, such as the eyes to see what is visible and ears to hear what is audible? . . . For example, because our eyes are delicate, they have been shuttered with eyelids which open when we have occasion to use them, and close in sleep; and to protect them from injury by the wind, eyelashes have made to grow as a screen; and our foreheads have been fringed with eyebrows to prevent damage even from the sweat of the head.[156]

Such design, Socrates argued, could also be shown in other ways: in the granting of human beings, as distinguished from other animals, both intelligence (derived from cosmic intelligence) and non-seasonal sex, that is, without a specific mating season. A whole range of other species were created by a divine "benevolent craftsman" specifically to serve human needs.[157]

In building on Socrates's thought, Plato did not directly advance the argument from design in the fashion of Xenophon's Socrates. He did, however, promote creationist ideas and a creationist physics. For the ancient Greek philosophers, matter was always the precondition for everything else. Hence, Plato's Demiurge or divine craftsman in *Timaeus* did not create the world *ex nihilo* (out of nothing). Rather, he relied on previously existing matter to generate order out of Chaos. The Demiurge designed the world on the model of "the perfect intelligible Living Creature." In this way Plato's Demiurge constituted the greatest of all causes and generated a world that was the finest of all possible worlds. In *The Laws*, Plato urged that those who were impious and attributed the world's coming into being to necessity and chance rather than design be treated as criminals and imprisoned or even executed.[158]

Gomperz was the first to discern the critique of Plato's *Timaeus* as fundamental to Epicurus's thought, a view that is now generally recognized.[159] In attempting to provide a materialist explanation of the emergence of the world/cosmos in all of its complexity, Epicurus, countering Plato's *Timaeus*, as Sedley points out, adopted a viewpoint that not only reduced the improbability of the cosmos developing in its present form, but made the actual causal development of such a cosmos a certainty. This was what Epicureans called "the power of infinity" associated with the assumptions of (1) infinite space, time, and matter; (2) an infinite number of worlds; (3) a mathematically smallest magnitude, connected in precise ways with other minimum magnitudes as inseparable "parts" of atoms (literally uncuttables); (4) a resulting finite number of possible atomic types/shapes derived from the arrangement of these smallest magnitudes; (5) a largest possible size to a world; and (6) the principle of *isonomia*, or distributive equality between like things. As a result of these mathematical assumptions (no doubt influenced by Polyaenus), together with the basic material postulates, Sedley argues, Epicurus was able to argue that anything possible was bound to happen in the universe at large, and anything necessary would happen in any given world.[160] Epicurus's swerve, moreover, went against a strict determinism and guaranteed that no world would be exactly like another. In short, a sophisticated argument of cosmic probability was used to bolster the case for a material explanation of the existing world. The development of the world/cosmos could be explained, according to this argument, entirely in materialist terms without the need for the intervention of a Demiurge.

Epicurus's biggest conflict with Plato, however, had to do with the latter's promotion of a new astral religion as the state religion, which was to gain influence in Hellenistic times as the dominant religious view. With the shattering of the Greek polis, the result of the rise of Macedonian rule and the wars of the Diadochi, the traditional political life of the polis had not only declined but also its religious life, in which the gods had been seen as connected to cities, each polis being associated with particular gods, as in the case of Athena and Athens.

Plato, who finished his dialogue *Timaeus* only a few years before the Social War between Athens and its revolting Ionian allies, and wrote *The Laws*, his last work, in the aftermath of that war, lived long enough to see the further decline of the Athenian polis. He witnessed the growing power of Phillip II's Macedonia and the expansion of the Persian Empire, as well as the weakening of the Greek states. His later works, therefore, in some ways prefigured Hellenistic times. Both *Timaeus* and *The*

Laws recognized two types of religion: the old traditional religion of the anthropomorphic gods, to which a kind of sufferance was given, since such forms of worship still had influence on the masses, and an astral religion (with Babylonian roots) that saw the worship of the heavenly bodies such as the sun, moon, stars, and meteors as divine powers. Here natural science in the form of astronomy backed by geometry and religion were seen as two sides of a single reality. The astral religion was to assume increasing dominance among the educated, often promoted as a state religion in late antiquity, sometimes taking a hybrid form, as in Plato's notion of Apollo-Helios. In the astral religion, the stars were seen as the embodiment of the soul and the source of human learning, particularly mathematics. Greek religion thus shifted from anthropomorphic gods in human form to cosmic sky gods.[161] In *The Laws* the Nocturnal Council enforced the harsh laws against impiety.[162] The early, exoteric writings of Aristotle supported Plato's notion of transcendent astral gods.

It was this notion of cosmic gods, conceived in terms of the regular cyclical movements of the sun, stars, and planets, seen as representing both divine intelligence and a fatalistic notion of inexorable destiny, presented in mathematical form, that engendered Epicurus's revolt. His *Principal Doctrines* refer numerous times to "the fear of the phenomena of the heavens," alongside mechanistic determinism as forms of fatalism that go against the notion of autonomous human agency.[163] His *Letter to Pythocles*, often seen as an epistle on meteorology, consisted of an emphasis on the limits of sense perception with respect to the cosmos and thus the existence of multiple possible causes of what was observed at a great distance.[164] Epicurus's goal at every point was to bring the heavens down to earth, in order to make a case for human agency as opposed to cosmic determinism. His most serious error in his *Letter to Pythocles*, and indeed, in all of his thought, was his contention that the sun was about the size it appeared to be. This view was motivated less by a serious attempt to address meteorology on Epicurus's part—indeed, he complained of the "slavish artifices of the astrologers"—than by the rejection of any notion of overwhelming power and divine intelligence in the cosmos, leaving room for humanity finding the source of freedom within itself.[165]

As Lucretius wrote of Epicurus in *De rerum natura*:

> It used to be that human life, polluted, was lying
> in the dirt before our eyes, crushed by the weight of religion,
> which stretched out its head on display from the regions of
> heaven,
> threatening mortals from above with its horrible-looking face.
> It was a Greek man who first dared to raise his mortal eyes
> against religion, and who first fought back against it.
> Neither the stories about the gods, nor thunderbolts, nor the sky
> with its threatening rumbles held him back, but provoked
> all the more the fierce sharpness of his mind, so that he desired
> to be the first to shatter the imprisoning bolts of the gates
> of nature.[166]

Plato had responded to Athens ruled by the demos with attempts to provide a philosophical and political basis for the reestablishment of aristocratic rule. This was symbolized most fully by his "noble lie" in *The Republic*, in which citizens were to be presented with the false parable of the metals, according to which, in generating human beings God had mixed gold in with some people (meant to be rulers), silver in others (the helpers or guardians), and iron and brass in still others (farmers and artisans), creating innate superiority and inferiority and generating social classes: rulers, guardians, and the ruled. It was in opposition to this view, so at odds with Epicurus's egalitarianism, Farrington states, that Epicurus was known to refer critically to Plato ironically as "the golden man," symbolizing his regressive, aristocratic views.[167]

In contrast to Plato's well-known concept of justice in *The Republic*, stemming from his aristocratic-class conception, in which the polis is considered an organic entity with each class playing its designated functional role (gold, silver, or iron and brass), Epicurus's concept of justice is based on reciprocity and the social compact: "There was never an absolute justice, but only an agreement made in reciprocal intercourse. . . . Justice is the same for all."[168]

Epicureanism is sometimes regarded as divorced from political praxis, representing a withdrawal from public life. This, however, has to be put in the context of the Hellenistic Age and the wars of the Diadochi. The Greek polis was no longer ruled by its citizens but by a foreign master, predominantly placed under Macedonian rule. In the collapse of the Greek order, irrationalism and insecurity prevailed and people sought a sense of freedom not in the state but in their inner selves. The fight was against fatalism, in which both mechanism and cosmic determinism were the enemies. Skepticism too was rife in this context and had to be resisted if an approach based on reason, materialism, and freedom was to be promoted. "At the dawn of the third century [BCE]. . . . [Epicurus's] age demanded of philosophy that it should provide a guide for the individual in the conduct of life at a period of social collapse."[169] The Epicurean community thus became a form of resistance, not simply in Epicurus's Garden, but extending over the Hellenistic and Roman realms, well into the second and even, to a diminishing degree, in the third and fourth centuries CE, thus persisting over the course of seven centuries.

Epicurus saw the end of Athenian democracy and the rise of the universal realm of kings in the Hellenistic Age. His work *On Kingship* undoubtedly dealt with the ethical basis of kingship and the avoidance of tyranny in the time in which he lived. Although direct knowledge of Epicurus's treatise is unknown, Philodemus's *The Good King According to Homer* retrieved from the Herculaneum papyri, reflected the Epicurean approach and may have used Epicurus's *On Kingship* as a basis. It is thought by some classicists that the source of Philodemus's critical references to Demetrius the Besieger (Poliorcetes) for his vanity—while ruling Athens, Demetrius had himself declared a god—may have come from Epicurus. Philodemus's *The Good King According to Homer* was an explicit attempt to cultivate a notion of kingship divorced from tyranny and civil war of the kind that prevailed under the Diadochi.[170] Lucretius's *De rerum natura* is explicit about the tyranny of kings and the folly of their perpetual pursuit of war.[171]

Demetrius the Poliorcetes's son, Antigonus Gonatas, was interested in surrounding himself with philosophers, particularly Stoics. We know from a letter from Epicurus to his brother Aristobulus, referred to by Diogenes Laertius, that Zeno of Citium sent two Stoic philosophers to reside at the court of Antigonus in Macedonia. However, Epicurus, to all appearances, kept his distance from the Antigonids.[172]

In the second century CE the quack prophet Alexander of Abonoteichus, a Paphlagonian mystic, claimed that the god Asclepius had been reborn as a serpent named Glycon and Alexander had built a temple from which issued oracles. He had a human head mask complete with a large tame serpent. His goal was to dominate and swindle a population caught up in superstition. As Lucian explained, Alexander's main opposition came from Epicureans and Christians, and it was the former that he feared most, who had exposed him before his audience. Alexander responded by staging a burning of books, committing Epicurus's *Principal Doctrines* to the flames. He declared through an oracle that Epicurus was in Hades "and with filthy slime he sits with leaden shackles on his ankles." Lucian wrote: "It was war to the death against Epicurus. And no wonder—what man had a better right to be the bitter enemy of a quack who loved humbug and loathed truth than Epicurus, the one who delved into the nature of things, the only one who discovered the truth of it all?"[173]

Indeed, *the revolt of nature* represented by Epicurus in the early Hellenistic Age took the form of an uncompromising materialism that insisted on the inner freedom of humanity in a time of social dissolution, constituting a message of defiance, resistance, and hope. In Farrington's words:

> The philosophical distrust of the sense[s], the philosophical teaching that feelings are evil in themselves, are part of the political theory that the just society can only exist if the few monopolize power and defend this monopoly by sponsoring or tolerating the belief in capricious and angry gods, whose will is expressed in the natural calamities in this life, and extends beyond the grave to rob even death of its peace. Epicurus attacked every aspect of this complex of ideas by a coherent philosophy expressed in a propaganda which brought it within the reach and the comprehension of the average man. This was to renew the foundations of society.[174]

CHAPTER THREE

Marx and Epicurus

Direct knowledge of Epicureanism disappeared in Western Europe during the medieval era. It was known only through fragments, usually critical, contained in the works of other writers. It was only in the Renaissance that key manuscripts of Epicurus—the three letters to Herodotus, Menoeceus, and Pythocles, and *The Principal Doctrines*, which were included in Book 10 of Diogenes Laertius's *Lives of Eminent Philosophers*, and Lucretius's *De rerum natura* (*On the Nature of Things*)—were rediscovered within Western philosophy.

The disappearance of Epicurean manuscripts during the medieval era was not surprising. Except for books recovered from the charred papyri of Herculaneum (ironically almost all Epicurean), which were first discovered in the late eighteenth century, and manuscripts retrieved in the late nineteenth and early twentieth century from a rubbish dump near the ancient Egyptian city of Oxyrhynchus, there are few surviving papyri from the ancient Greek and Roman worlds. Nearly all works that have reached us are copies of copies. Of Aeschylus's eighty to ninety plays and Sophocles's hundred and twenty, only seven of each survived. Epicurus's three hundred books (other than fragments from *On Nature*) were all lost, along with those of his closest followers, such as Metrodorus, Hermarchus, Themista, Leontion, and Colotes.

The destruction of the papyri can be mainly attributed to climate and pests, and thus the result of the workings of time. But some of the destruction was due to human action or inaction. The libraries of ancient Athens, and that of Alexandria, the greatest of the ancient world, along with the twenty-eight public libraries of ancient Rome, all vanished without a trace. On occasion, ancient manuscripts were deliberately destroyed, among them Epicurean ones, since they were seen as representing a dangerous atheistic threat. Of those ancient Greek and Roman manuscripts that did survive as copies, many were preserved in the East, particularly in Constantinople, and in the Islamic world. However, some ancient texts, mostly Latin, were copied and preserved by monks in medieval monasteries in the West.[1]

The Rediscovery of Epicurus and Lucretius in the Renaissance and Enlightenment

Lucretius's *De rerum natura* was copied by a monk in a scriptorium sometime in the ninth century, at a time when the ancient papyrus manuscript could still be read. That copy somehow survived for another five hundred years until it was found by the Renaissance humanist Gian Francesco Poggio Bracciolini in 1417, though it was not made publicly available for another twenty years.[2] Meanwhile, in 1421–23, Giovanni Aurispa made his famous trip to Constantinople, with the backing of the Pope and the support of the Byzantine Emperor, returning with 238 Greek classical works previously lost to Western Europe. In addition to all of the extant Plato, all of Plotinus, plays by Aeschylus and Sophocles, poems of Pindar, and volumes of Xenophon, this also included Diogenes Laertius's complete *Lives of the Eminent Philosophers*, containing Epicurus's three epistles and the *Principal Doctrines*—none of which were included in previous publications from Diogenes available in the West. Diogenes and Lucretius were first printed at about the same time in Latin in 1472 and 1473, respectively.[3]

It would be difficult to exaggerate the effect that the Renaissance recovery of major Epicurean works was to have on the European Enlightenment of the seventeenth and eighteenth centuries, and even into the nineteenth century. In all three areas of epistemology, physics, and ethics, Epicureanism was to have an enormous impact on the formation of modernity. In the seventeenth-century scientific revolution, such major figures as Giordano Bruno, Galileo Galilei, Francis Bacon, Pierre Gassendi, Thomas Hobbes, Walter Charleton, Robert Boyle, Isaac Newton, and John Locke, to name only some of the most prominent figures, were heavily influenced by Democritean and especially Epicurean epistemology and atomism. In seventeenth-century science, Epicureanism came to replace views derived from Aristotelian scholasticism.[4]

Bruno, the Italian materialist who helped disseminate Copernicus's teaching on the heliocentric universe, was burned at the stake by the Catholic Church in 1600, not so much because of his adoption of Copernicus's views as his (partial) adherence to Epicurean philosophy with its anti-theological implications.[5] Likewise, the Church's persecution of Galileo, in which he was forced to recant his views, had less to do with his promotion of a heliocentric cosmology than his adoption of Epicurean Atomism in his *Assayer* (1623), which was viewed by the Church as threatening the very foundations of Christianity.[6]

The influence of Democritus and Epicurus on Bacon was profound and can be found in much of his philosophical work, in which he went so far at points as to defend Atomism, though often protecting himself by justifying this in religious terms. He stated in *De Augmentis Scientiarum* (1623) that "the natural philosophy of Democritus and others [Epicurus and Lucretius],

> who removed God and Mind from the structure of things, and attributed the form thereof to infinite essays and proofs of nature . . . and assigned the causes of particular things to the necessity of matter, without any intermixture of final causes, seems to me (so far as I can judge from the fragments and relics of their philosophy) to have been, as regards physical causes, much more solid and to have penetrated further into nature than that of Aristotle and Plato; for this single reason, that the former never wasted time on final causes, while the latter were ever inculcating them.[7]

In his essay "Of Atheism," Bacon quoted from Epicurus's *Letter to Menoeceus*, presenting as a "noble" sentiment the statement (later quoted in the foreword to Marx's dissertation): "Not the man who denies the gods worshipped by the multitude, but he who affirms of the gods what the multitude believes about them is truly impious."[8]

Bacon, as Benjamin Farrington pointed out, was strongly influenced by Lucretius's statement, which opened Book 6 of *De rerum natura*, on the transformation of the mode of production from food-gathering society to food-production society. This was related to the picture of the goddess Ceres sowing grain, which his father commissioned and had placed above the fireplace in the dining hall of his home, the significance of which could hardly have failed to impress itself upon Bacon's mind at an early age.[9]

In France, Gassendi, in his *De vita et moribus Epicuri libri Octo* (1647) and other works was, in Karl Marx's words, "the restorer of Epicurean materialism" in modern times, becoming in the process one of the leading figures, along with Hobbes and René Descartes, in the development of the mechanical philosophy.[10] Gassendi accepted the notion of the senses as the basis of knowledge, along with Epicurean atomism, though remaining committed, unlike Epicurus, to the notion of an immortal incorporeal soul. Gassendi's analysis was spread to England by Walter Charleton, the physician to Charles I, in his *Physiologica Epicuro-Gassendo-Charltoniana* (1654).[11]

Hobbes constructed his own materialist philosophy largely on the foundations of Epicurean epistemology and atomism. He took from Epicurus the concept of the social contract central to his *Leviathan*. Boyle developed the corpuscular philosophy out of the ideas of the ancient atomists, a view that was to be adopted by Newton. Locke, whose work was impacted by Gassendi, introduced the hypothesis that thought could be derived from a material basis, superadded to matter, rather than a pure immaterial entity.[12]

In the eighteenth century, David Hume devoted a section of his *Enquiry on Human Understanding* (1748) to an imaginary speech of defiance and rebellion by Epicurus standing in for Hume's own views.[13] Voltaire (the *nom de plume* of François-Marie Arouet) had six different editions of Lucretius's *De rerum nature* on his bookshelves. "Lucretius," he observed, "is admirable in his exordiums, in his descriptions, in his ethics, in everything he says against superstition." Lucretius, Peter Gay explained, inspired much of Enlightenment discourse, including Voltaire, with his description of the role of Epicurus in bringing light to humanity, related to the conquest of religion by science.[14]

As Jonathan Kemp wrote in *Diderot, Interpreter of Nature*, "The work of Epicurus dominates the history of early materialism."[15] This is particularly the case for the eighteenth-century radical French materialists, Julien Offray de la Mettrie, Paul-Henri Thiry, Baron d'Holbach, and Denis Diderot. La Mettrie is known for advancing a mechanistic materialism in which everything could be traced to matter and motion. Notable among his philosophical works was *The System of Epicurus* (1750).

Holbach's *System of Nature* (1770) was an explicitly Epicurean work. To see God in nature, according to Holbach, was an unnecessary duplication since nature could be seen as arising of itself. "Morals and politics," he wrote, "would be equally enabled to draw from *materialism* advantages" that "the dogma of spirituality can never supply."[16] Holbach's work "was condemned by the *parlement* of Paris in 1770" for "'reviving' and expanding the 'system of Lucretius.'"[17] Diderot, the editor of the *Encyclopédie*, traced materialism in philosophy back to the Atomism of Democritus and Epicurus, and argued against all teleological conceptions of the natural world, insisting that the natural world came into being in the form of particular combinations of atoms, which pass away, in ceaseless cycles. He gave to this a dialectical conception arguing in a Heraclitean (and Epicurean) way that "all nature is in a perpetual state of flux. . . . There is nothing clearly defined in nature. . . . Everything is bound up with everything else."[18]

The German Enlightenment also showed the influence of Epicureanism. At first, this was largely negative. Gottfried Wilhelm Leibniz's ambitious monadic philosophy saw the world as made up of windowless monads conceived of as unextended, immaterial substances that, like atoms, were indestructible, persisting in bodies and forming the basis of composites. This was intended to fulfill the same role as atoms, while ensuring a direct connection to God. Since they were windowless, individual monads could not causally affect one another but rather were all products of a pre-established harmony. Though philosophically intriguing, Leibniz's monadology was to prove ineffective in countering materialism and Atomism within science.[19]

Immanuel Kant, in contrast to Leibniz, was directly influenced by Epicureanism. In his *Universal Natural History and the Theory of the Heavens* (1755) Kant wrote:

> I will . . . not deny that the theory of Lucretius, or his predecessors, Epicurus, Leucippus and Democritus has much resemblance with mine. . . . Epicurus asserted a gravity or weight which forced . . . elementary particles to sink or fall; and this does not seem to differ much from Newton's Attraction, which I accept. He also gave them a certain deviation from the straight line in the falling movement, although he had absurd fancies regarding the causes and consequences of it. This deviation agrees to some degree with the alteration from the falling in a straight line, which we deduce from the repulsion of particles.[20]

In the *Critique of Pure Reason*, Kant saw Epicurus as the dialectical counterpart of Plato in epistemology. "Epicurus," he wrote, "can be called the foremost philosopher of sensibility, and Plato that of the intellectual."[21] In his *Logic*, Kant described the Epicureans as "*the best philosophers of nature* among Greek thinkers" and compared them to Bacon as "the greatest student of nature in modern times."[22]

In the great philosophical debates over religion in Germany at the time, Epicurus came under attack as an atheistic materialist. In 1754, Hermann Samuel Reimarus, a natural theologian and deist, published *The Principal Truths of Natural Religion Defended and Illustrated, in Nine Dissertations: Wherein the Objections of Lucretius, Buffon, Maupertuis, Rousseau, La Mettrie, and Other Ancient and Modern Followers of Epicurus Are Considered, and Their Doctrines Refuted*. Reimarus's work was aimed at countering the ancient Epicurean critique of intelligent design and its modern representatives. Hence, Reimarus argued against what he called Epicurean "blind chance" and was in favor of God's "wisdom and design." The ultimate crime of Epicurean philosophy, he argued, was to "banish God into the *Intermundia*," leaving him with no relation to the world.

In the first five of the nine "dissertations" that made up his work, Reimarus devoted himself principally to attacking Epicurus's own arguments, while in the remaining four "dissertations" he addressed the modern followers of Epicurus (Georges-Louis Leclerc, Comte de Buffon, Pierre Louis Moreau de Maupertuis, Jean-Jacques Rousseau, and La Mettrie). Rejecting the notion of the spontaneous creation of life from the earth at some point in the past, Reimarus declared in direct opposition to Epicurus's view: "The origin of men and other animals from the earth cannot be accounted for in a natural way. . . . The earth has no title to be called the general mother of us all."[23]

Likewise, Georg Wilhelm Friedrich Hegel's *Lectures on the Philosophy of Religion* (1827) took aim at Epicurus, insisting, "As soon as one attributes true being to the finite, as soon as things are independent and God is excluded from them, then God is by no means omnipresent; for when one says God is omnipresent, then one is at the same time saying that God is actual. But God is not alongside things, in the interstices, like the God of Epicurus." Rather, God's "substantiality," as Spinoza said, is indicated by "the omnipresence of God in thought. . . . God is the absolute substance." Nothing could have been more opposed to Epicurus's view.[24]

Hegel's treatment of Epicurus in his *History of Philosophy* appears at first sight to be contradictory. He saw Epicurus as the defender of the finite and the material, and thus ultimately the enemy of speculative philosophy and religion, along with the universal Notion. He chastised Epicureanism for its "lack of thought, which has been made a principle" given its emphasis on the senses. Epicurus, he claimed, did not rise above "ordinary conceptions or even of sensuous existence."[25] Indeed, Epicureanism had set itself "up against Philosophy."[26] It was for this reason that Hegel declared: "We have no respect for the philosophic thoughts of Epicurus, or rather he has no thoughts for us to respect."[27]

Nevertheless, Hegel also praised Epicurus as "the inventor of empiric Natural Science, of empiric Psychology." He characterized "the practical philosophy of Epicurus" as depending "on the individuality of self-consciousness" and thus the Enlightenment in antiquity, constituting a precursor to the modern materialism of Bacon and others. "The physics of Epicurus," he wrote, "were . . . famous for the reason that they introduced more enlightened views in regard to what is physical, and banished the fear of the gods."[28]

The explanation for Hegel's seemingly contradictory assessment of Epicurus was that he saw the Garden as having abandoned universal, speculative philosophy for natural philosophy and empirical natural science. By adopting the criterion of the senses, Epicurus pointed to modern Enlightenment philosophy with its anti-teleological, empiricist, and deist views. This represented, in Hegel's view, the negation of speculative philosophy itself.

Marx's Epicurean Notebooks

Of all nineteenth-century thinkers, it was Marx who analyzed Epicurean philosophy most thoroughly and with the greatest penetration (setting aside the work of philosophers who were also papyrologists like Theodor Gomperz). Marx's deep interest in Epicurus was related to the left-Hegelian views of his time, coupled with his interest in Enlightenment thought. It is often asked why Marx wrote his doctoral thesis on Epicurus. This is a question that is difficult to answer if one assumes, as in the traditional interpretation of Western Marxism, that when he wrote his doctoral thesis Marx was an "uncritical" follower of Hegel, who had little respect for Epicurus's philosophy.[29] However, the mystery is dispelled if one recognizes that Marx was a child of the Enlightenment, particularly the French Enlightenment, which had intruded into his part of the Rhineland with Napoleon Bonaparte's army and had left a radical legacy. Marx's father was a follower of Voltaire, while his future father-in-law and mentor, Ludwig von Westphalen, to whom he dedicated his dissertation, was enamored with the utopian socialist Henri de Saint-Simon. Both were members of the Trier Casino Society, formed after the 1830 Revolution as a forum of oppositional thought.[30] Marx's birthplace, Trier, David McLellan writes, "was one of the first cities in Germany where French doctrines of utopian socialism appeared."[31] All of the French materialists had been influenced by Epicurus.

It is therefore not surprising that Epicurus was one of the first two philosophers (the other was Plato) that Marx mentioned in any of his extant writings. Thus, in his gymnasium examination paper in defense of Christianity, a virtual requirement of the time, Epicurus was presented, perhaps ironically, as Michael Heinrich says, as the great atheist in contrast to Christ.[32] Whether Marx was already attracted to atheism in 1835 when this was written we do not know. But a year or two later he was already tending to atheism, as can be seen from his poetry in 1836–37.[33]

When Marx began his intensive studies of Hegel, he approached this with considerable resistance—complaining that to succumb to Hegel's "grotesque craggy melody" was to fall "into the arms of the enemy," giving in to "an idol of a view that I hated." At the time he had already been reading Bacon and Reimarus, both of whom had centrally addressed Epicurus's philosophy, Bacon favorably, Reimarus unfavorably.[34] In his 1833 *History of Modern Philosophy from Bacon to Spinoza*, which Marx cited in his dissertation, Ludwig Feuerbach had insisted that Epicurus's materialism was much superior to the rendition of it provided by Gassendi, the modern restorer of Epicureanism, due to the more sensuous character of Epicurus's materialism.[35] For Hegel, as well as the young Hegelians, the key significance of Epicurus's philosophy (and Hellenistic philosophy in general) was that it represented the phase of "self-consciousness" in antiquity, a prerequisite to Enlightenment and self-determination.

In 1840, Marx's close friend in the Berlin Circle of Young Hegelians, Karl Friedrich Köppen, published *Friedrich the Great and His Opponents*, in which he declared, "All the figures of the Enlightenment are indeed related to the Epicureans in many respects, just as from the opposite point of view the Epicureans have shown themselves chiefly to be the Enlightenment figures of antiquity." Köppen dedicated his book to Marx and later explained that his ideas in this period were derived largely from him.[36] (Marx at this time had been composing his seven *Epicurean Notebooks*.) Marx himself concluded his dissertation by declaring, "Epicurus is . . . the greatest representative of [the ancient] Greek Enlightenment."[37] Later, Marx was to state that "Epicurus was the true radical Enlightener of antiquity."[38] In his doctoral thesis, Marx was to quote favorably the eighteenth-century French materialist Holbach, the foundation of whose outlook, as revealed in his *System of Nature*, was explicitly Epicurean.[39] Given its importance for British and French materialism, James White wrote in *Karl Marx and the Intellectual Origins of Dialectical Materialism*, "Atomistic philosophy . . . had strong political overtones, and these were well known to Marx when he embarked on his dissertation."[40]

In winter term 1839–40, Marx, as a doctoral student in Berlin, began doing preparatory work on his dissertation by composing his seven *Notebooks on Epicurean Philosophy*. The covers of the notebooks each carried the heading *Epicurean Philosophy*. The

Notebooks consisted of Marx's excerpts in the Greek and Latin, along with extensive commentary on Epicurus's extant works and that of his followers (chiefly Lucretius). The *Notebooks* also included fragments from other ancient authors commenting on Epicurus's thought and on Epicureanism more broadly.

The *First Notebook* and the opening section of the *Second Notebook* are devoted to notes and commentary with respect to Book 10 of Diogenes Laertius's, *Lives of Eminent Philosophers*, including the short summary of Epicurus's Canonic; the three epistles; and the *Principal Doctrines*. The remainder of the *Second Notebook* includes fragments from Sextus Empiricus, while ending with an examination of Plutarch's polemics against Epicurus. The *Third Notebook* is devoted exclusively to the analysis and criticism of Plutarch's polemics against Epicurus. The *Fourth Notebook* commences once again with Plutarch on Epicurus, but the bulk of the notebook is focused on Lucretius's *De rerum natura*, Books 1–3. The *Fifth Notebook*, of which pages are missing, is directed at Seneca's fragments on Epicurus, extracts from Joannes Stobaeus's compilations, and fragments from Clement of Alexandria. The *Sixth Notebook* is dedicated to Lucretius's *De rerum natura*, Books 4–5, and general philosophy. The *Seventh Notebook* is concerned exclusively with Cicero's references to Epicurean philosophy.

Marx's *Notebooks on Epicurean Philosophy* exhibit a process of genuine discovery. Although the 1839–40 *Notebooks* lack the fully worked out position of his 1841 doctoral thesis on the *Difference Between the Democritean and Epicurean Philosophy of Nature*, the range of issues addressed are wider than those taken up in the dissertation itself. The *Notebooks* thus serve to fill out the picture provided by the dissertation. In many ways, the *Notebooks* provide a perspective that is more profound, insofar as they are more directly concerned with the questions of human freedom and self-consciousness. Moreover, some of the most penetrating insights to be found in the dissertation related to Epicurus's own philosophy (independent of Democritus) are anticipated in the *Notebooks on Epicurean Philosophy*.

In his generally helpful exposition of Marx's *Epicurean Notebooks*, Michael Heinrich quotes a statement by Marx in the *Seventh Notebook*, in which Marx was addressing Cicero's views on Epicurus's philosophy, with which he strongly disagreed. Marx stated somewhat ambiguously in these passages that "Epicurus's philosophy of nature is basically Democritean." Quoting this, Heinrich observes that "there is no talk [in Marx's *Epicurean Notebooks*] of a fundamental 'difference'" represented by Epicurus's philosophy, as compared with that of Democritus.[41] Yet the distinctiveness of Epicurus is in fact emphasized in the *First Notebook*, which already raises the question of Epicurus's swerve, and thus his departure from Democritus. This is drawn out even more clearly, as we shall see, in the *Fourth Notebook*, where Marx does compare Epicurus, if briefly, directly to Democritus.

Still, a direct comparison between Democritus and Epicurus is, as Heinrich notes, scarcely visible in the *Notebooks*. Democritus is barely mentioned at all, which is a clear indication that Marx, though working on preparing a thesis on Epicurus, was not drawn to it initially as a result of a comparison of Democritus and Epicurus, but due to issues derived from his encounter with Epicurus directly. Moreover, although he indicates in the Foreword to his dissertation his intention to write about the Hellenistic philosophies in general, including Stoicism and Skepticism, only the slightest mentions of these philosophical traditions appear in his *Notebooks on Epicurean Philosophy* and his dissertation, indicating that his initial interest was squarely directed toward Epicureanism.

Commencing his systematic examination of Lucretius's *De rerum natura* at the beginning of the *Fourth Notebook*, Marx states, "It goes without saying that but little use can be made of Lucretius." Nevertheless, over the pages that follow Marx was to reverse this view, as he encountered the full impact of Lucretius's sensuous materialism.[42] Most scholars of Epicureanism from Marx's day to the present have seen Lucretius as accurately conveying Epicurus's philosophy.

The first two *Notebooks on Epicurean Philosophy* start off with a level of surety and penetration that suggests this was not Marx's first encounter with Epicurus's writings. Thus, it is significant how much emphasis Marx places from the start on those points that were later to stand out in his dissertation, and that were to affect the development of his thinking in general. Epicurus's philosophy, as Diogenes Laertius explained, was divided into Canon (epistemology), Physics, and Ethics. Marx in his *Notebooks*, however, chooses to approach the canonics first, the ethics second, and the physics last. This suggests that his original interest in Epicurus's philosophy lay in the ethics rather than the physics. However, he may have chosen to look at Epicurus's physics last in order to better understand how Epicurus's ethics were justified as emanating from it, via a materialist ontology.

Canonic

Marx takes almost no notes on Diogenes Laertius's biography of Epicurus, though writing down that Epicurus's favorite philosopher was Anaxagoras. Marx was certainly aware of the historical context of Epicurus's time dominated by the wars of the Diadochi, which he refers to later on in his work. But this does not enter into his *Notebooks on Epicurean Philosophy*.[43] Rather he jumps almost immediately into "The Canon," or Epicurus's epistemology, focused on the three standards of truth: (1) sensations, (2) preconceptions (or prolepses), and (3) feelings. Marx is primarily interested in the first two of these. In Epicurus's Canonics the truth of the senses is emphasized, and the senses themselves are "devoid of reason." Hence, sense perceptions are not immediately forms of knowledge but are combined with preconceptions so as to take conceptual form, allowing for order in knowledge, and the exercise of judgment. If the senses are seen as the source of truth, sense perceptions must in particular instances "await" confirmation.[44] At the same time, preconceptions constitute the generalizations from past human experience, necessary for the organization of the mental faculties. Marx in his doctoral thesis quotes Clement of Alexandria (ca.150–215 CE) as saying, "Without preconception, no one can either inquire, or doubt, or judge, or even argue [*argure*]."[45]

Marx's principal interest with respect to Epicurean epistemology is how such truth, derived from the senses, is supplemented by and interpreted through reason, a topic that recurs throughout his *Notebooks*, and is particularly emphasized in the first two. He thus quotes Diogenes's statement that in Epicurus's Canonics, "there are two kinds of *inquiry*, the one concerned with *things*, the other with the *mere word*."[46]

The relation between the senses that are "devoid of reason" and reason itself in Epicurus was, Marx knew, closely related to Aristotle's *De Anima*, in which Aristotle declared that "the perception of special sensibles is always true and is enjoyed by all animals, while thinking admits of being false and is enjoyed by no animal that does not have rationality."[47] With respect to Epicurus's views, the general relation of the sense perception to reason seems to be cleared up for Marx at a point in his *Second Notebook* where he refers to Aristotle's discussion in his *Metaphysics* of Anaxagoras's approach to reason. According to

Marx, "Aristotle says in the first book of the *Metaphysics* that he [Anaxagoras] uses the *νοῦς* [reason] like a machine and only resorts to it when he runs out of natural explanations. But this apparent dualism . . . must be understood more profoundly. The *νοῦς* is active and is resorted to where there is no natural determination." Reason is thus an "active and resorted to when there is no natural determinant. . . . The *νοῦς* is the philosopher's own *νοῦς*." By means of inference it is possible to go beyond what has been determined empirically through the senses and address what is objectively unknown.[48] It is evident that this notion of reason coming, where necessary, to the aid of the senses in Anaxagoras is meant to apply in Marx's conception to Epicurus as well. As Marx notes, Epicurus is compelled to supplement the senses with the "abstracting conception" of reason as "the criterion of truth." The world is viewed as "half sensuous, half reflecting consciousness."[49] Although Epicurus presents a "dialectic of sensuous certitude," according to Marx, he is ultimately concerned not with sensuous certainty or the pleasure of the senses, "nor with anything else except the freedom of the mind and its freedom from determination."[50]

There is a certain naïve quality, characteristic of ancient Greek philosophy, to Epicurus's treatment of reason, according to Marx. It did not have the developed quality of modern conceptions. Here it is worth recalling that Marx did not have access to those aspects of the philosophy of mind incorporated into Book 25 of *On Nature*. However, there was, Marx argued, a freshness and power arising from Epicurus's naturalistic basis that was lacking in much of modern philosophy. "The Kantians," Marx wrote, "are as it were appointed priests of ignorance, their daily business is to tell their beads over their own powerlessness and the power of things. The Epicureans are more consistent" in their approach to knowledge.[51]

Ethics

For Marx, it is "the freedom of the mind and its freedom from determination" coupled with the relation of this to the actual autonomy of the individual human being, as a sensuous intellectual, and also social being, that is at the heart of Epicurus's ethics and his philosophy as a whole. Marx notes proceed, therefore, not from Epicurus's epistemology, *The Canon*, to his physics, which is the logical order of his thought, but rather go directly to the ethics in the form Epicurus's *Letter to Menoeceus* followed by the *Principal Doctrines*. Marx commences here with the quote from Epicurus (also quoted by Bacon) that is later acclaimed in the Foreword to his doctoral thesis: "Not the man who denies the gods worshipped by the multitude, but he who affirms of the gods what the multitude believes about them is truly impious." This marks Epicurus's revolt against the Greek religion of his time. This revolt is carried out in the name of nature and thus materiality. Epicurus, Marx observes, follows this up with his famous declaration that "death is nothing to us," or the notion that devoid of the senses, there is only nothingness, and thus there can be no immortal soul, dispensing with the fear of Hades, and of everlasting torment. Marx, throughout his life, was to refer to this statement of Epicurus, and to the principle of materiality itself, rendered by Lucretius, "*mors immortalis*" (death the immortal).[52]

But state religion is not alone, in Epicurus's view, in constituting a threat to the conception of human freedom, since this can also be found in the rigid mechanism that characterizes the work of prior atomistic thinkers. Thus, given special stress in Marx's notes on the *Letter to Menoeceus* (with vertical lines beside it for emphasis) is Epicurus's rejection not only of teleology, but even more of the kind of fatalism associated with the mechanistic physics of Democritus, along with that of his more extreme followers (such as Nausiphanes). Thus, Epicurus writes, "It would be better to accept the myth about the gods than to bow beneath the yoke of fate imposed by the Physicists, for the former holds out hope of obtaining mercy by honouring the gods, and the latter inexorable necessity."[53] In this way, both divine teleology and mechanistic philosophy are depicted as enemies of Epicurean philosophy, the latter ultimately even more than the former, since denying human freedom. This was to become central to Marx's understanding of Epicureanism.

Marx took special note in his extracts from the *Letter to Menoeceus* and the *Principal Doctrines* of Epicurus's principle of *ataraxia* and the attempt to fathom those questions that "most alarm the mind." But Marx was to place his greatest emphasis in his treatment of the *Principal Doctrines* on Epicurus's doctrines on justice. He extracted all but one of the eight doctrines on justice (while splitting another in two), placing triple vertical strokes in the margins next to all of them. This was preceded by the statement: "The following passages represent Epicurus's views on . . . the state. The [social] contract he considers as the basis, and accordingly, only utility as the end."[54] The most important of these doctrines was the notion that justice is conditioned by changing historical circumstances. Thus, as indicated in *Principal Doctrines* number 38: "If objective circumstances . . . change, and the same things which had been just turn out to be no longer useful, then those things were just as long as they were useful for the mutual associations of fellow citizens; but later, when they were no longer useful, they were no longer just."[55] Marx underlined this quote and was later to use this proposition successfully in his speech in his own defense, in his trial in Prussia as editor of the *Neue Rheinische Zeitung*.[56] Marx was to lay stress throughout his work as a whole on the fact that it was Epicurus who had originated the concept of social contract.[57]

Physics

Only after engaging with Epicurus's epistemology as presented in *The Canon* (summarized by Diogenes Laertius) and his ethics in his *Letter to Menoeceus* and the *Principal Doctrines* does Marx turn to Epicurus's materialist physics, first in the *Letter to Herodotus*. Marx provides extracts on the main aspects of Epicurus's atomism. He then focuses near the end of the *First Notebook* on questions of dialectics, material motion, and the swerve, providing a concrete indication of where he was headed theoretically when he began his preparatory notes for his dissertation. Here he introduces the issue of Epicurus's "immanent dialectics" and his focus on "repulsion," as integral to the "law of the atom" embodied in the swerve (*clinamen atomi*), "the declination [of the atom] from the straight line."[58]

What is more, in depicting the invisible atom and the void as the dual basis of existence, Epicurus broke with the Ionian conception of the material world as manifested in the visible elements (such as earth, air, fire, and water) or in mixtures, as in Anaxagoras and Empedocles. Instead, he saw material essence, in line with the atomism of Leucippus and Democritus, as underlying the world of appearance, which was the realm of accident, a manifestation of conglomerations of atoms.[59] Atoms, as Marx emphasized in his dissertation, constitute in Epicurus "the *corporeal* in general."[60] The world of appearance thus has its *being* in "a form external to itself, the world of the atom." As Marx states with regard to Epicurus's immanent dialectics, "Epicurus was the first to grasp appearance as appearance, that is, as alienation of the essence, activating itself in its reality as such an alienation."

If the *essence* of material reality was the supersensible realm of the atom (and the void) and hence death the immortal, its corresponding *appearance* was the accidental form of this in life itself. Here sensuous existence could be seen "activating itself in its reality" as the alienation of the underlying essence. For Marx, the strength of Epicurus's philosophy brought this forward for the "first" time.[61]

At the end of the *First Notebook* Marx raises the question of the swerve based on Lucretius, with whom he was to engage much more fully in the *Fourth Notebook*. After quoting Epicurus on the relation of atoms as material bodies to the realm of the accidental, Marx suddenly writes—pointing to what lies at the center of his inquiry—that "it is a matter of certainty for Epicurus that repulsion is posited with the law of the atom, the declination from the straight line."[62] Lucretius is quoted as asking: "If the atoms never swerve so as to originate some new movement that will break the bonds of fate, the everlasting sequence of cause and effect—what is the source of free [will] . . . [?]"[63] This is of immense significance for Marx in two respects. First, the notion that the swerve originates "some new movement" points to "repulsion," which in Hegelian philosophy, particularly Hegel's *Philosophy of Nature*, is associated with being-for-self, self-consciousness, and individual freedom.[64] Second, breaking "the bonds of fate," as Marx following Lucretius indicates, points to the freedom of the will, breaking with a rigid conception of necessity or fatalism: "Only from the *clinamen*"—the declination or swerve— "does the individual motion emerge, the relation which has its determination as the determination of its self and no other."[65] Moreover, Marx depicts this as "the law of the atom." It is thus already clear from the first of his *Epicurean Notebooks* that Marx's main interest in addressing Epicurus's philosophy is the ontology of freedom and determination.

In the *Second Notebook*, Marx takes on Epicurus's cosmology in his *Letter to Pythocles*. Referring a number of times to Epicurus's "iron logic," Marx points to how Epicurus tries to bring the heavens down to earth, rejecting all divine, teleological principles. In absenting the notions of creation, divine motion, and the divinity attributed to the sun and stars, Epicurus was combating the "slavish artifices of the astrologers," and, as Marx notes, that of the astronomers themselves. The weakness of this view, from a scientific standpoint, is that it disregarded mathematical proofs, resulting in some absurdities like the affirmation that the sun, which to the senses seemed about two feet wide, was in fact that size.[66]

However, the strength of Epicurus's analysis, from a philosophical (and scientific) standpoint, as Marx noted, is in his rejection of disjunctive, or either-or propositions, that is, the principle of bivalence, adopting a more dialectical frame of analysis, adequate to the complexity of changing fluctuating material reality. Everything in the celestial sphere was seen as either impenetrable to empirical analysis or it admitted of many possible causes. As Epicurus wrote and Marx quoted: "We always hold fast to what is possible."[67] A supposed determinacy of a kind that pointed to the universe as the manifestation of the workings of the gods had no clear basis, since it had to encounter the indeterminate and unknown. The heavens were thus not to be viewed as themselves divine or as contradicting earthly existence and the supremacy of self-consciousness.

Epicurus explicitly opposed what he saw as creation myths. Here the critique of the heavens, in Epicurean philosophy, was a necessary part of the critique of the earth.[68] For Marx, Epicurus was the heir in his time to the Ionian materialist tradition in Greek philosophy. At the same time, Epicureanism constituted the final transcendence of ancient philosophy, overcoming the skeptics in that respect. "Antiquity," Marx wrote, "was rooted in nature, in materiality. Its [later] degradation and profanation means in the main the defeat of materiality, of solid life," in favor of the "spirituality" that has dominated within philosophy in the modern world.[69] Here he seems to have raised in his *Second Notebook* the issue of materialism versus idealism at a time when this had not yet emerged as the central issue it was soon to become.[70]

Marx's confrontation with Plutarch in the *Third Notebook* focuses on Plutarch's lecture *Reply to Colotes in Defense of the Other Philosophers* and his essay *That Epicurus Actually Makes a Pleasant Life Impossible*. These appear side by side in Plutarch's *Moralia*. The essay on Epicurus making a pleasant life impossible is traditionally published first (and accordingly appears first in Marx's notes), followed by the lecture on Colotes. However, the essay arose in direct response to discussions in Plutarch's school regarding the lecture, so the actual chronological order is reversed.[71] Both were replies, written centuries later, to Colotes's book *On the Point that Conformity to the Doctrines of the Other Philosophers Actually Makes It Impossible to Live*. Here Colotes, in line with Epicurus, argued that the dominant idealist and skeptical philosophies, represented by Plato in the Old Academy and Arcesilaus in the Middle Academy, denied the corporeal basis of existence and thus made it impossible to live in conformity with those philosophies.[72]

A key element in Plutarch's criticism of Epicurus and Colotes was his defense of the notion that philosophy should be "contemplative" in orientation in the sense that body is subordinate to the mind. Thus, Plutarch argued that Epicureans "lay the contemplative part of the soul flat in the body and use the appetites of the flesh as leaden weights to hold it down. In this way they are no better than stable hands or shepherds, who serve their charges with hay or straw or grass of one kind or the other as the proper food for them to crop and chew."[73] Instead, philosophers needed to exercise their faculty of contemplation, removed from material, bodily causes. The comparison of materialist philosophers, who started from the body, to grazing animals, was taken from Plato's *Republic* and was meant, in Plutarch's case, to convey a ruling-class disdain for Epicureanism as a plebeian materialism.[74]

Colotes famously declared in his book that Socrates in real life put food in his mouth not his ear.[75] What was meant by this was that in his real material life Socrates contradicted his professed ignorance along with his skepticism and idealism, and was forced to conform to real earthly conditions, needs, and limits, which according to Epicureanism should be the starting point of philosophy. As Marx wrote, taking the side of Epicurus and Colotes and against Plutarch: "Colotes makes a good joke when he offers Socrates hay instead of bread and asks him why he does not put food in his ear, but in his mouth. Socrates occupied himself with very trivial matters, this being a necessary consequence of his historical position."[76] The key here, for Marx, was precisely the focus on contemplation at the expense of corporeal existence. The skepticism of Democritus, Socrates, the Middle/New Academy , which succeeded Plato's Academy, and Plutarch himself was a diversion from real world, material conditions. So ineffective, in fact, were Plutarch's attempts to refute Epicurus and Colotes in the essay *That Epicurus Actually Makes a Pleasant Life Impossible* that the result is, contrary to Plutarch's intention, "a panegyric in favour of Epicurus."[77]

Plutarch's attempt in *The Reply to Colotes* to contradict Epicurus on the truth of the senses by saying, skeptically, that what is warm or cold differs from person to person and thus has no real basis, was dismissed by Marx as failing to capture what Hegel called "the dialectic of sense-certainty." In Hegel's terms, the "dialectic of sense-certainty" was "nothing else but the simple history of its movement or of its experience, and sense-certainty itself is nothing else but just this history."[78] Hegel used this notion both in response to a philosophy of pure immediacy, which he sometimes associated with Epicureanism, and, more importantly, as a way of countering skepticism. The latter was characterized by "invincibility" in its own terms because it rejected all determinism and universality and relied entirely on pure consciousness.[79] As Hegel said of the skepticism of the Middle/New Academy, which Colotes had attacked in his *On the Point that Conformity to the Doctrines of the Other Philosophers Actually Makes It Impossible to Live*, "All objective truth has really been denied."[80]

For Marx, all of this came down to a confrontation between Epicureanism and the Skepticism of the Middle/New Academy (and of Plutarch). "If one wishes to solve the dialectic of sensuous certitude in itself," Marx writes, "one must admit that the attribute is in the combination, in the relation of sensuous knowledge to the sensuous, and as this relation is directly differentiated, so must the attribute also be directly differentiated. Thus, the error will not be ascribed either to the object or to knowledge, but the whole of sensuous certainty will be considered as this fluctuating process."[81] The dialectic of sensuous certitude, for Marx, had to do with the correctness of the senses, when properly adjudicated by reason and experience, in line with knowledge obtained through the historical process. The senses, Marx argued against Plutarch, have no "fixed being," and cannot be treated as a mere predicate, but have to be seen as subject, in the sense of belonging to a material process that defies mere abstraction, since it is necessary to avoid separating "that which is not separated in sensuousness." It is clear that for Marx at this point, it is the sensuous that is real, living material existence, which is the subject. Introducing as early as 1839–40, in his *Notebooks on Epicurus*, an argument that he is usually thought to have acquired only later via Feuerbach's critique of Hegel, Marx wrote: "All philosophers have made the predicates themselves into subjects," thus inverting reality.[82]

It is in the *Fourth Notebook* that Marx focuses primarily on Lucretius's *De rerum natura*. Here he discovers, perhaps for the first time, the full power of Lucretius as "fresh keen, poetic master of the world." Lucretius gives to Epicurus's Atomism its full sensuous form as manifested material being. The atom and the void, according to Marx, constitute the fulcrum of "Epicurean materiality." Metaphorically speaking, "the formation of combinations of atoms, their repulsion and attraction, is a noisy affair. An uproarious contest, a hostile tension, constitutes the workshop and the smithy of the world. The world in the depths of whose heart here is such a tumult is torn within." Here free will arises in sensuous form out of the mechanical determinism/fatalism so often associated with atomistics, so that "One sees how the blind, uncanny power of fate is transposed into the arbitrary will of the person, of the individual and shatters the forms and substances."[83]

In this respect, Epicurus's swerve "is one of the most profound conclusions, and it is based on the very essence of Epicurean philosophy." In Hegelian terms, the swerve allows the individual "being-for-self," represented by the point, but negated by the fall of the atom in a straight line, to reassert itself through the swerve and repulsion, as a new movement.[84] It is at this stage in his *Notebooks on Epicurean Philosophy* that Marx first explicitly compares Democritus to Epicurus. Unlike Democritus's much earlier philosophy, from which Epicurus departs with the swerve, the philosophy of the Garden could be celebrated as the primary philosophy of the age in which it had emerged.[85] In Lucretius, Marx writes, one finds the "shape of being-for-self, a nature without god, and a god aloof from the world." The power of the swerve "is the defiance, the headstrongness of the atom," which transcends any notion of a "mechanical world."[86]

The Seventh Notebook, principally focused on Cicero's treatment of Epicurus, brings Marx's notion of the Garden as a philosophy of self-consciousness to the fore. Epicurus's whole philosophy is rooted in "being-for-self," that is, in individual self-consciousness, and free will, that seeks to break at every point from necessity, fatalism, and rigid determinism, though taking the determinism of the atom as its basis. Being-for-self arises out of "necessity in the totality of the [Epicurean] system." The result is that this philosophy ends in "actual self-consciousness." As Marx states, "By the fact that we acknowledge that nature is reasonable, our dependence on it ceases. Nature is no longer a source of terror to our consciousness, and it is precisely Epicurus who makes the form of consciousness, in its directness, the being-for-self, the form of nature. Only when nature is acknowledged as absolutely free from conscious reason and is considered as reason in itself, does it become entirely the property of reason."[87]

In the process of writing his *Notebooks on Epicurean Philosophy*, Marx provided in the *Sixth Notebook* a "Plan of Hegel's Philosophy of Nature" in three successive versions.[88] The editors of the Marx-Engels *Gesamtausgabe* (MEGA) judged this "Plan" to be unrelated to the content of Marx's notebooks and published it separately in the first volume of Marx and Engels's *Collected Works*, following the *Notebooks on Epicurean Philosophy* themselves. However, Marx twice observed in his versions of Hegel's "Plan" the position that "repulsion" occupied in Hegel's system, as well as noting Hegel's concept of "material being-for-itself." This suggests that the views expressed by Hegel in relation to these categories were very much on Marx's mind, if not spelled out either in his *Notebooks on Epicurean Philosophy* or in his dissertation.

With respect to attraction and repulsion, Hegel had written that "falling is attraction, the next step is repulsion." This conformed to Marx's interpretation of the role of attraction and repulsion in Epicurus's declination of the atom. Kant in his *Metaphysical Foundations of Natural Science* had explained attraction and repulsion as together constituting the motion integral to matter, and that "without repulsion, no matter is possible." Hegel, in contrast, argued against Kant that motion was separate from matter, and that therefore "what is attracted and repelled is already matter" (material-being-for-itself). Here the difference between Hegel's speculative view of matter, which also implied a certain abstract mechanism, and Epicurus's more consistently materialist and dynamic view, as depicted by Marx, where attraction, repulsion, and indeed the swerve are seen as properties intrinsic to the atom/matter—a position held by Kant as well—become clear.[89]

Marx's Doctoral Thesis on the Epicurean Philosophy of Nature

Marx's doctoral thesis on the *Difference Between the Democritean and Epicurean Philosophy of Nature* carried forward the analysis already developed in large part in his *Notebooks on Epicurean Philosophy*. It was submitted to the Faculty of Philosophy at the University of Jena in early April 1841, just a little over a year after he wrote the *Notebooks*. The Foreword to the dissertation was dated March 1841, and may not have been submitted with the completed dissertation, since it included what Michael Heinrich has called "a clear confession of atheism." The extant copy of the dissertation is in the handwriting of an unknown copyist with insertions in Marx's handwriting. The dissertation consists of two parts: "Part One: Difference Between the Democritean and Epicurean Philosophy in General" and "Part Two: On the Difference Between the Democritean and Epicurean Physics in Detail." The copy of the dissertation that survived is missing the texts of the fourth and fifth chapters of Part One (although the notes to these chapters are included in the extant copy) along with the text of an Appendix responding to Plutarch's polemic against Epicurus on the gods. The dissertation was first published in the main in Stuttgart in 1902, and in full in volume 1 of the *Marx/Engels Historisch-Kritische Gesamtausgabe* in 1927. The first translation in English was by Kurt Karl Merz in Melbourne in 1946. A more accessible English translation was published in 1967 in Norman D. Livergood's *Activity in Marx's Philosophy*.[90]

Epicurean scholar Elizabeth Asmis has referred to Epicurus as Marx's "hero" in his dissertation.[91] This is abundantly clear in the Foreword to Marx's treatise, where Marx declares, "Philosophy, as long as a drop of blood shall pulse in its world-subduing and absolutely free heart will never grow tired of answering its adversaries with the cry of Epicurus" calling for enlightenment and the rejection of a subservient belief in the gods.[92] He goes on to draw a comparison between Epicurus and the rebellious Titan Prometheus, who brought light, and with it enlightenment, to humanity, while defying the gods, quoting a stanza from Aeschylus's *Prometheus Bound*, where Prometheus says to the "servants of the gods, Hermes": "Be sure of this, I would not change my state / Of evil fortune for your servitude. / Better to be the servant of this rock / Than to be faithful boy to Father Zeus." Marx stated that "Prometheus is the most eminent saint and martyr of the philosophical calendar."[93] It is this sense of Epicurus as a heroic figure, who defied the myth of the gods as the rulers of humanity, and was a proponent of human self-consciousness and freedom, that pervades Marx's entire dissertation.

Louis Althusser contended in *For Marx* that "if we exclude the doctoral dissertation, which is still the work of a student, the Young Marx *was never strictly speaking a Hegelian*."[94] Yet, in his dissertation, which was anything but the work of a mere student, Marx, as Frederick Engels would declare, demonstrated his "perfect independence of Hegel."[95] To be sure, Marx's doctoral thesis is "Hegelian" in much of its method, in the sense of adopting Hegel's general dialectical notion of the main ideas within history of philosophy emerging in relation to the development of society. Marx also employs Hegelian terminology and that of German speculative philosophy more generally, including such categories as "abstract individuality," "being-for-self," "self-consciousness," "dialectic" (in the Hegelian sense), and "negation of the negation." Yet the subject, content, and conclusions of Marx's dissertation are distinctly non-Hegelian, departing from Hegel's own dismissive treatment of Epicurus, and having altogether different objectives, related to questions of materiality, freedom, and the critique of religion. Hegel himself, as Marx frequently noted, had misinterpreted Epicurus.[96] Thus, Marx establishes from the start, in his doctoral thesis, his freedom from Hegel.

Marx was at this point the most radical and materialistically inclined of the Young Hegelians, barring Feuerbach, whose work on modern philosophy is cited in Marx's dissertation and whose *Essence of Christianity* was published in the same year that Marx's doctoral thesis was submitted. For Marx, Epicurus's importance lay not in his contribution to speculative philosophy, so much as in his departure from it, and as a forerunner of materialist natural science and the modern Enlightenment. Indeed, according to Marx, it is precisely because philosophy in Hegel's conception was confined to speculative philosophy, placing the Notion ahead of the senses, that Hegel short-changed Epicurus's significance for the evolution of philosophical thought.[97]

Part One of Marx's thesis seeks to differentiate Epicurus from Democritus before him. Despite the widespread influence of Epicureanism in the Hellenistic and Roman ages, and the enormous impact of the Epicurean philosophy of nature on the Renaissance and the Enlightenment, it had come to be accepted within nineteenth-century philosophy that Democritus was the greater thinker within ancient Atomism. As Marx put it, Epicurus was seen as having provided a "syncretic combination" of a misappropriated Democritean physics with a hedonistic Cyrenaic ethics. Epicureanism was thus characterized as full of "arbitrary vagaries."[98] Marx was the first modern thinker to turn this upside down, demonstrating conclusively that Epicurus was by far the more significant philosopher. Writing in 1928 in his "Karl Marx on Greek Atomism," Cyril Bailey explained, "Almost as a pioneer he [Marx] rejects the . . . tradition . . . that Epicurus adopted the Atomism of Democritus wholesale, changing it here and there for the worse." Instead, Marx called "attention in a very arresting way to the real difference between Democritus and Epicurus, and to the genuine originality of the later thinker."[99]

The differences between Democritean and Epicurean physics were significant, if not always fully appreciated. For Democritus, atoms had two properties: size and shape. Epicurus added weight. In Democritus's case, atoms could potentially be any size. For Epicurus, the number of variations in the size of the atoms was incomprehensibly large, but not infinite, since atoms could never be so large as to cross the threshold into the realm of perception. In Epicurus, atoms, while remaining "uncuttables," contained within them minima, or minimum parts. In Democritus, atoms move in every direction. For Epicurus they fall toward the earth in parallel lines—except for minimal, chance swerves.[100]

It is here that the most important feature of Epicurus's Atomism, differentiating it from Democritus, arises, that is, in

Epicurus's declination or swerve (in Latin, *clinamen*) of the atom from the straight line. This is the topic of the opening chapter of Part Two of Marx's dissertation. The swerve is a property of the atom, which is "the substantial premise . . . the exclusive, the immediate principle," so, like the atom itself, it needs no causal explanation.[101] In terms of Epicurean physics, the swerve meant that atoms, despite falling in parallel lines, could collide with one another and were subject to attraction and repulsion, the latter representing a new movement, and leading to conglomerations or assemblages of atoms. In terms of human agency, the swerve was a departure from Democritean mechanism and fatalism, as well as religious teleology, signifying that non-human and human animals could initiate their own actions. The swerve, as Marx following Lucretius emphasized, broke "the bonds of fate."[102]

Equally important for Marx in differentiating Democritus and Epicurus was their respective philosophies of knowledge, or their epistemologies. Democritus's Atomism was of a completely mechanical sort, presented as a hypothesis on the structure of reality beyond the senses. But the effect, in his philosophy, was to reduce the phenomenal world of the senses to a mere "subjective semblance" of reality and thus to belie the senses. This, as Marx explained, introduced a skepticism into his philosophy that went hand in hand with his mechanistic view and an unending, contradictory search for empirical, positive knowledge.[103]

In contrast, Epicurus saw the phenomenal world of appearance as the *active alienation* of essence of the atom; appearance as appearance was the alienation of essence (constituting the nature of time itself). The world of the senses, of *appearance*, of combination, was therefore the world of life. The atom (and the void) represented inexorable *essence,* or *mors immortalis*, death the immortal. Marx emphasized how this was evident in Epicurus's distinction between the atom as *arche* (ἀρχή) and *stoicheion* (στοιχεῖον), akin to the distinction between matter and form and essence and existence. The atom as it manifests itself in the phenomenal world of existence is *stoicheion*, as opposed to *arche*, where it is invisible essence.[104]

Epicurus's philosophy, Marx explained, was thus designed to emphasize the realm of freedom, sensual existence, and *ataraxia*, focusing on life itself. "The whole of the Epicurean philosophy," Marx wrote in his *Notebooks on Epicurean Philosophy*, "swerves away from the premises; so, pleasure, for example, is the swerving away from pain. . . . Determinism is swerved away from by accident . . . God swerves away from the world, it does not exist for him, and therein is he God."[105]

In opposition to Democritus's rigid necessity, and in contrast to the author (pseudo-Plutarch) of *Placita Philosophorum* who was to attribute all to "*fate*, *right*, *providence*, and the *creator of the world*," Epicurus boldly stated that confronted with "Destiny [Necessity], which some introduce as sovereign over all things, he [the wise man] laughs to scorn affirming rather that some things happen of necessity, others of chance, others through our own agency. For he sees that necessity destroys responsibility and that chance or fate is inconstant; whereas our own actions are free."[106] If chance, for Democritus, was seen as a mere roll of the dice, and was the same as necessity, in Epicurus's case, contingency represented possibility.[107]

The swerve of Epicurus was, for Marx, the negation of the negation, negating the fall of the atom in the straight line, which itself had negated the atom as a fixed point (pure abstract individuality). It thereby initiated *new movement* or repulsion, leading to the emergence of new contingencies and new combinations within material existence.[108] "In the repulsion of the atoms," Marx writes, "their materiality which was posited in the fall in a straight line, and the form-determination, which was established in the declination, are united synthetically."[109] "It is from repulsion and the ensuing conglomeration of the qualified atoms that the world of appearance now emerges." Echoing the emergentism in Epicurus, Marx writes, "Atoms . . . are the substance of nature out of which everything emerges, into which everything dissolves."[110] The world of physical phenomena and all that is qualitatively new emerges through the "combination" of atoms in a myriad of different ways.[111]

In Epicurus's philosophy, Marx observes, "motion is established as self-determination." Hence, the "*repulsion*" embedded in Epicurus's "law of the atom," he adds in a Hegelian vein, "*is the first form of self-consciousness*," corresponding therefore to that self-consciousness that conceived itself as immediate being, as abstract individual, but is now realized in the form of free motion. "Epicurus was therefore the first to grasp the essence of the repulsion—even if only in sensuous form, whereas Democritus only knew of its material existence. Hence, we also find the more concrete forms of repulsion," as the synthesis of determinism and free will, "applied by Epicurus. In the political domain there is the *covenant* [social contract], in the social domain *friendship*, which is praised as the highest good."[112]

Marx quoted the fictional Epicurean Velleius in Cicero's dialogue, *On the Nature of the Gods*, who states, "By Epicurus we have been . . . set free"—redeemed from fate. Capturing what he called Epicurus's "iron logic," Marx therefore discovered in the philosophy of the Garden an argument for free will and human agency, rooted in materialism, that rejected all fatalistic determinations.[113] The *locus classicus* of this argument was to be found in Lucretius's treatment of the swerve in *De rerum natura* and its relationship to human freedom and conscious action.

What is remarkable is that Marx, alone in his time, anticipated many of the major conclusions of today's modern scholars of the classics, such as David Sedley and Tim O'Keefe, on Epicurus on free will and determinism (see chapter 2 of this book). Moreover, Marx developed his understanding of Epicurus's philosophy as one of human freedom without having access to the passages from Book 25 of Epicurus's *On Nature* conveying the Epicurean philosophy of mind, which has led modern scholars to interpret Epicurus as a materialist philosopher of free will and self-determination. Central to Epicurus's philosophy, in Marx's view, was his emphasis on freedom that forever breaks the bonds of fate. This was evident in Epicurus's statement, quoted by Seneca in his *Epistles*, and noted by Marx: "'It is wrong to live under necessity; but no man is constrained to live under necessity. . . . On all sides lie many short and simple paths to freedom; and let us thank God that no man can be kept in life. We may spurn the very constraints that hold us.' Epicurus . . . uttered these words."[114] "To serve philosophy," Epicurus wrote, was to "seek true freedom."[115] For Marx, Epicurus was "always turning the argument" of Democritus's mechanism and rigid determinism "inside out."[116]

Marx's interpretation of Epicurus and freedom in his *Notebooks on Epicurean Philosophy* and his doctoral dissertation was fully in accord with Epicurus's then unknown Book 25 of *On Nature*, which stated: "From the very outset we always have seeds directing us some towards these, some towards those, some towards these *and* those, actions and thoughts and characters, in greater and smaller numbers. Consequently, that which we develop—characteristics of this or that kind—is at first absolutely up to us."[117]

It was the sensuous character of Epicurus's materialism that, together with his conception of human freedom, gave the philosophy of the Garden its active, dialectical character. Epicurus's philosophy, Marx wrote, "makes the contradiction between matter and form the characteristic of the nature of appearance," or of phenomena as perceived by the senses. This contradiction between matter and form, such that material form is perceived as the coming into being and passing away—though, according to the principle of conservation, nothing comes from nothing, and nothing being destroyed is reduced to nothing, but rather remains part of matter—is most evident in Epicurus's conception of time.[118] For Epicurus, in Marx's words, "*Human sensuousness is . . . embodied time, the existing reflection of the sensuous world in itself.*" Consequently, "It is necessary to keep firmly to the *Enargie* [standard of judgment based on a clear vision] . . . for sensuous perception reflected in itself is time itself, and there is no going beyond it. . . . *The temporal character of things* [their motion] *and their appearance to the senses are posited as intrinsically one. . . . Hence, the senses are the only criteria in concrete nature, just as abstract reason is the only criterion in the world of the atoms.*"[119]

All of this means that there is a constant "interconnection between time and sensuousness." Hence, "the dialectic of sensuous certitude" is associated with perception of changing material forms, as manifestations of the alienation of matter.[120] As Marx put it, in his account of Epicurean materialism, "In hearing nature hears itself, in smelling it smells itself, in seeing it sees itself. Human sensuousness is therefore the medium in which natural processes are reflected as in a focus and ignited into the light of appearance."[121] Here Marx was commenting on Epicurus's notion of the *eidola* [εἴδωλον, eidolon, pl. eidola], better known today in relation to Lucretius's Latin term, *simulacra*. As Marx put it, "The *eidola* are the forms of natural bodies which, as surfaces, as it were, detach themselves like skins and transfer these bodies into appearance. These forms of the things stream constantly forth from them and penetrate into the senses and in precisely this way allow the objects to appear." Today, Epicurus's concept of *simulacra* is seen as a fundamentally ecological (and dialectical) conception of the interpenetrating particle flows of organic and inorganic matter, in which everything is in reality process.[122]

Epicurus's boldest move was his critique of the heavens in his attack on the astral religion, whereby he strongly affirmed his materialism, naturalism, and humanism. The significance of this was not lost on Marx, who from his gymnasium student days had seen Epicurus as the opponent of religion. "Even Aristotle," Marx observed, "takes the stars for gods."[123] Indeed, "Worship of the celestial bodies is a cult practiced by all Greek philosophers. . . . The religious attitude of the *Pythagoreans, Plato and Aristotle* to the heavenly bodies is well known." In contrast to this, "Epicurus's theory of the celestial bodies and the processes connected with them . . . stands in opposition . . . to the opinion of Greek philosophy as a whole."[124] All attempts to see stars, the sun, the planets, the moon, eclipses, the heavens in general, as eternal and immortal, connected to the gods and creationism, or in the case of Democritus (it seems) as gigantic atoms, were rejected by Epicurus as mythical and superstitious, generating confusion in human souls. He, therefore, used every argument against this, severing all such connections, and seeing the cosmos as material forms, for which there were no firm, apodictic explanations, beyond sensuous knowledge. The gods themselves lived in the *intermundia* between the worlds and were divine beings that had no relation either to the earth or the constellations but were models of *ataraxy*.[125]

Epicurus's critique of the heavens was thus aimed at a materialist conception of humanity as connected to the earth, devoid of the interference of the gods. The immortality of the soul was denied on the grounds that the soul was material and could not exist apart from sensuous existence.[126] The third of Marx's *Notebooks on Epicurean Philosophy*, along with an Appendix to his dissertation, of which there are some notes and fragments, were concerned with Plutarch's criticisms of Epicurus on religion. Plutarch, as Marx pointed out, regarded fear as integral to religion and to maintaining political-class power, views that Epicurus opposed. Epicurus, as Marx stated, believed that "no good for man lies outside himself," that is, he opposed humanism to the "theologising intellect."[127] There could be no security and contentment "while the things above and below the earth . . . remained as objects of suspicion" and sources of terror.[128]

It is at the end of Chapter 5 on "The Meteors" that Marx concludes his dissertation, with Epicurus's break with the astral religion, and his emphasis on earthly self-consciousness: "As the world becomes philosophical, philosophy also becomes worldly, [such] that its realisation is also its loss."[129] Epicurus represents philosophy turning toward worldly, materialist natural science, and away from the pure ideal of Plato in particular. Atomistic matter is the ground for its own alienation in the phenomena of the world and human freedom and development, the swerving away from all rigid determinism and teleology. The combinations that make up material phenomena, the world of the senses, are to be viewed as emergent forms of reality. As Marx emphasized, "Epicurus is therefore the greatest representative of Greek Enlightenment. . . . In *Epicurus* . . . *atomistics* with all its contradictions has been carried through and completed *as the natural science of self-consciousness*."[130] All of this marks, in a sense, the death of speculative philosophy, transformed by the movement toward natural science.

Marx concluded his dissertation by indicating that for Epicurus, in contrast to Democritus, the atom was the "active [*energisches*] principle" of nature.[131] Here he linked Aristotle's concept of *energeia* (ἐνέργεια), often translated as *actuality* but more accurately seen as *activity*, to Epicurus's core conception of nature. For Aristotle, as Marx wrote elsewhere, the principal ontological principle was a "divine energy," an outlook that Marx clearly saw as overlapping with Epicurus's materialism. Herein lay the ambiguity of Epicurus's philosophy, which embodied a conception of nature as active and changing, swerving away from all rigid determinism and fatalism, while promoting a praxis of the active cultivation of friendship and community in a chaotic world. Still, rather than seeking to change the world as a whole, as *homo faber*, the answer was a rebellious retreat, a largely defensive action, that nonetheless still emphasized *energeia*, rooted in human freedom and the sensuous interaction with nature.[132]

In Lucretius, one finds the sensuous character of Epicurus's materialism brought to the fore, in a work of poetic art, which was to have a vast influence on the development of early modern science. This sensuous naturalism also carries with it a definite ecological sensibility, recognizing material limits. Life, we are told, comes from the earth and does not descend from the skies. It is subject to inevitable decay and returns to its atomistic elements, reappearing in new forms. "Until up to the extreme limit of growth," Lucretius explains, "nature, the maker of all things," brings finishing touches. But once a peak has been reached and the "arteries of life" are no longer amply fed, with the result that "no more is now given into the arteries of life than what flows out and passes away—at this point the life of all things must come to a stand, [and] . . . nature by her power curbs back growth."[133]

If environmental destruction can be seen as in the nature of things, since all things eventually decay, it is also affected by human actions and changes to the landscape. Cultivated land is superior to uncultivated land in providing food, indicating that agriculture is subject to improvement. Human communities can plant vineyards and forests, learning from nature.[134] But all of this can also be neglected or undermined. Plagues, it is intimated by Lucretius, are in part human caused, related to the destruction of reason and rational action. Extinction of species occurs when animals and plants are maladapted to their environment, and when humanity does not intervene on their behalf for their preservation, as in the case of some domesticated animals.[135] All of nature, according to Lucretius, and as noted by Marx in his *Notebooks on Epicurean Philosophy*, is interconnected and is subject to renewal and decay, including earth and sky. Only matter is eternal. In this, Marx found a "negative dialectic," the dialectic of death the immortal, which was the precondition of life (and love).[136]

Epicureanism, as Marx said, taught that "the world is our friend." The path to a life of *ataraxia* was to live in accord with nature and with other human beings. The object of philosophical wisdom was thus the realization of contentment among a community of friends, one rooted in reciprocity. This required the development within individuals of enlightened self-consciousness free of the gods, the cultivation of self-sufficient existence, and a conception of human freedom and self-determination based on the recognition of the material basis of reality. As Vanessa Christina Williams wrote in *Marx's Ethical Vision*, one can see in the doctoral dissertation "Marx's overarching interest in defending what he recognizes as a brand of materialism that can accommodate freedom, conscious activity, and intervention into the material world."[137]

Marx had planned in the process of completing his doctoral thesis to go on to write a work that would address all three Hellenistic philosophies: Epicureanism, Stoicism, and Skepticism, viewing them as capturing all aspects of the Hegelian dialectic in their time: materialism, idealism/the spirit, and non-positive dialectical philosophy. The systematic studies of

Stoicism and Skepticism, however, were never completed—if begun at all.[138]

It is often viewed as an anomaly that Marx in the first half of 1840, while he was working on his doctoral thesis on Epicurus, made an excerpt from Aristotle's work *De Anima* (*On the Soul*), which included extensive translations. It was assumed by the MEGA editors that this mainly has to do with Marx's considerable interest in Aristotle.[139] But there can be little doubt that it was also related to Marx's dissertation, both due to the numerous references to Aristotle in that work, and the fact that it was in the later biological studies, and particularly in *De Anima*, that Aristotle moved toward a more materialist philosophical position. Thus, it is remarkable, as Marx no doubt recognized, that Aristotle wrote in *De Anima*: "The soul neither suffers nor acts without the body. . . . Thinking seems a possible exception. But if thinking is a kind of imagining, if it cannot be carried on without mental images, then this too is impossible without the body. . . . We conclude that all affections of the soul are inseparable from the material substratum of animal life."[140] Moreover, though it was once believed that Epicurus did not have access to Aristotle's later, esoteric writings, evidence obtained in the late twentieth century has shown this to be false, something that Marx may well have suspected.[141]

Marx's doctoral thesis was clearly a complex, transitional work, in which, while critically employing Hegelian methods of analysis, he became deeply engaged with the philosophy of the greatest materialist thinker of Greek and Roman antiquity, arriving at conclusions that were to point to his own later development. What is undeniable, as Ernst Bloch wrote, is that throughout his exploration of Epicurus's philosophy, Marx had "materialism germinating in him," leading him to broadly materialist conclusions.[142]

Berlin or Jena?

Marx did his doctoral studies at the University of Berlin. But when it came to submitting his doctoral thesis, he sent it to the University of Jena for approval rather than Berlin. It was an accepted practice at the time for smaller universities to confer doctorates "in absentia" upon the submission and approval of the thesis along with information on completed course work and the payment of a fee—and without an oral examination. This was a way in which the faculty at the smaller universities received support, since student fees were not sufficient to maintain the faculty. There are no extant records, however, that would explain why Marx chose this route rather than submitting his dissertation at the University of Berlin where he had done his studies. Explanations as to why he submitted his thesis in absentia in Jena rather than in Berlin therefore rely on inference and speculation.[143]

The dominant explanation for Marx's choice of Jena in which to submit his dissertation has been that with the royal succession of King Friedrich William IV of Prussia in 1840 Hegelianism was out of favor in Berlin, and Marx was concerned that his dissertation would not have been accepted, or at the very best would not have been well received.[144] Jena, however was outside the Prussian authority, and was thus not directly affected by the accession of the new Prussian king. Heinrich argues that this explanation for Marx's decision to choose Jena is not convincing. The appointment by the Prussian King Friedrich Wilhelm of Joseph Schelling as Prussian privy councilor and member of the Berlin Academy and his arrival in Berlin to deliver a series of lectures, in an attempt to overturn the Hegelian philosophy, did not commence until November 1841.[145] Although it is sometimes erroneously suggested that Marx may have been induced to submit his dissertation in Jena because his friend Bruno Bauer had his appointment to the theological faculty rejected in Bonn, this could not have affected Marx's decision in April 1841, since the rejection of Bauer's appointment occurred a year later in spring 1842.[146]

"In the spring of 1841," Heinrich writes, "nothing had changed as far as the composition of the faculty of philosophy [in Berlin], and Marx could have stuck to [Georg Andreas] Gabler, Hegel's successor, which Bruno Bauer had already recommended in March of 1840. Furthermore, Marx had not yet emerged publicly; his doctorate would not have been a political issue attracting greater attention." Heinrich offers a set of practical explanations:

> In Jena, the doctoral tuition fees were considerably lower than in Berlin and Marx had little money. Further, there were the exam conditions in Berlin: Marx would have had to translate his dissertation into Latin. The oral examination would have been conducted at least partially in Latin and would have required some preparation time. After Marx had finished his dissertation considerably later than planned, he probably did not want to wait even longer for the exam.[147]

Heinrich's explanation, which turns to practical considerations, naturally shares the belief with the dominant account, that Marx's doctoral thesis was primarily a Hegelian work and would be judged in those terms. Thus, the presumption is that Marx only had to fear an anti-Hegelian political bias with respect to his dissertation, which Heinrich claims would not yet have come into play at the time at the University of Berlin. But if it is credible to assume that Marx would have been apprehensive with respect to the reception of his dissertation due to its Hegelian character at a time of growing repression of such ideas in Germany—even if this did not yet bear on the University of Berlin—the question arises: Why then did he choose to send his thesis to Jena, where the faculty of philosophy were strongly *anti-Hegelian*? Setting aside the practical considerations mentioned by Heinrich, would not this have been a dangerous political-intellectual move for a young Hegelian, one that Marx would not have been so naïve as to fail to recognize?

Here the figure of Carl Friedrich Bachmann, dean of the faculty of philosophy at the University of Jena, enters the story. It was Bachmann to whom Marx submitted his doctoral thesis on April 6, 1841, writing: "I send you herewith a dissertation for a doctor's degree on the difference between the natural philosophy of Democritus and the natural philosophy of Epicurus." Bachmann was not only dean of the philosophy faculty at Jena, but also one of its foremost figures.[148] He had "sat at the feet" of both Hegel and Schelling. Bachmann had an interest in mineralogy, and in 1832 was appointed director of the Grand Ducal Mineralogical and Zoological Museum in Jena.[149]

Bachmann was originally a follower of Hegel, but in the 1830s he was to gain notoriety mainly as a result of his critiques of Hegel. In 1833 he had published a work titled *On Hegel's System and the Necessity of a Further Transformation of Philosophy*. This was followed in 1835 by his treatise *Anti-Hegel*. Bachmann's criticisms of Hegel were written from the standpoint of "anti-idealist realism," taking a broadly materialist position akin to the eighteenth-century French physiologist and materialist philosopher Pierre Jean Georges Cabanis, who argued in an explicitly Epicurean vein that life and intelligence were rooted in sensibility.[150] The foremost defense of Hegel in response to Bachmann's *Anti-Hegel* was Feuerbach's 1835 *Critique of the Anti-Hegel*, written from a Hegelian idealist standpoint.[151]

Significantly, Feuerbach was to criticize Bachmann for his arguments with respect to Hegel's identity theory, depicting the identity of thought and being, along with Bachmann's insistence on the materialist basis of mind.[152] Marx W. Wartofsky explains in his *Feuerbach* that Bachmann "attacked Hegel from the 'left'; that is, from the point of view of empiricism and materialism."[153] It was through the critique of Bachmann that Feuerbach developed much of his own materialism, drawing shortly after on some of the very ideas for which he had criticized Bachmann. He later justified this on the grounds that his defense of Hegel in his own transitional analysis was due to his refusal to subscribe to the views of the "half-philosophers" who challenged Hegel's work in a halfway manner. Nevertheless, some of the ideas of these "half-philosophers," particularly in the case of Bachmann, were soon to become Feuerbach's own and led to his enduring fame.[154]

Bachmann's position, as Wartofsky sums it up, "was that spirit, mind, thought, depended on matter and organization—a clearly materialist thesis." Feuerbach charged in his 1835 *Critique of the Anti-Hegel* that this was a "thoughtless empirical standpoint." Nevertheless, it was a view with which Feuerbach himself was later associated. "It is clear retrospectively," Wartofsky writes, "that the very issues of the relation of eating and drinking to consciousness, of matter to thought, and of sensing, feeling, worrying—the finite conditional modes of bodily existence [emphasized by Bachmann]—are the issues around which Feuerbach is to build his own philosophy."[155]

Bachmann had argued, along the lines of the materialist-empiricist tradition dating back to Epicurus, that sensing and perceiving precede and are the basis on which thought emerges. Feuerbach encountered Bachmann at "the peak of his [own] objective idealism."[156] This was shaken by his encounter, via Bachmann, with a materialism rooted in the senses, something that Feuerbach had previously encountered in relation to

Gassendi's restoration of Epicurus. All of this led to the development of Feuerbach's own sensuous materialism. As Feuerbach conceded in a letter to Arnold Ruge in 1841, "When the Anti-Hegel [Bachmann] detected the absence of realism in Hegel, this was based on a crude but correct instinct."[157]

If Bachmann was a critic of Hegel coming from a materialist and realist standpoint, he was not the only virulently anti-Hegelian thinker in the faculty of philosophy at Jena, which also included Jakob Friedrich Fries, who was a post-Kantian, a precursor to neo-Kantianism, and a founder of psychologism.[158] Fries was a liberal bourgeois thinker, but he was also known for his anti-Semitism. Fries was ultimately a more significant figure from the standpoint of philosophy than Bachmann, though lacking the latter's more direct administrative role as well as his prestige as a mineralogist. There is no doubting that Fries was an adamant opponent of Hegel's philosophy, which he notoriously said (in a private letter) "grew not in the gardens of science but on the dunghill [manure pile] of servility."[159]

Fries's position, contrary to Schelling and Hegel, was that nature had to be viewed entirely in mathematical and mechanical terms, in line with the Newtonian/Kantian concept of nature, and that "all material forces have to be traced back to two fundamental forces, one a force of attraction and the other of repulsion." In Epicurean terms, Fries argued, "You should arrange all our social relations in the most rational way, [and] each should regard the other as his equal." As Terry Pinkard explains, in Fries's conception "the highest 'formula of subsumption' (Fries's language) of 'right' is: 'People ought to recognize (*anerkennen*) each other as rational [agents] in their interaction with each other."[160]

Fries was a favorite target of Hegel himself, who criticized him in his *History of Philosophy*, his *Logic*, and his *Philosophy of Right*. In the Preface to the *Philosophy of Right* Hegel quoted Fries as declaring "in a speech on 'The state and constitution': 'In the people ruled by a genuine communal spirit, life for the discharge of all public business would come from below, from the people itself; living associations, indissolubly united by the holy chain of friendship, would be dedicated to every single project of public education and public spirit,' and so on." In criticizing Fries's statement, Hegel charged that Fries's psychologistic views were similar to those of "Epicurus, holding a similar view" on "'"immediate sense perception and the play of fancy," and were based on nothing more than "subjective action and opinion." Freedom, for Fries, according to Hegel, was "nothing else than . . . empty self-activity." (Here it is important to note that Hegel is making a more materialistic criticism of Fries than might first appear. For his critique is that such high-flown sentimentalist language is inadequate to thinking about the objective "architectonics" of the state and civil society, which only a perspective grounded in dialectical totality can grant us.) Hegel condemned Fries by referring to the Mephistopheles of Johann Wolfgang von Goethe's *Faust* who said that to despise reason and give way to the senses and feelings meant "thou hast surrendered to the devil and to perdition art doomed."[161] In his *History of Philosophy* Hegel characterized Fries as a "hedonist" and a proponent of "the subjectivity of arbitrary will and ignorance."[162] In his *Logic*, Hegel charged Fries's *System of Logic* with having "anthropological foundations" and thus constituting an "insignificant publication."[163]

Another major figure at Jena attached to the philosophy faculty was the historian Heinrich Luden, an admirer of Rousseau, a good friend of Goethe, and a leading figure in German Romantic-nationalist folk history. Luden's greatest work was his German history, *Geschichte des Teutschen Volkes*, published in twelve volumes, only reaching the year 1237. Marx had studied Luden's German history at University of Berlin.[164]

Once it is recognized, as Heinrich points out, that at the time Marx submitted his doctoral thesis the philosophical faculty at the University of Berlin would not have viewed it adversely on account of its supposed Hegelianism, the standard argument that Marx chose Jena in order to get around the growing anti-Hegelian sentiment in Berlin is greatly weakened. Once it is also recognized that the philosophy faculty at Jena was dominated by thinkers such as Bachmann and Fries who were virulently anti-Hegel, the shoe is suddenly on the other foot. If Marx had political-intellectual reasons for preferring Jena over Berlin and was concerned about the reception it would have received in Berlin, as opposed to Jena, this quite likely had to do with the incendiary and non-Hegelian (even at points anti-Hegelian) character of his doctoral thesis. The probable reasons for this should by now be clear. Marx wrote a doctoral thesis on Epicurus that was openly atheist in character, praising and explicitly identifying with the leading materialist thinker of antiquity, the figure most notorious and most widely vilified over the entire history of Christianity, and the most antithetical to philosophical idealism. In the process Marx swerved away from Hegel's interpretation of Epicurus, seeing him as the greatest representative of the ancient Enlightenment, and as a materialist thinker who nonetheless emphasized self-consciousness and human freedom. Nor did the dissertation back off from criticism of later Hegelians.

Here it is important to appreciate that although Marx's thesis may appear largely Hegelian today, from a considerable distance in time, due to the methods of analysis and concepts employed, this would not have been the case in the same way in Marx's day, especially where content rather than form was concerned. In the context of the Hegelianism of Marx's day, the subject, content, and conclusions of his dissertation would have been recognized as anti-Hegelian *in substance*, or at least heretical from the standpoint of Hegelian philosophy, very clearly showing Marx's independence of Hegel. If Hegel's last major work was his *Lectures on the Philosophy of Religion*, Marx's thesis, with its focus on Epicurus, was entirely antithetical to these *Lectures*, which had singled out Epicurus as the principal enemy of the notion of God's actuality on earth.[165]

Indeed, Marx's dissertation stood in opposition to the main thrust of Hegel's philosophy, arriving at a conclusion in which empiric natural science, materialism, and Epicurus as the radical Enlightener of antiquity were all strongly praised. This was a reversal of the Hegelian system. As Paul M. Schafer observed in his introduction to *The First Writings of Karl Marx*, "The substantive core" of Marx's dissertation, "that is, its atomist or materialist content," with which it was closely identified, was "Epicurean, while its analytical approach, that is, the dialectical method utilized to think those core ideas through," was "Hegelian." Naturally, it was the substantive core rather than the dialectical method that would have been the main concern at the time.[166]

Marx therefore had every reason to choose Jena over Berlin, where the dominant figure, at least administratively as dean of philosophy, was Bachmann, whose work criticized Hegel's speculative philosophy from the standpoint of a sensuous materialism related to Epicureanism. Moreover, in Jena, the overall sentiment (if we include Fries as well as Bachmann) was highly critical of Hegelian speculative philosophy. Marx, with his usual intellectual thoroughness, would have been well aware of Bachmann's *Anti-Hegel* and no doubt Feuerbach's *Critique of the Anti-Hegel* before he wrote to Bachmann. Nor could Marx have failed to perceive the conflict between Fries and Hegel, since Hegel had strongly highlighted it in his *History of Philosophy*, his *Logic*, and the *Philosophy of Right*, works that Marx had studied closely.

Bruno Bauer, who Marx had close relations with at the time, was shocked by the brazen character of Marx's dissertation, where he criticized Hegelians, both left and right, with an argument that pointed in a materialist direction. "What sort of berserker rage (*Berkserkerwurth*) has seized you again?" he wrote to Marx, the same month that Marx submitted his dissertation to Jena. "What is it that pushes you and worries you?" Bauer warned against provocations of Hegelians.[167]

Those like Heinrich and Sven-Eric Liedman, who are aware of the profound contradictions involved in Marx sending a supposedly Hegelian doctoral dissertation to anti-Hegelian Jena, have attempted to explain this away on various grounds. Heinrich's practical explanation carries a certain weight. Getting his thesis accepted in absentia in Jena rather than in Berlin would have saved Marx money, of which he had a shortage, and time. He desired to join Bauer quickly at the University of Bonn where he hoped to pursue a career.[168] None of this, however, seems adequate to explain Marx's choice, given his rebellious political-intellectual character, the effort he had put into his dissertation, and his concern with its reception, even acceptance.

Heinrich downplays the contradiction by noting that while Bachmann "had emerged a few years earlier as a vehement critic of Hegel," he did so as a "Kantian critic," which hardly seems to capture the nature of Bachmann's philosophical critique.[169] He speculates that "we do not know if Bachmann noticed the Hegelian references of the dissertation," and, in the event he had missed these, Bachmann would have been more inclined to be receptive toward the dissertation itself.[170] However, this suggestion is not at all credible. Bachmann was a serious and accomplished philosopher, attuned to the controversies of his time, and particularly cognizant of anything relating to Hegel, with whom he had studied and against whom he had directed two critiques. The idea that he could have read Marx's doctoral thesis without recognizing the various allusions to Hegel and the use of Hegelian concepts is implausible. More likely, as Marx would have anticipated, Bachmann saw in Marx's dissertation an approach that was not only independent from but critical of Hegel, an analysis that in some ways paralleled his own emphasis on the senses as the basis of knowledge, and that pointed in the direction of empiricism and materialism, and away from speculative philosophy. Although there is no sign that Marx was ever influenced in the slightest by Bachmann, there were some broad affinities.

Liedman's discussion of why Marx decided to submit an allegedly Hegelian dissertation to a virulently anti-Hegelian philosophical faculty that was led by Bachmann, the author of *Anti-Hegel* (not to mention Fries), is less straightforward than that of Heinrich. Liedman begins by claiming that Bachmann should by all rights have reacted negatively toward Marx's dissertation, not simply because of its supposed Hegelian character, but also because Marx in his footnotes had criticized some post-Hegelian thinkers, a category that, Liedman oddly contends, would have included Bachmann. Here the assumption seems to be that Marx's theory represented a Hegelian outlook in both form and substance (even if Hegel was somewhat repurposed) and would have been read in that way by the Jena philosophy faculty. Hence the Hegelianism of the dissertation, coupled with the criticisms that Marx leveled in his footnotes at those who had parted from Hegel, should have led to the dissertation being rejected, if personal and political bias entered in at all. Marx, Liedman suggests, submitted his dissertation to Jena in a politically naïve manner, heedless of the fact that his dissertation would likely be shot down due to its very Hegelianism.[171] For Liedman, Marx was probably motivated by a perception of an "indulgent" approach to dissertations on the part of the faculty at Jena.[172]

Yet, against Liedman's interpretation stands Marx's actual independence of Hegel's system revealed in his doctoral thesis on Epicurus's philosophy of nature. The fact that Bachmann had sought to transcend Hegelianism from an empiricist, realist, and materialist perspective, the very direction in which Marx's dissertation pointed, could only have induced a favorable reading on his part. It would have been quite unlike Marx to have submitted his dissertation simply counting on the "indulgence" of Bachmann and the other faculty at Jena.

As it turned out, the decision of Bachmann, backed by the other members of the Jena faculty, was not simply to accept Marx's dissertation on Epicurean natural philosophy but to approve it with distinction, which was fairly rare. On April 13, one week after Marx submitted his dissertation, Bachmann wrote to his philosophy colleagues that "in Herr Carl Heinrich Marx from Trier" he was presenting a "very worthy candidate," whose thesis "testifies to intelligence and perspicacity as much as to erudition, for which I regard the candidate as preeminently worthy." Here the key word was "preeminently," which few doctoral candidates received. Other candidates that same summer term in 1841, who had their dissertations approved, were given the designations "meets requirements" or "worthy." Marx's dissertation on Epicurus's natural philosophy, designated as "preeminently worthy," was thus rated much higher. Bachmann and his colleagues at Jena, including Fries and Luden, signed the approval of the doctorate. Marx's diploma was issued on April 15.[173]

The Alliance of Nature and Praxis

It is often said that Marx's doctoral thesis took an atheistic stance and evinced a view that challenged authority but was not actually materialist in orientation. Such an interpretation, however, does not stand up in terms of an analysis of Marx's thesis systematically, in detail, and in historical context. What is unquestionable is that Marx chose to write his thesis on the most notorious, if not the greatest, materialist philosopher in all of Western philosophy. Moreover, his treatment of Epicurus, in contradistinction to Hegel, was altogether favorable. Epicurus, in Marx's reading, concentrated on how, starting from a mechanistic Atomism, a realm of human freedom and natural contingency arose, allowing the emergence of new human realities. In Epicurus, Marx found a materialism rooted in the senses, and that therefore took on a sensuous quality. All knowledge came originally from the senses. With the swerve Epicurus had broken the bonds of fate, rejecting both rigid mechanism and teleology (as well as skepticism). The gods in Epicurus's philosophy had no relation to the world and were an ideal in human form. Fate did not determine humanity. Human free will was seen as consistent with a causal determinism. Epicurus's treatment of the swerve in terms of repulsion (and attraction) in his physics reflected the self-consciousness that pervaded his epistemology and his ethics.

All of Epicurus's philosophy was geared to materialism as the philosophy of "death the immortal," setting the stage for human life. In Epicurus, Marx found an "immanent dialectics" emanating from an emergent materialism. The emphasis that Marx drew from Epicurus was that of a humanism that was also a naturalism and a naturalism that was also a humanism. Marx thus portrayed Epicurus as a revolutionary figure in philosophy, one who broke with speculative philosophy. In ending his dissertation, Marx, as we have seen, acclaimed Epicurus not only as "the greatest representative of [the] Greek Enlightenment" but also the leading representative of "*the natural science of self-consciousness*," seeing the atom as its "active [*energisches*] principle." In Epicurus, Marx was to discover the very definition of a critical materialism, but not yet a materialist conception of history.

It is possible to argue about whether Marx identified himself as a critical materialist at this point, given the lack of an unequivocal declaration to this effect on his part. However, there cannot be the slightest doubt as to where his thought was headed.

As Engels wrote in *Ludwig Feuerbach*:

> The question of the relation of thinking to being, the relation of spirit to nature . . . that question, in relation to the [medieval] Church, was sharpened into this: "Did God create the world or has the world been in existence eternally?"
>
> The answers which the philosophers gave to this question split them into two great camps. Those who assert the primacy of spirit to nature, and, therefore, in the last instance, assumed world creation in some form or other—(and among the philosophers, Hegel, for example, this creation often becomes still more intricate and impossible than in Christianity)—comprised the camp of idealism. The others, who regarded nature as primary, belong to the various schools of materialism.
>
> These two expressions, idealism and materialism, primarily signify nothing more than this.[174]

It is absolutely clear as to which of these "two great camps" Marx belonged at the time that he finished his dissertation. He had entered into the contradiction between thought and being at its deepest level and had developed a deep understanding of the essential aspects of a critical materialism, sharply differentiated from mechanical materialism, one that asserted the role of human freedom.

Marx, it has long been recognized, publicly emerged as a materialist thinker in 1842, only months after the approval of his dissertation, and after he had given up on a professorial career.[175] This materialist turn is usually attributed to the combined effect of Feuerbach on his thought along with Marx's new role in October 1842 as the editor of the *Rheinische Zeitung*. The publication of Feuerbach's *The Essence of Christianity*, the same year as the approval of Marx's dissertation, had a strong effect on Marx. However, rather than seeing it as the determinant factor in the formation of his materialist outlook, it is more reasonable to assume that Feuerbach and Marx were at this time moving in parallel directions. This can be seen, with reference to 1839, the year of Feuerbach's "Toward a Critique of Hegel's Philosophy" and Marx's commencement of the writing of his *Notebooks on Epicurean Philosophy*. It is also indicated by the fact that Feuerbach's *History of Modern Philosophy* was cited by Marx in the writing of his dissertation, making it clear that he had carefully studied Feuerbach's treatment of Gassendi's great restorative work on Epicurus.

Hence, the alacrity with which Marx took up Feuerbach in 1841–42 reflects that they were working on nearly identical problems. In January 1842, a mere nine months after the submission of his dissertation, Marx's enthusiasm for Feuerbach's materialist critique of Hegel was at its height. In "Luther as Arbiter Between Strauss and Feuerbach," he wrote: "And I address you speculative theologians and philosophers: free yourself from the concepts and prepossessions of existing speculative philosophy if you want to get at things differently, as they are, that is to say, if you want to arrive at the *truth*. And there is no other road for you to *truth* and *freedom* except that leading *through* the stream of fire [the *Feuer-bach*]. Feuerbach is the purgatory of the present times."[176]

Feuerbach's overturning of both Christian theology and Hegelian speculative philosophy relied on his famous method of *inversion* of subject and predicate in which all conceptions of God/Spirit were shown to be mystified objectifications, with their true grounding found in human species-being (the existence of "man" as a generic being). Thus, the suffering attributed to God in religion (as in Christ's suffering) was a manifestation of actual human suffering and had no real meaning beyond human suffering. Undergirding this new philosophical anthropology was a *sensuous materialism*, in which knowledge and reason, as in Epicureanism, were ultimately grounded in the human senses and feelings (such as love), and in generic concepts/categories (related to Epicurus's preconceptions) that were synonymous with the development of human species-being in the realm of thought. Underlying Feuerbach's anthropological materialism was his genetico-critical (or genetico-analytical) method. Feuerbach sought to account for the grounds of all propositions of speculative philosophy in the actual material needs and feelings of human beings.[177]

As Engels was to recall decades later, Feuerbach's work appeared in a context in which "the main body of the most determined young Hegelians" were, by the practical necessities of the fight against positive religion, being "driven back to Anglo-French materialism. . . . While materialism conceives of nature as the sole reality, nature in the Hegelian system" represented "merely the 'alienation of the absolute idea.'" Here "the idea" was seen as "primary, nature the derived element":

> Then came Feuerbach's *Essence of Christianity*. With one blow it pulverized the contradiction, in that without circumlocutions it placed materialism on the throne again. Nature exists independently of all philosophy. It is the foundation upon which we as human beings, ourselves, products of nature, have grown up. Nothing exists outside nature and man, the higher being our

> religious fantasies have created are only the fantastic reflection of our own essence.
>
> The spell was broken. . . . Enthusiasm was general; we all became at once Feuerbachians. How enthusiastically Marx greeted the new conception and how much—in spite of all critical reservations—he was influenced by it, one may read in *The Holy Family* [1844].[178]

However, it soon became apparent that Feuerbach's abstractly sensuous nature, despite the brilliance and passion with which it was evoked, lacked any underlying conception of organic nature independent of anthropological nature, while the notion of the social (and the historical) and of human agency also remained undeveloped. This was to give his conception of human sensuousness and freedom a particularly abstract form. His critique thus remained in the halfway form of a negative inversion of Hegel that failed to move forward beyond Hegel. This was due to the far more abstract character of his analysis as compared with the Hegelian system, which always emphasized the identity of thought and active being, even if subsuming the latter in the former, and which was always directly historical in form. Hegel's speculative philosophy extended into the political realm and incorporated a notion of active agency and of human labor, together with the state, even if all of this was subsumed within spirit/thought. In the case of Epicurus, Marx had already emphasized at the close of his dissertation the role of human agency, or an *active principle*, in the philosophy of the Garden, creating a conception of human freedom that in its implications went far beyond that of Feuerbach.

Thus, the paradox of Marx's response to Feuerbach in 1842–44 was that while much of Feuerbach's sensuous materialism (adapted from Epicurean philosophy) and his methods of inversion and genetico-criticism strongly influenced Marx, countering both idealism and mechanical materialism, Feuerbach's philosophy was, for Marx, in many ways lacking. The abstract character of Feuerbach's philosophical anthropology, in which Hegelian philosophy was merely turned on its head, meant that Marx was forced back to ancient and early modern materialism, and to Hegel's dialectical philosophy, in the attempt to generate a more substantial and practical critique.

The limitations of Feuerbach's materialism were to become quickly apparent to Marx when, beginning in October 1842, he assumed the position of editor of the *Rheinische-Zeitung*, an academic career having been blocked. The requirements of political journalism, for example the need to understand the widespread arrest of peasants for pursuing their customary right to collect dead wood from the forests, were to propel him in a materialist and political-economic direction. In 1859, Marx recalled that as editor of the *Rheinische Zeitung*, "I first found myself in the embarrassing position of having to discuss what is known as material interests."[179] In response to this newfound need Marx wrote both his *Critique of Hegel's Philosophy of Right* (1843) and his *Economic and Philosophical Manuscripts* (1844).

On March 13, 1843, only days before his resignation as the editor of the *Rheinische Zeitung* in response to the iron controls imposed by Prussian censorship, Marx wrote to Arnold Ruge that Feuerbach's argument in his *Preliminary Theses on the Reform of Philosophy* (1842) seems "to me incorrect only in one respect, that he refers too much to nature and too little to politics. This, however, is the only alliance"—that is, the alliance of nature with politics or praxis—"by which present-day philosophy can become truth."[180] Feuerbach had played a preeminent role in the critique of heaven. Yet, as Marx stressed, "The criticism of heaven turns into the criticism of earth, the *criticism of religion* into the *criticism of law* and the *criticism of theology* into *the criticism of politics*."[181] If Feuerbach's naturalism, in opposition to theology and speculative philosophy, was to be meaningful, not simply an abstract materialism, it needed to contribute to the dialectical alliance of nature and praxis as the only firm guide to truth.

In the *Economic and Philosophical Manuscripts* of 1844, Marx provided his first attempt to synthesize the critique of bourgeois political economy and the critique of Hegelian philosophy with a sensuous, corporeal materialism, derived from a long materialist tradition extending from Epicurus to Feuerbach. What was unique in Marx's analysis was the alliance of nature and praxis. Thus, the reality of alienated human labor, rooted in the last instance in the alienation of human, sensuous, corporeal existence, of the human relation to nature, formed the material basis of his analysis. Although the initial structure of the 1844 manuscripts was derived from his critical engagement with political economy, particularly Adam Smith, the whole analysis turned to the concept of alienated labor, which Marx related to alienated nature (the estrangement of nature from labor). This was accompanied by the insistence, in Epicurean and Feuerbachian terms, on the indissoluble link between humanism and naturalism, and the sensuous, corporeal nature of human existence and agency. Hegel in his dialectical philosophy—as Marx argued in his critique of Hegel's *Phenomenology of Spirit* at the end of the *Economic and Philosophical Manuscripts*—had recognized the centrality of human labor. But this was conceived by Hegel only in terms of thought, not in corporeal terms, and not in relation to human production; not in terms of human beings as objective beings with their needs outside of themselves. In this way, Marx constructed the essential elements of his worldview that were to lead to his materialist conception of history, rooted in a materialist conception of nature.

The two works by Feuerbach that resonated most with Marx during the writing of the *Economic and Philosophical Manuscripts*, and on which he placed his main emphasis, were Feuerbach's "Preliminary Theses on the Reform of Philosophy" (1842) and his "Principles of the Philosophy of the Future" (1843). In ancient Greece within Western philosophy, Feuerbach observed in his *Principles*, it was first argued that knowledge began with "the *sensuous*, i.e., *unadulterated* and *objective* sensuous perception of the sensuous or the real," something that the modern era was only then rediscovering. With this, humanity "has also found its way *back to itself*, for a man who occupies himself only with creatures of the imagination and abstract thought, is not a *real*, not a truly human being."[182]

For Feuerbach, ancient materialist philosophy constituted a dialectic of "thought and being" rather than subsuming the latter within the former. It left "matter" as "a residue" outside of itself, "the substratum of reality." In this respect, the philosophy of antiquity was humanist as well as naturalist in orientation. "The ancient philosophers were men *whose wisdom still had reference to the world* . . . they were . . . *anthropologists*, not theologians," who saw the world of phenomena as emanating from sensuous, corporeal being.[183] As Feuerbach wrote of Epicurus, in terms replicated by Marx, his "atoms are absolute atheists or at least free spirits, which care as little about God as the God of Epicurus about the world and the atoms . . . they tolerate no co-regent, they are a world for themselves." As "indissoluble, the indivisible first and last of the world," the atom represents "time, eternal and immortal" and thus the whole basis of sensual existence.[184]

"Feuerbach," Marx wrote, "is the representative of *materialism* coinciding with *humanism* in the *theoretical* domain."[185] Humanism was one with naturalism. Both science and freedom, in Feuerbach's view, depended on the adoption of a sensuous materialism and thus a naturalist anthropology. "All science," he stated in his "Preliminary Theses," "must be grounded in *nature*. A doctrine remains a *hypothesis* as long as it has not found its *natural basis*. This is true particularly of the *doctrine of freedom*. Only the new philosophy will succeed in *naturalizing* freedom, which was hitherto an *anti-hypothesis*, a *super-natural hypothesis*."[186] However, Feuerbach's philosophy, while rejecting all super-natural beings, was able to replace this only with an abstract anthropological being, without history, without agency, and without politics. His philosophy thus came up short, as Marx recognized almost from the start, when it came to the question of the alliance of nature and praxis.

The Anthropology of the Senses

The *Economic and Philosophical Manuscripts* of 1844 stand out in Marx's intellectual corpus as representing a critical transitional period in his thought. They begin with critical notes on political economy, which he then seeks to dialectically mediate through the concepts of human species being and estranged labor. This establishes a broad materialist philosophical anthropology that concludes with a critique of Hegel's *Phenomenology*. Attempts to relegate the *Economic and Philosophical Manuscripts* to an "early Marx" before Marxism have been shown to be myopic, because in these early analyses the foundations of Marx's critical materialism governing his inquiries for the rest of his life are found—although with significant methodological shifts as he moved from primarily philosophical concerns to more economic ones.[187]

Hence, while the *Economic and Philosophical Manuscripts* are often seen as the culmination of Marx's "Feuerbachian" phase, this is misleading in several respects. Already, Marx was developing his nascent critique of political economy, based on the centrality of labor and with it a new conception of praxis, all of which was entirely missing in Feuerbach's work. Marx's *Critique of Hegel's Philosophy of Right*, while also seen as belonging to his Feuerbachian stage, addresses mainly politics, which was outside the purview of Feuerbach. Indeed, Marx was constantly moving beyond Feuerbach, forcing his own analysis back to a consideration of Hegelian idealism and ancient Atomism, in the process of developing a materialist critique that transcended the more limited bases of Feuerbach's critique of Hegel.[188] What is clear is that Marx's materialism, even at this stage, was far deeper and more profound than what is to be found in Feuerbach's philosophical anthropology, not simply because of its grounding in labor, but also because Marx constantly drew on ancient Epicurean materialism with its immanent dialectic.

Feuerbach's abstract philosophical anthropology, though based like Epicurean materialism on the senses, belonged neither to the materialist conception of nature nor to the materialist conception of history, lacking, in its mere inversion of the theologizing consciousness, both natural history and historical praxis. Hence, Feuerbach, though crucial in advancing an abstract, corporeal materialism that was the inverse of theologizing intellect, nonetheless did so without ever confronting nature or history concretely. Crossing "the fiery brook" represented by Feuerbach was necessary, in Marx's view, but it led to a *terra incognita* on the other side, where the problem became one of articulating a more concrete and historical materialism and class relations.[189] As Karl Korsch remarked, Marx's identification with Feuerbach lasted at most only "for an extremely short period of time."[190] Marx's materialism was in many ways more advanced than that of Feuerbach both in terms of natural history and social history, along with political economy. With all of his brilliance, Feuerbach's materialism had little to offer (substantively) to

Marx, resulting in constant echoes in Marx's writing at this stage to Epicurus (and Aristotle's *De Anima*) as well as Hegel.[191]

If Feuerbach took on a sensuous materialism as a result of his encounter with Gassendi's work on Epicurus, thus giving life to his analysis, in which he humanized nature and naturalized humanity, Marx was able to tap into this at a much deeper level through his penetrating studies of Epicurean philosophy itself. Thus, we find Marx in his *Economic and Philosophical Manuscripts* observing, in contrast to Hegel, that "*human nature*," the human being, is not "equivalent to *self-consciousness*." Rather, self-consciousness is rooted materialistically in the human relation to nature. The world of appearance, of lived existence, is a quality of "human nature, eye, [ear], etc.," of knowledge derived from the senses, "for man is a part of nature."[192] All of this derives from Marx's explication of Epicurus's materialism in his doctoral thesis, where he wrote: "In hearing nature hears itself, in smelling it smells itself, in seeing it sees itself. Human sensuousness is therefore the medium in which natural processes are reflected as in a focus and ignited into the light of appearance."[193] The relation of human beings with nature as a whole is thus a reflexive one, rooted in sensuous perception.

If the "alienation of self-consciousness" "establishes *thingness*" for Hegel, Marx sees such "thingness" as a manifestation of an "*alienated self-consciousness*." Self-consciousness, in its true, unalienated form, entails the recognition that human beings are sensuous, corporeal objective beings who came to consciously relate to the "*real sensuous objects*" outside of them as the necessary basis of their existence. Human beings were intrinsically connected to the world through the exercise of their senses and through productive activity in the process of the pursuit of life itself, and as *homo faber*. In the naturalism that Marx found in Epicurus, and in the materialist dialectic in general, he therefore found the basis of perceiving essential human powers and of human freedom as praxis: "Only naturalism," he writes, "is capable of understanding the process of human history." Yet a complete naturalism, for Marx in his early writings, is also a complete humanism.[194]

The materialism that Marx evokes in the *Economic and Philosophical Manuscripts* is already fully dialectical. In Epicurus, the soul is material and mortal since it cannot exist, nor the mind, severed from the sense organs and thus sensual perception. On this basis, he was able to found his ethics on the materialist principle that "death is nothing to us." Marx would refer to this throughout his life, not simply in relation to the reality of death, which he, like all human beings, faced in the course of his life, but also as the principle of materialism, in Lucretius's words, "death the immortal."[195] This materialist view that outside our senses there is no connection to the world, which then is literally nothing to us, led Marx to write in the *Economic and Philosophical Manuscripts*: "*Nature* . . . taken abstractly for itself, and fixed in its separation from man, is *nothing* for man. . . . *a nothing proving itself to be nothing*, [since] it is *devoid of sense*."[196] Ontologically, epistemologically, and also socially, above all in their production, human beings are engaged in sensuous interaction with the world around them, and only in this way does nature become real, living existence for us. In words that resonate with his depiction of Epicurean materialism as the highest form of the development of self-consciousness with respect to natural science to be found in antiquity, Marx states: "Only when science starts out from *sensuous* consciousness and *sensuous* need—that is, only when science starts out from nature—is it *real* science."[197]

Marx's epochal advance in the *Economic and Philosophical Manuscripts* was his conception of alienated labor. Although the notion of estranged labor was already present in Hegel, it was in the form of alienated intellectual labor. For Marx, however, it emerged as the essence of a materialist critique of capital. This is evident in his four moments of alienation: (1) from the object of labor (and thus from oneself as an objective being), (2) from the process of labor, (3) from human species-being, and (4) from other human beings (pointing to class divisions).[198] Although each of the moments dialectically implied all of the others, the defining element in Marx's conception of the alienation of labor, since the most ontologically centered, was alienation from species-being, or estrangement from the transformative productive powers of humanity as a species, distinct from other animals.[199]

Drawing on Reimarus, Hegel, and Feuerbach, Marx associated human species-being with the notion of humanity, as the "self-mediating being of nature."[200] Although other animals interacted with nature in complex and changing ways, often involving conscious action, human beings as *homo faber* and as the "tool-making animal" did so in more universal ways, via social production and developed language capabilities, reflecting *generic consciousness*.[201] The actuality and potentiality of human freedom was thus a product of the human capacity to swerve away from any rigid determinism, via social intercourse. Just as in Epicurus/Lucretius, human freedom from the war of all against all in the age of kings was made possible through a social revolt and a renewal of the social compact. Moreover, this principle could be seen, Marx argued, as operating more generally. The potential for human freedom or autonomous action in relation to the totality of the natural-material world—if always partial and dialectical—was embodied in *energeia* and was a product of *social praxis*.

Human species-being, that of the self-mediating being of nature, was, as Marx emphasized, alienated in class society, and above all in capitalist class society. The very existence of a class society meant that humanity was estranged from its own labor and production, and from its interdependent relation to the natural-material world. In the fully proletarianized society of industrial capitalism, this meant that workers were separated from the earth as the natural-material basis of production.[202]

The alienation of labor was therefore grounded in the alienation of nature. In his *Economic and Philosophical Manuscripts*, reflecting his early political-economic investigations while editor of the *Rheinische Zeitung* with respect to the removal of the common rights of the peasants, and his studies of the ground rent theory of classical political economy, Marx had already come to the realization that behind the alienation of labor lay the alienation of nature and of the entire objective world outside of humanity.[203] Hence, the *Economic and Philosophical Manuscripts* are already suffused with a deep ecological perspective, arising from both Epicurean materialism and the critique of capitalist property relations.

Epicurus and Greek antiquity in general, existing in an age when craft production was dominant, saw the relation between humanity and nature as a kind of organic/inorganic dialectic, with human organs conceived as natural tools for interacting with the environment, while the tools created by human beings were simply extensions of the human body in this respect.[204] Hence, the relation between nature was an organic one mediated by tools. Humanity and nature were, in a sense, one. As Marx, conveying this sense of things wrote: "Nature is man's *inorganic body*, that is to say nature in so far as it is not the human body. Man *lives* from nature, i.e. nature is his *body*, and he must maintain a continuing dialogue with it if he is not to die. To say that man's physical and mental life is linked to nature simply means that nature is linked to itself, for man is a part of nature."[205] Given the alienation of nature, as a precondition of the alienation of human production in class society, the only revolutionary solution for

Marx was the reconciliation of humanity with nature, according to which unalienated "*society* is . . . the perfected unity in essence of man with nature, the true resurrection of nature, the realized naturalism of man and the realized humanization of nature."[206]

The ecological critique that emanates from Marx's *Economic and Philosophical Manuscripts* is thus profound. Environmental degradation and estrangement are to be found in the division of labor between town and country, in the division of labor within production itself, and in the alienated inversion of naturally given human needs. All of this is for Marx unalterable within the present system:

> Even the need for fresh air ceases to be a need for the worker. Man reverts once more to living in a cave, but the cave is now polluted by the mephitic and pestilential breath of civilization. Moreover, the worker has no more than a precarious right to live in it, for it is for him an alien power that can be daily withdrawn and from which, should he fail to pay, he can be evicted at any time. He actually has to *pay* for this mortuary. A dwelling in the *light*, which Prometheus describes in Aeschylus as one of the great gifts through which he transformed savages into men, ceases to exist for the worker. Light, air, etc.—the simplest *animal* cleanliness—ceases to be a need for man. *Dirt*—this pollution and putrefaction of man, the *sewage* (this word is to be understood in its literal sense) of civilization—becomes an *element of life* for him. Universal *unnatural* neglect, putrefied nature, becomes an *element of life* for him. None of his senses exist any longer, either in their human form or in their *inhuman* form, i.e. not even in their animal form. . . . It is not only human needs which man lacks—even his *animal* needs cease to exist. The Irishman has only one need left—the need *to eat*, to eat *potatoes*, and, more precisely, to eat *rotten potatoes*, the worst kind of potatoes. But

England and France already have a *little* Ireland in each of their industrial cities.[207]

The Materialist Conception of Nature and History

In 1845, Marx and Engels published *The Holy Family, or Critique of Critical Criticism*, aimed at the views of Bruno Bauer in particular, and which included a brief outline of Enlightenment materialism by Marx titled, "Critical Battle Against French Materialism." For Marx, "French and English materialism was always closely related to *Democritus* and *Epicurus*." In the seventeenth century, Thomas Hobbes was closely connected to Gassendi, the French "restorer of *Epicurean* materialism" and the enemy of Cartesian metaphysics.[208] Descartes had sharply divided physics and metaphysics, reducing the former simply to matter (extension) and to mechanical motion and reducing the latter to the realm of the spirit. The result was divergent, if overlapping trends in materialism between Cartesian mechanism and Epicurean-derived "sensualism."[209]

The English materialist tradition, running through Bacon, Hobbes, and Locke, had all drawn inspiration directly from the ancient Greek materialists, particularly Epicurus, thus presenting a sensualist materialism. For Marx, "The real progenitor of *English materialism* and all *modern experimental science is Bacon*. To him natural philosophy is the only true philosophy, and *physics* based on the experience of the senses is the chiefest part of natural philosophy. *Anaxagoras* and his *homoeomeriae* [identity of the elements/atoms of a substance with its observed properties], *Democritus* and his atoms, he often quotes as authorities."

Marx may have been unaware of Bacon's quotations from Epicurus on materialism in some of his works—Epicurus was a figure Bacon referred to less frequently than Democritus, no doubt due to his atheist reputation, but who clearly influenced Bacon's emphasis on the senses. Nevertheless, for Bacon, according to Marx, "The *senses* are infallible and the *source* of all knowledge," a view squarely in line with Epicurus. "In *Bacon*, its first creator [in modern times]," Marx wrote, "materialism still holds back within itself in a naïve way the germs of a many-sided development. On the one hand, matter, surrounded by a sensuous, poetic glamour, seems to attract man's whole entity by winning smiles. On the other, the aphoristically formulated doctrine pullulates with inconsistencies, imported from theology."[210]

It was Hobbes, who, according to Marx, took Bacon's materialism forward, giving it a more consistent and systematic character in his *Elements of Law, Natural and Politic* (1640)—the two parts of which, *Human Nature* and *De Corpore Politico* are often published as separate works—and even more important in his *De Corpore* (1655).[211] It was the later work on which Marx seems to have relied directly.[212] If more systematic in nature than Bacon, Hobbes's materialism, according to Marx, loses some of the vividness present in the former. Summarizing Hobbes, Marx writes:

> If all human knowledge is furnished by the senses, then our concepts, notions, and ideas are but the phantoms of the real world, more or less divested of its sensual form. Philosophy can but give names to these phantoms. . . . But it would imply a contradiction if, on the one hand, we maintained that all ideas had their origin in the world of sensation, and, on the other, that a word was more than a word. . . . An *unbodily substance* is the same absurdity as an *unbodily body*. *Body*, *being*, *substance*, are but different names for the same *reality*. It is impossible to separate thought from matter *that* thinks. This matter is the substratum of all changes going on

> in the world.... Only material things being perceptible, knowable to us, we cannot know *anything* about the existence of God.[213]

What Hobbes lacked, however, was any proof of "Bacon's fundamental principle" of "the origin of all human knowledge and ideas from the world of sensation." This necessary step, Marx wrote, was left to Locke, "who in his *Essay on Human Understanding*, supplied this proof. . . . Locke founded [in modern times] the philosophy of *bon sens*, of common sense, i.e., he said indirectly that there cannot be any philosophy in variance with the healthy human senses and reason based on them."[214]

Although Marx's contention on Locke's role in the development of materialism might occasion some surprise, recent scholarship has strongly pointed to him as a "weak materialist," compatible with property dualism, whose analysis was based on what he called the two "very touchy subjects": (1) thinking matter, and (2) the immortality of the soul. Both of these were addressed, if hesitantly, in ways that differed from standard Christian doctrine, in Locke's *An Essay Concerning Human Understanding*. Although Locke tried, in the still religious context of the times, to introduce materialist views in these areas as innocuously as possible, he ended up being strongly criticized on both scores, by Leibniz and others.[215]

There could be hardly any doubt as to the ultimate Epicurean source of these "touchy subjects." As Locke recognized in his journal, written when he was working on the first unpublished draft of his *Essay*, to suppose the soul is immortal because immaterial and indestructible, though the body be deprived of sensation and therefore thought, would be to say that in such a case the soul would be nothing to us. "To prove that immortality of the soule simply because[,] it being not naturally to be destroid by anything [,] it will have an eternall duration which duration may be without any perception[,] is to prove noe other immortality of the soule than what belongs to Epicurus's atoms, viz that it perpetually exists but has no sense either of happyness or misery."[216]

Locke questioned but did not deny the possibility of the immortality of the soul but clearly saw it as a proposition that did not apply meaningfully to this world, even if God having infinite power could create a personal immortality in "another world."[217] However, more important than all of this to Marx was undoubtedly Locke's anti-Cartesian hypothesis of "thinking extended matter." This notion of *thinking matter*, or a capacity for thought "superadded" to matter, rooted in sense and perception led to the virulent attacks on Locke's materialism by Leibniz and others, but nevertheless raised the issue of materialism directly, denying the Cartesian ontological dualism of matter and mind.[218] Locke, Marx explained, played the crucial role in showing how knowledge arose from sense perception.

It is therefore significant that it was Locke rather than Descartes who, outside of natural science, was the most important source inspiring the development of French materialism. Locke directly influenced the eighteenth-century philosophers Étienne Bonnot de Condillac and Claude Adrien Helvétius. For Condillac, Marx wrote, "the art of sensuous perception" along with the whole development of the individual was the result of "*experience* and *habit*." Helvetius related Locke's sensuous materialism directly to social life. In later French materialists, notably La Mettrie and Holbach, we find an attempted "synthesis of Cartesian and English materialism," also reaching back to Epicurean materialism.[219]

French materialism, in the sensuous strand derived from Locke, Marx contended, led directly to the realms of theory and practice and "to *socialism and communism*. There is no need for any great penetration to see from the teaching of materialism . . . how necessarily materialism is connected with communism and socialism. If man draws all his knowledge, sensation, etc., from the world of the senses and the experience gained in it, then what has to be done is to arrange the empirical world in such a way that man experiences and becomes accustomed to what is truly human in it" and becomes self-conscious.[220] "For socialist man the *whole of what is called world history* is nothing more than the creation of man through human labour, and the development of nature for man, he therefore has palpable and incontrovertible proof of his self-mediated *birth*, of his *process of emergence*."[221]

The utopian socialists thus proceeded directly from materialism, Charles Fourier from the French materialists, Robert Owen from the English materialists, utilitarians, and empiricists. In Germany, speculative philosophy, evolving out of the seventeenth-century metaphysics of Descartes, Leibniz, and Spinoza, culminated in Germany in Hegel's "universal metaphysical kingdom." Feuerbach represented the return of materialist philosophy in Germany. "Feuerbach," Marx wrote, is the representative of *materialism* coinciding with *humanism* in the *practical* domain," upending Hegel's system. As his *History of Modern Philosophy from Bacon to Spinoza* demonstrated, Feuerbach had engaged with the main materialist theorists. He learned about Epicurean materialism from Gassendi.[222]

Summarizing the theoretical relation of materialism to socialism in the *Economic and Philosophical Manuscripts*, Marx had written: "Socialism no longer needs such mediation," that is, the materialist critique of religion as the basis of the critique of earth. "Its starting point is the *theoretically and practically sensuous consciousness* of man and of nature as *essential beings*. It is the *positive self-consciousness* of man, no longer mediated through the abolition of religion." Materialism, which Marx encountered in his studies of Epicurus and the later Aristotle, and carried forward to modern times, ushered in the theory and practice of socialism "necessary for the next period of historical development, in the emancipation and recovery of mankind."[223]

This "new stage of historical development" represented by socialism demanded, as Marx intimated as early as the *Economic and Philosophical Manuscripts*, a new kind of materialism, grounded in history and praxis, a materialist conception of history to accompany the materialist conception of nature promulgated by all previous materialisms. It was this that Marx took up in his 1845 *Theses on Feuerbach*. Here he wrote: "The chief defect of all hitherto existing materialism (that of Feuerbach included) is that the thing, reality, sensuousness, is conceived only in the form of the *object or of contemplation*, but not as *sensuous human activity*, *practice*, not subjectively. Hence, in contradiction to materialism, the *active* side was developed abstractly by idealism—which, of course, does not know real, sensuous activity as such."[224] By all previous materialism, Marx meant the ancient materialism of Democritus and Epicurus, in particular, all the way to seventeenth- and eighteenth-century English and French materialism, as well as the nineteenth-century materialism of Feuerbach himself, who was Marx's immediate subject. "Feuerbach," Marx wrote, "not satisfied with *abstract thinking*, wants *contemplation*," concerned with the sensuous relation to the objective world, "but he does not see sensuousness as *practical*, human-sensuous activity."[225]

A similar criticism might be leveled at Epicurus's more active materialism, in that it was primarily contemplative in the sense of being confined to a limited praxis of human friendship and community in the context of the demise of the Greek polis. To be sure, in antiquity, Epicureanism, as Marx was well aware, was viewed as the principal opponent of contemplative philosophy in that it commenced with the body and sensuous existence rather than with the mind and abstract contemplation. Life and thought were seen as emerging from matter and motion, in opposition to all notions of divine creation and a supreme *Logos*. It was for this reason that Plutarch charged that Epicurus "lay the contemplative part of the soul flat in the body." Thought, in the Garden, was seen as dependent on the health of the body.[226] Yet Epicurus promoted contentment or *ataraxia*, and a philosophy of *enough* as the end, rather than material change or political action. For Epicureanism, praxis was thus mainly confined to establishing a climate of security amid the chaos engendered by the decline of the polis and the wars of the Diadochi.

Indeed, the materialist conception of nature, associated with the philosophy of nature and natural science, from Democritus to Bacon, generally had this limitation, characteristic of natural science, of being aimed at contemplation of the world, thereby falling short of what was required of a more transformative social praxis.[227] According to Marx's critique, Feuerbach had been compelled by his *mere inversion* of the Hegelian idealism to replace the spirit with the human essence. He thus focused on species-being as the human essence, lacking any concrete relation to what human beings did, how they produced, and the nature of historical change. What was lacking in Feuerbach was any concrete notion of the *social*, and of the *practical-historical* dimension. This, moreover, raised the question of the necessity of developing a ruthless critique of the current order. As Marx stated in his Eleventh thesis on Feuerbach: "The philosophers have only *interpreted* the world in various ways; the point is to *change* it."[228]

In advancing this position in his *Theses on Feuerbach*, Marx was not abandoning the more contemplative materialism of ancient and modern philosophy and of natural science, but rather insisting that human nature was "the ensemble of social relations" and thus ever changing and developing with history. This was in line with the role of human beings as the self-mediating beings of nature. The materialist conception of nature was incomplete without a dialectically related materialist conception of history that dealt with the *active* role of human beings. What was needed was an alliance of nature and revolutionary praxis. Ernst Bloch wrote in his chapter on "Epicurus and Marx" in *On Karl Marx* (1968): "The First and Eleventh theses of Feuerbach are already present *in statu nascendi* in the references to Epicurus" in Marx's dissertation. Marx's Eleventh thesis was thus anticipated by the "energizing principle" with which he had ended his doctoral thesis.[229]

The new focus on *practical materialism* was to be worked out by Marx with Engels in *The German Ideology* in 1846, a work for which they were unable to find a publisher, and which was left to "the gnawing criticism of the mice," but served its "main purpose" of "self-clarification."[230] *The German Ideology* begins with a materialism presented in "corporeal" terms, in this respect going back to Marx's doctoral thesis on Epicurus and to his critique of Hegel's *Phenomenology of Spirit* at the end of his *Economic and Philosophical Manuscripts*—in both of which the corporeal, sensuous aspect of Marx's materialism stood out. For Epicurus, the corporeal realm consists of the atoms (as opposed to the void) and of compounds emerging from the attraction and repulsion of atoms. "It is impossible to conceive anything that is incorporeal," Epicurus wrote, "as self-existent, except empty space. And empty space cannot itself either act or be acted upon, but simply allows body to move through it. Hence, those who call soul incorporeal speak foolishly."[231] Similarly, for Marx in his critique of Hegel's *Phenomenology* in the *Economic and Philosophical Manuscripts* human beings were corporeal, sensual beings and thus objective beings, who depended for their existence and the satisfaction of their needs on objects outside of themselves.[232]

The turn toward a materialist conception of history rooted in human corporeal being constitutes the critical breakthrough of *The German Ideology* in 1846, where Marx begins by declaring:

> The first premise of all human history is, of course, the existence of *living* human individuals. Thus, the first fact to be established is the *corporeal organization* of these individuals and *their consequent relation to the rest of nature*. . . . Men can be distinguished from animals by consciousness, by religion or anything else you like. They themselves begin to distinguish themselves from animals as soon as they begin to *produce* their means of subsistence, a step which is conditioned by their corporeal organization.[233]

As Joseph Fracchia argues in his great work *Bodies and Artefacts: Historical Materialism as Corporeal Semiotics* (2022), Marx's materialist conception of history had human corporeal organization, and thus naturalism, as its foundation. This provided the "guiding thread of a historical-materialist *Wissenschaft*. It was at all times an analysis that was 'up from the body.'" Although Marx, Fracchia writes, had "discussed dimensions of corporeality in the *Manuscripts*, this positing" in *The German Ideology* "of human corporeal organization as the 'first fact' for historical theory and writing marks a radical corporeal turn."[234] This, as Engels was later to recall, was Marx's first great discovery, "the law of evolution in human history" rooted in human corporeal being and its necessary relation to labor and production.[235]

Yet, what is important in the beginning of *The German Ideology* is not simply Marx's reference to the corporeal, which had been present in his thinking from his doctoral thesis on Epicurus onward, but rather the connection developed between the materialist conception of nature and the materialist conception of history, both of which were linked to human corporeal being and human production. Marx went from the reality that human beings had objective bodily needs external to themselves, meaning that their mere human existence was dependent on external objects for the satisfaction of their needs, to the necessity of human production. From there arose in quick succession the social character of production, its development in specific historical modes of production, the division of labor, and finally the rise of class society, particular class formations, culture, and ideology.

The World Is My Friend

Part 1 of volume 1 of *The German Ideology* was titled "Feuerbach. Opposition of Materialist and Idealist Outlooks." But the analysis at this point scarcely dealt with Feuerbach at all, since his materialism focusing on the human essence was immediately superseded by a more concrete, corporeally based, historical materialism, aimed at praxis or free human activity (*energeia*). It is on this basis of *The German Ideology* that Marx and Engels first outlined the main features of the materialist conception of history, going beyond the earlier materialist conception of nature, dating back to antiquity. Human nature was no longer seen, as Marx explained in the *Theses on Feuerbach,* in terms of a fixed essence inhering in every human individual but as "the ensemble of social relations" emerging in a process of historical development. "All [human] history," Marx was to write in 1847 in *The Poverty of Philosophy*, "is nothing but a continuous transformation of human nature."[236]

If *The German Ideology* is primarily known for its clear rendition of Marx's materialist conception of history in volume 1 on

Feuerbach, and also to some extent for its critiques of Bruno Bauer and of "true socialism," it was the critique of the Young Hegelian Max Stirner (the pseudonym of Johann Kaspar Schmidt) in his *The Ego and Its Own* (1844) that took up the great majority of the work. Stirner's work was highly critical of Feuerbach's notion of the human essence for being a mere inversion, which replaced God with abstract humanity, thus not escaping the theological form. In this limited respect his critique of Feuerbach corresponded with that of Marx. But Stirner sought to carry the life of the spirit on to the notion of the individual corporeal ego, to the unique "I," divorced from material conditions, history, and society, creating an abstraction that removed the very notion of historical humanity.

This part of *The German Ideology* is extremely challenging to the reader, due to Marx's sardonic mirroring of Stirner's language of myth, ghosts, aphorisms, and neologisms, and the conflict between rationalism and irrationalism. This calls for a close back-to-back look at the arguments of both thinkers, while wading through Stirner's fantastical style and Marx's deep irony. Yet Marx's critique of Stirner has special significance since it constituted a critique of irrationalism and a state of nihilistic consciousness based on the spirit of the individual corporeal ego. Here Stirner sought to supersede "the modern," anticipating in many ways the postmodernism of the late twentieth and early twenty-first centuries. Marx's goal seems to have been to defend the broad German tradition represented by Hegel and Feuerbach from its debasement into an openly egoistic spiritualism in which "philosophical categories . . . lost the last vestige of connection with reality, and the last vestige of *meaning*."[237]

The Ego and Its Own both opens and closes with a statement that reads like a nihilistic parody of Epicurus's famous "death is nothing to us," replacing it with "all things are nothing to me."[238]

For Stirner, the ancients were above all concerned with sensuousness, with the world, and with things. The ancients, he contends, "did not know *thought*," spirit.[239] They were materialists, realists, and naturalists. The development of the ego in history meant that the world was to be abandoned for the spirit, and then the spirit for corporeal or material ego, rising above mere worldly existence and all notion of the human essence.

Stirner proceeded quickly to a discussion of the ancients, followed by a treatment of the moderns. In commenting on ancient philosophy, he focused almost entirely on the Hellenistic philosophies of the Epicureans, Stoics, and Skeptics, seeing them as representing the death of the philosophy of antiquity, and the beginning of the transition to the modern. Stirner's whole intention was to argue that the ancients, while primarily materialists/realists concerned with the world, nature, and things, had ended up in the Hellenistic period in "repelling the world" altogether. Democritus, Epicurus, the Stoics, and the Skeptics, he argued, had all rejected the world.[240] But in putting forward this argument Stirner fell into gross errors and contradictions at every stage, as Marx was to point out.

Marx was particularly concerned with the distortions of Epicurus. Stirner mistook the principle of materialism in Epicurus as that of "an active life." Marx replied that for the Epicureans "the principle of the concept of nature is the *mors immortalis* . . . and, in opposition to Aristotle's divine energy, divine leisure is put forward as the ideal of life instead of 'active life.'"[241]

In his dissertation Marx had associated *energeia* with the atom, which Epicurus had transferred in his philosophy to human beings in a materialist context, requiring activity for the sake of establishing friendship, community and an accord with nature, culminating in *ataraxia*. Intent on refuting Stirner, however, Marx downplayed the active element in achieving equanimity in life, emphasizing death the immortal and divine leisure as the concepts defining Epicurean ethics. He went on to point out that Stirner did not recognize the centrality of *ataraxia* in Epicurus, attributing the concept simply to the Stoics and Skeptics, while reducing Epicureanism to crude hedonism and failing to understand, as Marx pointed out, that for the Epicureans *ataraxia* is "placed higher than the 'hedone' [ἡδονή, pleasure]."[242]

More to the point for Marx was Stirner's claim that the Epicureans were in their "*practical philosophy* trickier and more deceitful" and "shrewd" than the Stoics, insofar as the Epicureans argued "the world must be deceived, for it is my enemy." Coupled with this was Stirner's contention that the "Stoics were unable to say anything about the spirit." To which Marx replied with respect to the Stoics, who advanced not only the spirit but also the speculative method, that this was "so little true that even *seeing spirits* originated from them." This in fact had caused Epicurus's later Roman followers to ridicule the Stoics for their groundless spiritualism. Marx declared: Stirner "enriches us with a new dictum of the Epicureans: 'the world must be deceived, for it is my enemy.' Hitherto it was only known that the Epicureans made statements in the sense that the world must be *disillusioned*, and especially freed from fear of gods, for the world is my *friend*." (As Alexander Herzen was later to write, Epicureanism had "a certain fraternal affection for all things living.") Stirner, Marx claimed, mistranslated from the Greek, turning the phrase "peace of mind" into "rejection of the world." He was thus unable to understand the positive reconciliation of nature and humanity within Epicurean philosophy.[243]

Stirner made the mistake, according to Marx, of seeing the Skeptics as representing "a philosophy more radical than Epicurus" even though the Skeptics reduced the theoretical relation of people to things to *appearance*, denying "actuality," while "in practice they left everything as of old." The Epicureans, in contrast, were far more radical than both the Stoics and Skeptics, attacking all state religion.[244] "To give our saint [Stirner] some indication of the real base on which the philosophy of Epicurus rests," Marx writes,

> it is sufficient to mention that the idea that the state rests on the mutual agreement of people, on a *contrat social*, is found for the first time in Epicurus. . . . Epicurus was the true radical Enlightener of antiquity; he openly attacked the ancient religion, and it was from him, too, that the atheism of the Romans, in so far as it existed, was derived. For this reason, too, Lucretius praised Epicurus as the hero who was the first to overthrow the gods and trample religion underfoot; for this reason among all church fathers, from Plutarch to Luther, Epicurus has always had the reputation of being the atheist philosopher *par excellence*, and was called a swine; for which reason, too, Clement of Alexandria says that when Paul takes up arms against philosophy he has in mind Epicurus alone. Hence we see how "cunning, perfidious" and "clever" was the attitude of this open atheist to the world in directly attacking its religion, while the Stoics adapted the ancient religion in their own speculative fashion, and the Sceptics used their concept of "appearance" as the excuse for being able to accompany all their judgements with a *reservatio mentalis*.[245]

For Marx, the irrationalism of Stirner lay in his complete abandonment of materialism, humanism, naturalism, Enlightenment, reason, and history in favor of an abstract, in fact spiritualized/idealistic ego. So intent was Stirner on characterizing the ancient world as the world of the child that he had to exclude any consideration of the encyclopedic work of Aristotle altogether. A materialist and historical perspective, in contrast, would recognize that the materialism and realism of ancient philosophy, particularly with respect to the natural world, remained vital. This provided the essential grounds from which to develop the conception of human beings as the self-mediating beings of history, that is the creator—if not under conditions entirely of their own choosing—of their historical world. The materialist conception of nature, of natural science emerging over thousands of years, needed to be complemented in the more revolutionary era of the nineteenth century by a materialist conception of history. The individual was a social individual, not a mere ego.

Real materialism, for Marx, meant true humanism, encompassing universal humanity and culminating in socialism. In its materialism and its ethics, that is, its emphasis on freedom, equality, and justice, if not exactly in its praxis of self-sufficiency and *ataraxia*, Epicureanism had prefigured modern socialism. As Marx wrote in his *Seventh Epicurean Notebook*—using a metaphor that was later to become increasingly important to him, drawn from Hegel and William Shakespeare—what was revealed in the study of Epicurus was the "silent, persevering mole of real philosophical knowledge" struggling to emerge to take "its place in history."[246] In Epicurus, the mole represented the emergence of materialism for the first time as a *social* doctrine, one in which the individual human being was both a material being and a social being, and therefore needed to struggle to be free.

Dialectic as the Abstraction of Movement

Over the course of the two decades between the publication of *The Poverty of Philosophy* in 1847 and the publication of *Capital* in 1867, Marx was to devote his theoretical efforts almost entirely to the critique of political economy, leaving philosophical discussions as such largely behind. This did not, however, constitute an abandonment of philosophy. Rather, Marx's main conclusions with respect to materialist philosophy, dialectics, the conception of human freedom, and the interconnections between nature and society as an emergent form of nature were incorporated into his work at every stage. Historical materialism needs a historical naturalism as its basis.

Thus, in his famous "Second Observation" in *The Poverty of Philosophy*, Marx concluded a discussion on the dialectical connection between the forces and relations of production and the production of ideas by emphasizing the ubiquity of motion: "There is a continual movement of growth in productive forces, of destruction of social relations, of formation in ideas; the only immutable thing is the abstraction of movement—*mors immortalis*."[247] Here what Marx had referred to in *The German Ideology* as Epicurus's "principle of the concept of nature," utilizing Lucretius's famous phrase, is rendered the *abstraction of movement*, of *energeia*, underlying all existence, matter in motion. Later, in 1870, responding to a statement by Friedrich Lange, a critic of materialism and the founder of neo-Kantianism, Marx wrote, in a letter to Louis Kugelmann, that Lange's reference to Marx's adept handling of "'the free movement of matter,'" was "nothing but a paraphrase for the *method* of dealing with matter—the *dialectic method*."[248] In this view, it was precisely because matter is continually in motion, destroying what came before, while constantly creating new combinations out of the old, as emergent forms, that an *immanent dialectic*, a form of abstraction aimed at capturing this entire movement, is necessary. Marx's own treatment of that immanent dialectic of matter had begun with his doctoral thesis on Epicurus.

The insights that Marx gained from Epicurus, and from Aristotle's *De Anima*, on the philosophy of nature helped to ground all of his subsequent thought, which always had a deep ontological and epistemological materialism/realism as its basis. In *Capital*, Marx quoted Lucretius on the *principle of conservation* basic to all materialism and emphasized above all in Epicurean philosophy: "What Lucretius says is self-evident: '*nil posse creari de nihilo*,' out of nothing, nothing can be created."[249] Likewise, in addressing the material basis of production, Marx cited the Italian political economist, historian, and philosopher Pietro Verri, who, drawing on the same principle, declared: "All the phenomena of the universe, whether produced by the hand of man or indeed by the universal laws of physics, are not to be conceived of as acts of creation but solely as a reordering of matter."[250] It was this reordering or organization of matter, however, that constantly created the new within society as well as universal nature. Thus, in *Capital* Marx wrote of the cooperative organization of labor that it leads to the "creation of a new productive power, which is intrinsically a collective one," a new emergent phenomenon arising through the reordering of previous relations.[251]

In his complex historical causality, Marx often pointed to residual historical factors, not part of the dominant relations, existing in the pores of the world, expressing alternative possibilities. Here he referred symbolically to "the gods of Epicurus" who lived in the *intermundia* between the worlds.[252] He rejected, in line with Epicurus and dialectics in general, the absolute rule of disjunctive either/or propositions (the principle of bivalence), and thus the crude misapplication of the formal contradictions to relations that were in flux and historically evolving. Here Marx emphasized the role of contingency, as in the Epicurean swerve, which *broke the bonds of fate*, and pointed to human freedom. Marx similarly rejected all fatalistic notions, while adhering to causal determinism, always holding on to what is objectively possible. Whereas for Epicurus, in the age of the Diadochi, a praxis of survival was seen as culminating in *ataraxia*, to be achieved socially through friendship in the Garden, for Marx, in an age of revolution, a meaningful praxis entailed the reconstitution of the social totality through the class struggle of the oppressed in the interest of universal human development.

In his encounter with Epicurus's materialist philosophy Marx first discovered the "rational kernel" in the Hegelian mystical shell, or the immanent materialist dialectic.[253] Epicurus as the Enlightenment figure of antiquity was the enemy of the religious alienation of humanity and of philosophical idealism. Matter in motion, according to Marx's interpretation of Epicurus, became "*embodied time, the existing reflection of the sensuous world in itself.*"[254] Hence, "Epicurus," in his concept of the swerve, Marx wrote, "was . . . the first to grasp the essence of repulsion—even if only in sensuous form, whereas Democritus only knew of its material existence."[255] Likewise, Epicurus was "the first to grasp appearance as appearance, that is, as alienation of essence, activating itself in its reality as such an alienation."[256] In this way, Epicurus pointed to the whole critical dialectical method, which permeated all of his thought. Epicurus was thus Hegel inverted. When Marx famously wrote in *Capital* that with Hegel the dialectic "is standing on its head. It must be inverted, in order to discover the rational kernel in the mystical shell," he was deliberately echoing Epicurus's observation, coming to us from Lucretius, that the Skeptic (or idealist) is an individual who "has stood with his own head where his feet belong."[257]

Indeed, for Marx, Epicurus was a materialist and dialectical thinker of the first order. It is possible that in his later years Marx may have had some second thoughts, as to whether what he saw appearing systematically in Epicurus was actually a reflection of himself and that it could not be proved on the basis of the available fragments. He wrote to Ferdinand Lassalle, responding to the latter's work on Heraclitus, that there was a good deal of difficulty of being sure as to one interpretation when dealing with fragments. Here Marx used his own work on Epicurus as an example, though in the case of Heraclitus the problem of working with fragments is magnified many times. Marx indicated that this was a problem of conceiving a complete system from fragments, and that what he had found in that respect with regard to Epicurus may well have been "*implicitly* present" but "not consciously as a system."[258]

Nevertheless, as we saw in the previous chapter, contemporary scholarship on Epicureanism, in the work of such thinkers as David Furley and Sedley, with considerably more in the way of primary sources at its disposal, particularly the text from Book 25 of Epicurus's *On Nature*, has arrived at results that now independently confirm Marx's interpretation, where the questions of the swerve and freedom and determinism are concerned. Sedley's notion of emergence in Epicurus is consistent with Marx's early nineteenth-century interpretation. More important, though, from the standpoint of Marxism, is that it is now clear that his study of Epicurus played a crucial role in the development of Marx's own dialectical synthesis.

In Epicurus's ethics Marx encountered a sophisticated theory of needs, distinguishing basic and non-basic needs on which the whole notion of the Garden as a community of *ataraxia* was grounded. It was close attention to essential needs and the requirements of self-sufficiency that allowed Epicurus to save his community by doling out beans during the siege of Athens by Demetrius the Besieger. Just as *ataraxia* was placed higher than *hedone*, so social/community needs were placed higher than individual hedonistic ones. Epicurus's critique of the unending pursuit of wealth, his grasp that accumulation is the real poverty, and his notion of the proper apportioning of needs, allowing for human development, clearly influenced Marx's analysis of both a rich world of needs, and the "hierarchy of . . . needs."[259] As Marx wrote in the *Grundrisse*, "The childish world of antiquity" was opposed to the acquisitive movement, culminating in capitalism, which sacrifices "the human end in itself to an entirely external end. This is why the childish world of antiquity appears . . . as loftier." Moreover, "It really is loftier in all matters where closed shapes, forms and given limits are sought for," only in the relentless manufacture of new needs associated with the development of production does it fall short.[260] The difficulty in the modern era is once again making the "human end" supreme, but in a context of constant historical change.

Attention to the whole materialist conception of nature to be found in Epicurus and carried forward in the seventeenth-century scientific revolution, meant that the deep structure of Marx's thought always took an ecological form, rooted in the complex, dialectical interaction of humanity with the earth. In the early 1850s, Marx's close friend, the physician-scientist-communist Roland Daniels (to whom Marx dedicated *The Poverty of Philosophy*), wrote his work, *Mikrokosmos*, in which he introduced, based on the scientific revolutions occurring at the time, an early ecological systems perspective.[261] As Daniels stated:

> It is not only the individual that owes its entire existence to an ongoing metabolism [*Stoffwechsel*]; but rather, the entire animal and plant worlds exist side by side and mutually condition each other through the steady exchange of materials and elements. . . . In this manner the whole of nature stands in the closest harmonious connection, indeed still more: the bodies mutually guarantee each other their existence. Animals and people could not exist without plants, and indeed, not without the now living genera and species; and both have their [living] conditions in precisely this

> specific nature. . . . Only matter is immortal in its eternal circulation [Lucretius, 3.865-69].[262]

The close connection of the metabolism concept of nineteenth-century science to Epicurus/Lucretius's ancient atomistic philosophy, brought out by Daniels, is fairly obvious. As Lucretius wrote, "So the sum of things is renewed always, and mortal creatures live by mutual exchange."[263]

There is no doubt that the close relations between Daniels and Marx helped spark this element of Marx's own analysis, leading to his heavy emphasis on his concept of *social metabolism* (as well as the "universal metabolism of nature"), which was to play such a large role in his ecological critique. Daniels died as a result of an illness he had contracted while in prison in connection with the Cologne Communist Trial. Marx was thus the only reader of his book manuscript, which was not published until the 1980s. Inspired by Daniels, Marx incorporated the notion of metabolism into his thought, as a regulative principle of natural relations out of which the human social metabolism in the form of production arose.[264] What impressed Marx was that the concept of metabolism could be extended into what today would be called an ecological systems theory that also embraced human society, leading Marx to develop the concept of "social metabolism" as the distinctly human metabolic relation to nature formed by labor and production.[265] Eventually, via the work of Justus von Liebig on the robbery of the soil in industrialized agriculture, Marx was to come to the conclusion that the alienated social metabolism in capitalism had created a fatal contradiction between capitalism and the earth: an "irreparable rift in the interdependent process of social metabolism, a metabolism prescribed by the natural laws of life itself."[266] As with Daniels, Marx's statement resonated with Lucretius's *De rerum natura*. Thus it corresponds with

Lucretius's famous description of death/destruction as a "fatal rift" or "fatal disunion" through the violation of a "natural condition" of either inorganic or organic nature.[267]

Marx in *The Holy Family* followed Epicurus in arguing that the human individual was not an *atomistic individual* and therefore contentless like the atom itself, but a *social* individual, living and developing in society, and to be judged in those terms. Unlike Feuerbach's materialism, Epicureanism had explicitly introduced historical and social change and development, with the concept of the *social contract*, and notions of social justice. For Epicurus, justice was based on reciprocity and the requirements of justice changed with changing social conditions, since it depended on what was efficacious for humanity in general. It was the Epicurean argument on justice that Marx was to employ in his own defense in his political trial in Prussia as editor of the *Neue Rheinische Zeitung*, faced with charges of insulting a public prosecutor and hurling calumnies at police officers.[268] In line with Epicurus's definition of justice, Marx declared:

> Society is not founded upon the law; that is a legal fiction. On the contrary, the law must be founded upon society, it must express the common interests and needs of society—as distinct from the caprice of individuals—which arise from the material mode of production prevailing at the time. . . . You cannot make the old laws the foundation of the new social development, any more than these old laws created the old social conditions. They were engendered by the old conditions of society and must perish with them. They are bound to change with the changing conditions of life.[269]

Marx never lost his deep affinity for Epicurus. Heraclitus, for him, was the originator of dialectics in antiquity, while Aristotle was the greatest, most encyclopedic mind. But Epicurus represented the break with the dominant political/class structure of antiquity, and its alienated character. His natural philosophy was the real progenitor of modern materialism. Like Hegel, Marx agreed that Epicurus had nothing to offer speculative philosophy. He was rather its antithesis. Epicurus thus represented a break with philosophy, in Hegelian terms. The immanent dialectical principle of materialism he found in Epicurus, not Feuerbach, remained foundational throughout Marx's life. In 1874, Marx provided Engels with passages from the ancient atomists, translated from the ancient Greek, which would form part of Engels's notes on "The Ancient Outlook on Nature," constituting preparatory materials for *The Dialectics of Nature*.[270] Engels was particularly interested in how John Dalton had, in a sense, revived ancient Atomism within modern chemistry.[271]

As Engels indicated, Marx in 1857 had wanted to write the article on "Epicurus" for the *New American Cyclopaedia* co-edited by Charles A. Dana, managing editor of the *New York Tribune*, for which Marx was the European correspondent. However, the job of writing that article was given instead to the U.S German émigré Hermann Raster. It is true that Raster provided a relatively credible article on Epicurus, in which he indicated "No other ancient school of philosophy has evinced a cohesive power equal to that of Epicurus."[272] Yet he discounted the whole question of Epicurus's swerve, failing to comprehend Epicurus's concepts of freedom or emergence, thus missing what Marx had recognized as most important in Epicurean materialism, subsequently confirmed by the work of Gomperz.

Upon Marx's death Engels observed that when confronted with death Marx responded: "'Death is not a misfortune for him who dies, but for him who survives' . . . quoting Epicurus."[273] Behind this lay not only the reality of mortality, of death the immortal, but a whole revolutionary materialist dialectic, bolstered by a critical *Wissenschaft*, in which life was struggle, and the object of that struggle was a *real humanism* and a *real naturalism*, the reconciliation of humanity and nature and the *disalienation of the world*. As Marx well understood, Epicurus's message in his time was a revolutionary one, to be compared to Prometheus's defiance of the gods in Aeschylus.

CHAPTER FOUR

Marxism and Epicureanism

Frederick Engels, like Karl Marx, had a deep respect for Epicurus as the leading materialist of Greek antiquity. As he wrote in 1882 in "Bruno Bauer and Early Christianity": "While classic Greek philosophy in its last forms—particularly in the Epicurean school—led to atheistic materialism, Greek vulgar philosophy led to the doctrine of a one and only God and of the immortality of the human soul."[1] In 1893, Alexei Mikhailovich Voden, a twenty-three-year-old scholar who had studied at St. Petersburg University and the University of Berlin and was attached to Russian Social Democracy, visited London to pursue research at the British Museum on the history of English philosophy. Leading Russian Marxist philosopher Georgi Plekhanov had given him a letter of recommendation to Engels. Voden was invited by Engels to his home on ten occasions to discuss issues of philosophy and politics. When the young Russian scholar visited Engels on the last of these occasions in July 1893, Engels was deeply engaged with Marx's unpublished 1841 doctoral thesis on the *Difference Between the Democritean and Epicurean Philosophy of Nature*, which he had found among Marx's papers, but which was not published until almost a decade later in 1902.

After inquiring into whether Voden was interested in the history of ancient Greek philosophy, Engels offered to present the gist of Marx's thesis. He then proceeded to quote from heart not only from Marx and Epicurus, but also from various ancient Greek authors, including Diogenes Laertius, Sextus Empiricus, and Clement of Alexandria, whom Marx had referred to in this work. Engels indicated that Marx's thesis had overturned the views of both ancient and modern writers who claimed that Epicurus's work had failed to "cognize the cause of things." Marx, in contrast, had reconstructed the "immanent dialectics" of the Epicurean system. Engels indicated that Marx had spoken to him of his desire to return to and publish his research into Hellenistic philosophy.[2]

When Voden asked Engels if Marx had ever been "a Hegelian in the strict sense of the word," Engels replied that Marx's dissertation on Epicurus, written at a time when he had "completely mastered Hegelian dialectics and had not yet been obliged by the course of his studies to replace it by the materialist dialectical method," already showed "perfect independence of Hegel in the application of Hegel's own dialectics, and that in the sphere in which Hegel was strongest—the history of thought." Hegel, representing an idealist standpoint, had in fact issued various "scornful opinions" with regard to Epicurus's philosophical system as distinct from his contributions to natural science and empiricism, while, in Marx and Engels's time, Friedrich Lange's *History of Materialism* had fallen far short even of Immanuel Kant's eighteenth-century treatments of materialism and Epicurus. Engels concluded his conversation with Voden by expressing "the desire" that he "should find out and report to him whether any viewpoint resembling Marx's in any way was current in literature on the subject" of Epicurus, that is, any that explored the immanent dialectics of Epicurus's materialist philosophy along the lines that Marx had developed.[3]

It is doubtful that Voden ever responded directly to Engels's request. He burned all of his correspondence with Engels a few months later in autumn 1893, just before the arrival of the French police, who were on the lookout for revolutionaries. Engels died in 1895, the year before Voden returned to London.[4]

What Voden would have discovered in examining the general scholarship on Epicurus in the early 1890s, when Engels made his request, was a body of work that could hardly have been more in conflict with Marx's 1841 dissertation. At the time that Marx wrote his doctoral thesis and for decades after his death, the dominant view was that Epicurus was a secondary figure, greatly inferior to Democritus, whose physics he had copied at best and deviated from at worst. According to Heinrich Ritter's *The History of Ancient Philosophy* (1838), to which Marx referred several times in his dissertation, "We don't see in the totality of Epicurus's doctrines a whole whose parts fit together. It is evident that the canonic and physics of Epicurus are nothing but a clumsy appendix to his morality. But who could praise Epicurus's morality, either the virtues it contains or its originality, or finally the logical series that reigns there? In the first place, we don't find it in the least original. . . . We can't say that it is a well tied together doctrine. . . . This doctrine appears to us to be of little scientific value."[5] In the words of Eduard Zeller, considered in the late nineteenth century to be the leading German authority on ancient Greek philosophy, "The scientific value and capacity for development of Epicureanism are out of all proportion to its extensive diffusion and the length of time during which it continued to flourish. No other system troubled itself so little about the foundations on which it rested. . . . But this philosophical sterility, the mechanical handing down of unchangeable principles, places the intellectual value of Epicureanism on the lowest level."[6] For Lange in his *History of Materialism*, Epicurus's notion of the swerve of the atom was of no real significance, mentioned only in passing as "an incalculable element" and "error" that logically marred his materialism.[7]

However, a deeper inquiry, if Voden had been able to pursue it, might have led him to the profound but highly specialized research of Theodor Gomperz in the 1870s based on the recovery of parts of Book 25 of Epicurus's *On Nature*. Gomperz argued that Epicurus's work established the compatibility of free will with causal determinism.[8] Gomperz's initial discoveries were eventually to lead, particularly over the last half-century, to the intensive study of Epicurus's Book 25 by classicists, and to a remarkable recovery of Epicurus's concept of freedom that was consistent with Marx's argument in his dissertation, written more than a century before.

Voden, it is evident, never directly investigated Gomperz's work on Book 25 of Epicurus's *On Nature*. Nevertheless, he continued to pursue the question of Marx's dissertation and the significance of Epicureanism for the development of historical materialism, first raised in his final conversation with Engels, which clearly occupied a central place in his thinking over the next four and a half decades. Thus, it is Voden who is credited with having "prepared the German and Russian editions of Marx's dissertation" for publication, the first full version of which appeared in volume 1 of the *Karl Marx and Friedrich Engels Gesamtausgabe* (MEGA) in 1927, complete with editorial notes.[9]

Moreover, in the last year of his life (1938-39), Voden wrote an article on Epicurus for the Russian *Granat Encyclopedic Dictionary* that reflected the development of his thinking in this area and pointed to the close connection between historical materialism and ancient Epicurean philosophy. In that article Voden, following Marx, discussed Epicurus's swerve, indicating that this was not simply a postulate of a random movement, but rather constituted the basis for all voluntary action and creative change. The historical conditions in which Epicurus's philosophy arose were, he noted, those of "the decline of socio-political life" in the Hellenistic period. Epicurus saw philosophy as necessarily constituting a "practical activity," ensuring that a free, secure, and contented life was possible. An active role in philosophy was extended by Epicurus to all people, including women and slaves. Language was conceived as a historically emergent fact, while society and state were rooted in a social contract. In these and other ways, Voden validated and extended Marx's argument in his dissertation and *The German Ideology*. He also quoted V. I. Lenin's *Philosophical Notebooks* on Epicurus's materialism. In writing his article, he utilized nearly all of the most up-to-date works in Epicurean scholarship (including Hermann Usener, Ettore Bignone, and Cyril Bailey). He referred to materials recently unearthed from the Herculaneum papyri and the inscription of Diogenes of Oenoanda. However, missing was any treatment of Gomperz's work on Book 25 of *On Nature*, representing a position close to Marx's own, and based on the new evidence from the Herculaneum papyri.[10]

Engels had clearly expected Voden to convey to Plekhanov that it was in relation to ancient philosophy and not to French mechanistic materialism that Marx had developed his materialist dialectics. But Plekhanov, who informed Voden that he had wasted his time talking to Engels about Epicurus rather than the French materialists, clearly did not get the message.[11] Searching for an adequate basis of Marx's materialism, Plekhanov finally derived the fiction of its basis in the work of Baruch Spinoza, ignoring Marx's many criticisms of the latter.[12] No doubt Plekhanov's lack of interest in what Engels had to say on Marx and Epicurus, despite being told that Marx had devoted his dissertation to the ancient Greek materialist, was influenced by the prejudices in the history of philosophy in his day.

However, in the view of Marx's contemporary Alexander Herzen, the Russian revolutionary Narodnik, socialist, and philosopher, Epicurus was a central figure. As Lenin was to observe, Herzen "went further than Hegel, following Feuerbach to materialism." He "came right up to dialectical materialism and halted—before historical materialism."[13] In his *Letters on the Study of Nature* ("Letter Four" on "The Last Epoch of Ancient Science"), Herzen depicted Epicureanism as "the last, purely Greek attempt to reconcile thought with life and the individual with his environment," that is, with nature. Devastating in its materialist critique, "Epicureanism dealt the death blow to paganism" in religion. Moreover, Epicureanism was, for Herzen, intrinsically dialectical. "Lucretius begins *à la* Hegel from being and non-being as active first principles which interacted and coexisted." The motion of atoms led to the emergence of "whole worlds where the conditions for their formation exist and worlds perish where these conditions do not." Epicurus's philosophy was known for its "love for life" and its "affection" for "all things living," along with its "scorn for death." Referring to "Lucretius's fiery heart," Herzen subscribed to his view that "Epicurus was the greatest of the Greeks" and that "morality—conscious morality, human morality—to which all pagan religion constitutes an obstacle—starts with him [Epicurus], and that, since then, man himself is the measure of morality, etc."[14]

Lenin was a close reader of Herzen's *Lectures on the Study of Nature* and would have been well aware of his treatment of Epicurus. However, in his 1908 *Materialism and Empirio-Criticism*, he followed Adolphe Franck's 1844 *Dictionnaire des Sciences Philosophiques*, which confusedly classified Epicureanism as belonging to "moral sensationalism" rather than "objective sensationalism," or materialism—later regarded as a false distinction. Nevertheless, Epicurus, for Lenin, was clearly seen as holding to the fundamental materialist proposition on the sensual basis of existence and knowledge: "Only the sensuous exists; there is no other being than material being."[15] As was common at the time and has remained so, Lenin presumed that Marx when he submitted his dissertation was a "Hegelian idealist." It is unlikely that he had read Marx's dissertation on Epicurus, and hence he was unaware of the atheism and materialism embedded in it and the complex dialectical relation to Hegelian idealism evidenced there.[16]

In his 1915 notes on Georg Wilhelm Friedrich Hegel's *Lectures on the History of Philosophy* in his *Philosophical Notebooks*, Lenin contended that Epicurus provided "a guess work of genius and *sign posts for science*" in his pioneering materialist conjectures. He quoted Hegel's statement: "It may be said that Epicurus is the inventor of empirical natural science, of empirical psychology. In contrast to the Stoic ends, conceptions of the understanding, is experience, the sensuous present. There [with the Stoics] we have abstract, limited understanding, without truth in itself, and therefore without the presence and reality of nature; here [in Epicurus] we have this sense of nature, which is truer than these other hypotheses." In response to this, Lenin had written, in caps: "(THIS ALMOST COMPLETELY APPROACHES DIALECTICAL MATERIALISM)."[17]

It is surely no mere coincidence, although he would not have been aware of it, that Lenin, via his Marxist-materialist reading of Hegel's comment on Epicurus, reached a conclusion with respect to Epicurus similar to that of Marx himself at the end of his dissertation, where Marx had written: "Epicurus is . . . the greatest representative of Greek Enlightenment. . . . In *Epicurus* . . . *atomistics* with all its contradictions has been carried through and completed *as the natural science of self-consciousness*." Hence "self-consciousness" becomes the "absolute principle."[18] For Lenin, via Hegel, Epicurus approached the very core of dialectical materialism. In response to Hegel's criticism that in the case of Epicurus's Atomism, the mere material can give rise to thought, Lenin wrote that Hegel was simply eluding "the essence of *materialism* and materialist dialectics."[19] Indeed, Lenin's entire section on "The Philosophy of Epicurus," in his 1915 "Conspectus of Hegel's Book, 'Lectures on the History of Philosophy,'" where he dialectically counters Hegel's views, amply demonstrates his own deep appreciation of Epicurus as a thinker, and as a forerunner of dialectical materialism. At this stage too, it is clear that Lenin had thoroughly studied Diogenes Laertius's Book 10 on Epicurus.[20]

Lenin's "Conspectus" of Hegel's Book, 'Lectures on the History of Philosophy,'" was not published until 1930. However, the combination of the publication of the full version of Marx's doctoral thesis in 1927 and the publication a few years later of Lenin's "Conspectus" on Hegel's *History of Philosophy* (part of his *Philosophical Notebooks*) had the effect of bringing Epicureanism to the fore in Soviet philosophy—just prior to the purges that decimated the most vital parts of the early Soviet philosophical tradition. According to the remarkable work *A Textbook of Soviet Philosophy* published under the direction of Mikhail Shirokov in 1931, the ancient materialist philosophy of Epicurus had provided a concept of "emergence" that had attracted Marx. Here "emergence is the uniting of atoms; disappearance their falling apart." This served to explain a process of self-generation, "the origin and development of the solar system, the movement of the human soul, etc." Out of this had arisen the fundamental materialist view. In materialist dialectics, there is "ceaseless emergence and annihilation of the forms of . . . movement," which continued to reproduce themselves "in ever new movement and in ever new qualities."[21]

The first notable and influential, if flawed, assessment of Marx's dissertation was a seven-page analysis provided by Franz Mehring in his biography *Karl Marx: The Story of His Life*, published in 1918.[22] Mehring was a leading figure in the left opposition within the German Social Democratic Party, together with Rosa Luxemburg, Karl Liebknecht, and Clara Zetkin, and joined with them in the Spartacist League, founded in 1916. Just short of two weeks after the murder of Luxemburg and Liebknecht in January 1919, Mehring, who had been ill, died. Published the year before his death, his biography of Marx was for many decades the authoritative guide to Marx's life. At the time that Mehring was considering Marx's dissertation, it had been published only in part, since it was missing all of the notes, which were vital. Moreover, the *Notebooks on Epicurean Philosophy* were not published, even in part, until almost a decade later. Much of the material surrounding Marx's dissertation was thus unavailable to Mehring.

On the dissertation, Mehring provides only a confused and in some places derisive account. "Marx," he writes, "is still completely on the idealist basis of the Hegelian philosophy." Epicurus's swerve and his whole physics are presented by Mehring as absolute absurdities. Marx was flatly wrong in thinking that Epicurus was the greater philosopher than Democritus: "Democritus," Mehring declares, "was the pioneer and not Epicurus." Marx supposedly claimed that Epicurus's emphasis on self-consciousness and Enlightenment, in Mehring's words, "neutralizes all real and authentic science"—a view that contradicts Marx's own praise of Epicurus as the Enlightenment figure of antiquity who brought natural science into the light of self-consciousness. Nevertheless, Mehring clearly understood that what Marx found most positive in Epicurus was an argument for free will against rigid determinism or fatalism. Moreover, "what drew him [Marx] to Epicurus," Mehring states, was "the 'energizing principle'" that Epicurus's whole philosophy represented, and Epicurus's "Promethean" enlightenment outlook.[23]

The publication in full of Marx's dissertation on Epicurus in 1927 drew attention to it within classical scholarship. In 1928, Bailey, the leading English classical scholar specializing in Hellenistic philosophy and particularly Epicureanism, wrote a review of Marx's dissertation for *The Classical Quarterly*. Bailey had translated Lucretius in 1910 and Epicurus's extant works in 1926 and was the author in 1928 of *The Greek Atomists and Epicurus*. He played the leading role in the revival of English scholarship on Epicurus in the early twentieth century. Writing on "Karl Marx on Greek Atomism" in *The Classical Quarterly*, Bailey exclaimed that "it is almost astonishing to see how far he got considering the materials then available." Not only did Marx demonstrate "a penetrating acquaintance with the two philosophers," Democritus and Epicurus, but he was "the first to perceive" Epicurus's positive departure from Democritus, based on an entirely different theory of knowledge, recognizing Epicurus's "genuine originality." Bailey questioned whether Marx's more theoretical assumptions about Epicurus's philosophy were entirely correct, with respect both to his interpretation of the swerve and conceptions of human freedom, and his depiction of Epicurus's philosophy as a conscious system. Marx, according to Bailey, had fallen prey at times to the temptation of reading too much of his own contemporary viewpoint into Epicurus. Nevertheless, "any student of Epicurus," he wrote, would benefit from Marx's thesis.[24] Bailey's own work, which drew on the extensive collection of fragments on Epicurus from antiquity compiled by Hermann Usener, along with the work of Gomperz and others in decoding the Herculaneum papyri, was to lead to enormous advances in Epicurean scholarship in the twentieth century and up to the present.

Epicurus and Marxian Classicism

Beginning in the 1930s, partly inspired by Bailey's important work on Epicurus, and partly by the publication of Marx's doctoral thesis, there was a flowering of work by English-speaking classicists on Epicurus as a precursor of modern and particularly Marxist materialism. The leading roles in this respect were played by Benjamin Farrington and George Thomson. In 1942, Farrington, then a professor of classics at University College, Swansea, in Wales, was attending the meetings of the Classical Association in Cambridge when one of the leading classicists in Britain, Francis Macdonald Cornford, holder of the Laurence Professorship of Ancient Philosophy at Cambridge University, delivered a paper on "The Marxist View of Ancient Philosophy."[25] Farrington later wrote "I . . . could hardly believe my ears," sitting there and realizing the main target of Cornford's attack, the arch-villain of the piece, was his own 1939 book *Science and Politics in the Ancient World*. The secondary target of Cornford's polemic was George Thomson's 1940 *Aeschylus and Athens*. Both were strongly condemned by Cornford as Marxists for taking the side of Ionian materialist philosophy, and particularly Epicurus against Plato, who had been the primary subject of Cornford's scholarship. Yet, while Thomson was, as Cornford noted, an "avowed Marxist," Farrington in 1942 was not, and had little acquaintance with the materialist conception of history.[26]

Although an Irish nationalist and generally on the left, having been inspired by the International Brigades in the Spanish Civil War, Farrington did not have a deep knowledge of historical materialism when he wrote *Science and Politics in the Ancient*

World and had approached his subject "rather as a rationalist than as a Marxist." In 1939, despite the fact that the second half of his book was devoted to Epicurus, he had not read Marx's doctoral dissertation or even Bailey's review of it. Farrington later recalled, "This was one omission I had to repair when I found myself exalted to the position of a Marxist authority on the subject." Although his book had been well received by Marxists, it had made no mention of Marx or Marxism. Oddly, the "ignorance of Marxism in some circles in Britain" was then so great, Farrington wrote, that a figure as prestigious as Cornford could seek "to demolish Marxism by attacking a book which never mentions it."[27]

Cornford commenced his criticism by quoting at length from Engels's *Anti-Dühring* in which Engels said that the materialist conception of history meant that it was necessary to reexamine past history as a history of class struggles. Marxists were then accused of crudely imposing an "economic interpretation of history" on the classical world.[28] Concerned mainly to defend Plato against criticisms that both the *Republic* and *The Laws* were oligarchic and class-repressive in character, Cornford chastised Farrington for using the common translation of the "noble lie" in relation to Plato's *Republic*, claiming that it was being used as "poisonous propaganda." Ironically, Cornford wrote that rather than "lie" a better word would have been "propaganda."[29] In his own acclaimed translation of *The Republic* published posthumously a few years later, Cornford was to render "noble lie" into the more innocuous "convenient fiction," establishing a precedent that was to be followed by later translators.[30] None of this of course altered the nature of Plato's parable of the metals with its outright advocacy of what it depicted as a deliberate untruth, aimed at justifying a class hierarchy. Here, the rulers were said to be mixed by God with gold, separating them from the guardians, mixed with silver, and from farmers and artisans, mixed with iron and brass. The oligarchic nature of Plato's philosophy, as Farrington later observed, was something that "British scholarship habitually suppressed."[31]

Going on the attack against the "Marxist view" of Epicurus, Cornford insisted, supposedly showing the emptiness of Marxist economism in this area but only demonstrating his own ignorance of historical materialism, that Epicurus, rather than being a representative of science, modernity, and capitalism, was actually an enemy of endless acquisition. Cornford thus pointed out that Epicurus saw "the pursuit of wealth as a misuse of human energy, no less disastrous than the pursuit of power. He had no wish to control, or to exploit, the forces of Nature." Cornford believed that this put Epicurus completely at variance with Marxism, which he identified with Prometheanism in the sense of extreme productivism. Epicurus, Cornford told his audience, would not have been interested in "the steam engine, the power loom, and the tractor" and "would have felt more sympathy with Mr. Gandhi" than the modern capitalist, who was of so much concern to Marxists. Epicurus's denial of an immortal soul, Cornford added with a nod to the Church of England, not only removed the fear of Hades, but "the joy of heaven," and was thus antagonistic to the Christian worldview.[32] In this sense, Epicurus was portrayed as a negative figure.

Cornford naturally made no mention of Marx's doctoral thesis on Epicurus of which he seems to have been completely oblivious. His polemic induced Farrington to begin to explore Marx's analysis, but upon turning to the dissertation for the first time he found it difficult reading due to what he called its "Hegelian German" (an English translation was not published until 1967).[33] Nevertheless, it was no less illuminating and was to inspire some of his later analysis of Epicurus. Although much of Farrington's work was on Greek science, he was less interested in Epicurean physics and Marx's discussion of that than he was in the political, historical, and ethical aspects of Epicureanism.

Mehring's early dismissal of the dissertation, Farrington discovered, had been "much too hasty" and was amply contradicted by Bailey's expert opinion. What he noticed immediately was "a marked independence of Hegel" demonstrated in Marx's dissertation. So deep and profound was Marx's treatment of Epicurus that it in many ways "anticipated the direction in which Epicurean studies have proceeded in the last hundred years."[34]

The editors of the first volume of the MEGA, in which the complete dissertation was published for the first time, characterized Marx's work then as atheist, not yet materialist.[35] In contrast, Farrington, with his deep knowledge of Greek materialism and science, was clear that Marx was at the time of his dissertation deeply engaged with materialist philosophy. Marx's choice of Epicurus as the subject of his dissertation represented "a real affinity of spirit. His delight in the thought of Epicurus and Lucretius is visible in every page of his work."[36]

Most important, for Farrington, was Marx's development of the Epicurean notion of freedom. "The conception of the atom," he wrote, "allowed both for the development of a world of nature under the rule of law and a human society that was both part of nature, yet distinguished from it by being the theatre of human will": "While Democritus was a determinist, Epicurus championed the free will." Epicurus thus "sought to construct not simply a philosophy of nature but a philosophy of man. He sought to account for the fact not simply that *nature* had emerged from the play of atoms in the void but also *society*; not simply man as animal, but man as that unique thing, a moral being."[37]

Over the course of his studies, Farrington came to the conclusion that Epicurus and Lucretius not only offered to Marx a materialist philosophical basis, mediated by modern science, but also a source of inspiration for his materialist conception of history. Going beyond Marx's dissertation, Farrington emphasized the proto-historical materialist aspects of Book V of *De rerum natura*, which Marx certainly studied carefully, although he left no notes related to his readings. Here was to be found the broadest picture of the Epicurean system, allowing one to perceive the general outlines of Epicurean anthropology, history, and sociology. Lucretius indicated that only rational philosophy (or *ratio*, standing for the Epicurean method) could allow one to perceive the world as it was prior to property, walled towns, war, and commerce.[38] Lucretius, in Farrington's account, therefore described an early way of life in which human beings had arisen out of the feral state of wild beasts to inaugurate

> a regime of friendship (*tunc et amicitiem coeperunt iungere*) by a mutual contract to avoid doing injury. This marked the end of a time when each man had relied for his safety on his own strength (*valere et vivere doctus*, 961) and the substitution for it of the rule of pity for the weak with the special obligation to respect women and children. It is not claimed that this union of hearts (*concordia*) was perfectly realized; but it is argued, it must have been respected for the most part or the human race would have exterminated itself before now. Such was the regime of friendship which characterized the older way of life.[39]

Justice in this community of friendship (known as *vita prior* or before recorded history) was based directly on reciprocity and a mutual covenant.[40] The stage of human social development that succeeded the regime of friendship, according to Lucretius, was the period of kings and the death of kings. This was followed by the city-state bound together by a system of laws, establishing justice as legally sanctioned, while also leading to organized political warfare, and the military slaughter of tens of thousands in a single day.[41] The class state corresponded to the rise of accumulated wealth and a money economy, of which Plato's political philosophy was a dramatic illustration. As Richard Seaford has explained, the fact that Greek society was the first historical formation to introduce a systematic money economy based on coinage led to an early recognition of social alienation.[42] The response of Epicurus was profound: "The wealth demanded by nature is both limited and easily procured; that demanded by idle imaginings stretches on to infinity." He added: "Nothing is sufficient for him to whom what is sufficient seems little"—thus "unlimited wealth is great poverty."[43] The disruption due to the development of private property, acquisitive commerce (*chrematistics*) instead of *oikos* (household management), the unrestrained pursuit of wealth, state religion, and war were all associated with the new alienated political society.

In *The Faith of Epicurus* Farrington quotes Philodemus (ca. 110–35 BCE) as stating in his *Rhetoric*, in Epicurean terms, with respect to friendship and the state:

> If a man were to undertake a systematic enquiry to find out what is most destructive of friendship and most productive of enmity, he could find it in the regime of the *polis*. Witness the envy felt for those who compete for its prizes. Witness the rivalry that necessarily springs up between competitors. Witness the division of opinion that accompanies the introduction of fresh legislation and the deliberate organization of faction fights which set not only individuals but whole peoples by the ears.[44]

The Epicurean doctrine, it will be remembered, was a historical product of "a period of social collapse."[45] Epicurus developed his philosophy in response to the demise of the Athenian polis (and of the Greek poleis) during the wars of the Diadochi. Although Epicureanism was to continue for centuries afterward, what could be called its second flowering occurred at the time of the breakdown of the Roman Republic. In each case, there was a growth of political alienation and withdrawal from public life.

Epicurus and Lucretius presented this as the product of long historical development. The decline of a society rooted in friendship and the unity of the heart had given way to one based on force, class divisions, and the state, which eventually succumbed to its own disunity. The only real answer to the social malaise that followed was to reestablish community based on human unity and friendship. In Epicurus's view, as explained by Farrington, "Friendship was the supreme virtue. These considerations explain the remarkable fact that, when Lucretius discusses the evils of society, what he lists is not the crimes but the punishments—the execution cell, the horrible hurling down from the rock, the cat-o'-nine-tails, the rack, the pitch-cap, the brandings, the torches (III, 1014–17). What the Epicureans say about justice ceases to be unsatisfactory when we remember that, according to them, what the world needed was not more justice, but more love."[46]

Indeed, the reason for the transition to the city-state and the society of laws, following the wars of kings and civil unrest (which succeeded the early regime of friendship) in Epicurus and Lucretius—Farrington explained—was the fear of death. Greed and fear are described by Lucretius as "wounds of life," which are "fed by the fear of death" or the struggle for existence. "To be despised and poverty-stricken," according to Lucretius, "is felt to be a sort of tarrying before the gates of death." Driven by this fear, human beings engage in a war of all against all, seeking their personal advantage. Such fear "overcomes the sense of honor, tears asunder the bond of friendship, and abolishes respect of man for man." State religions, as in Plato, took advantage of this fear by inculcating a fear of the afterlife.[47]

Hence, confronted with the demise of the society founded on the polis, and by the Platonic proposal to reconstruct the state on the basis of hierarchy and coercion, Epicurus provided an entirely different answer. "It is the specific originality of Epicurus," Farrington wrote, "that he is the first man known to history to have organized a movement for the liberation of mankind at large from superstition."[48] Epicureanism was a movement that sought "to overcome the evils of a class-divided society" by means of "voluntary community." It saw its enemy within the realm of philosophy in "the myths which were devised by Plato and others to buttress" a hierarchal state through state religion. Yet Farrington conceded in his "Second Thoughts on Epicurus" (1953) that Epicureanism was not in its time a forward-looking perspective. Rather, it was a philosophy that looked to the past, with the result that the Epicureans were 'in the strictest [cultural] sense reactionaries." In this respect, it was true, Farrington conceded in the face of Cornford's criticism, that the outlook of Epicureans in antiquity had as much in common with Gandhi and the notion of a society of self-sufficiency as it had with Marx, who looked forward to a revolutionary future made possible by changing human relations to production.[49]

However, in 1967, when Farrington published his influential *The Faith of Epicurus*, his perspective changed once again, emphasizing the radical implications of Epicurus's thought. Here what stood out for him was how Epicurus's materialist analysis, which was trapped in its own historical times and thus could provide no other solution than voluntary communities, reemerged, mole-like, more than a millennium later, in a more radical form. Incorporated into Marx's analysis, it was to feed into a revolutionary materialist perspective. As Farrington wrote at this time:

> The Epicurean conception of nature, which saw it as a theatre of law and removed it from miracle, from the arbitrary interference of the deity, helped the seventeenth century to clear the path for the new birth of science. Two centuries later the searching Epicurean critique of the inherent injustice of state power set Karl Marx dreaming of the day when the state would wither away, when the freedom of each individual would be the condition of the freedom of all, and the truly human period of history would begin.[50]

What *The Faith of Epicurus* demonstrated was that although Epicurus had encouraged his followers to refrain as much as possible from politics, what this meant was to remove themselves from the normal public life as it existed at the time, which was dominated by class, corruption, militarism, and state-religion. This did not mean a denial altogether of the responsibilities of citizenship or that Epicureanism was passive in a political and ideological sense. Here the central thrust initiated by Epicurus was the struggle against state-religion, particularly astral religion of the kind promoted by Plato, which was the greatest impediment to human freedom as well as to *ataraxia*. The critique of religion, moreover, required a critique of the earth, that is, an explanation of the human relation to the earth and through it to society. In a famous struggle in the ancient world, recounted by Lucian in his *Alexander the False Prophet* and noted by Marx, Epicureans led in the fight against the Paphlagonian mystic, who had a large following in Rome and had tried to impose the worship of Asclepius, the god of healing reborn in the form of a serpent. Exposed by Epicureans, who opposed him both in mass and as individuals, Alexander declared the "unmitigated Epicurus" to be "his worst enemy," and publicly set fire to Epicurus's *Principal Doctrines*. He sought to have those Epicureans who defied him stoned to death. Lucian, who wrote his critique of Alexander partly to defend Epicurus, praises the courage of the Epicureans in combating this mystical religion, in contrast to the acceptance of Alexander offered by those from the Academy and the Stoics.[51]

For Farrington, Epicurus was not devoid of praxis but was "a reformer in the making."[52] He opposed the political order of the Hellenistic states at the time of the wars of the Diadochi from without rather than within. He offered his renewed regime of friendship as an alternative to the type of coercive "justice" promoted by Plato's *Laws* and to a "sick society," as Farrington put it. Opposing Plato's (the "golden man's") notion of the noble lie or the parable of the metals, justifying a class order of society, Epicurus provided an egalitarian vision based on human community and friendship. "The astonishing thing," Farrington wrote, "is that so uncompromising a creed should have met with wide success."[53]

Farrington was also a noted scholar of Francis Bacon, having translated some of his work from Latin into English. He highlighted Bacon's recognition of Lucretius's (Epicurus's) argument on the transformation of the mode of production associated with historical change. Central to Bacon's analysis in the *New Atlantis* and other works, Farrington explained, was progress in the industrial arts and changing modes of production, in which Bacon was strongly influenced by Lucretius (Epicurus). In *Novum Organum* Bacon quoted from memory (slightly misquoting) the opening sentence of Book VI of *De rerum natura*:

> To man's frail race great Athens long ago
> First gave the seed whence waving harvests grow,
> And re-created all our life below.[54]

In the eyes of Bacon, Lucretius's passage was closely related to the painting that his father, Nicholas Bacon, had commissioned to go over the fireplace, symbolizing the changing mode of production with the growth of agriculture. As Farrington explained in *Francis Bacon, Pioneer of Planned Science*:

> *The New Atlantis* is an idealization of the England that Bacon hoped to assist in creating. It differs from [Thomas] More's *Utopia* principally in this, that More seemed able to think only in terms of a more equal distribution of existing wealth, while Bacon dreamed of the creation of an age of plenty by a transformation of the means of production. He remembered in his father's dining hall the picture of Ceres introducing to mankind the art of agriculture. He remarked, with reference to this, that the new arts are new creations, and that the Roman poet Lucretius has said of the introduction of agriculture that it *re-created* the life of primitive men. The invention of the new arts was, he wrote, a sort of imitation of the work of the Creator, a means to refashioning the life of man.[55]

According to Farrington, it was this overall perspective, going back to Bacon's childhood, that had induced him to justify his new philosophy of works by reference to the origins of agriculture in Lucretius's great poem.

Marx, who studied Lucretius carefully along with Epicurus, was clearly aware of Lucretius's account of the historical development of production. Epicurus's reference to changing forms of social intercourse affecting the development of justice was highlighted by Marx and used, as previously indicated, in his own defense when he was on trial in Prussia for his role as editor of the *Rheinische Zeitung*. For Farrington, there was a line that ran, albeit with changing historical conditions and analyses, from Epicurus to Bacon to Marx.

If Cornford in his "The Marxist View of Ancient Philosophy" concentrated his fire mainly on Farrington, he was in some ways even more vehement in his attacks on Thomson for his criticisms of Plato's "noble lie" and his defense of Epicurean materialism. As with Farrington, Thomson saw Epicurus as "the heir to Ionian materialism." Epicureanism could be defined as a theory of "the freedom of the will" and "that the human consciousness was capable of reacting on its environment," generating a complex dialectic, in which "matter not mind is the *prius*."[56]

Thomson was a prodigious classical scholar of Greek antiquity. As Seaford declared in "George Thomson and Ancient Greece" in 1997, in works such as *Aeschylus and Athens*, *The First Philosophers*, and *Marxism and Poetry* Thomson demonstrated that "he was the greatest Hellenist of his generation," even though "not even made a Fellow of the British Academy," undoubtedly for political reasons.[57] What made Thomson's work so important, according to Seaford, was his ability to address big ideas, such as "how did drama come into being," and his mastery of such areas as historical methods, dialectics, ancient languages, ethnology, philosophy, logic, and aesthetics. Ironically, he was in many respects the successor and "culmination" of the Cambridge School of Hellenists, better known as the Cambridge ritualists, the leading founders of which were Cornford and British classical scholar Jane Harrison.[58]

The Cambridge ritualists had dug into the history of Greek religious rites, in a Durkheimian-vein, in order to reveal the origins of Greek philosophy and art. But it reached an impasse due to the limitations of its method, which in the case of Harrison, with all her brilliance, did not extend to historical analysis. "The Cambridge School," Seaford writes, "was unable to explain fundamental change."[59] Cornford later turned away from the tradition he had helped found, even clearly distancing himself from it in his "Marxist View of Ancient Philosophy."[60] He recognized that the method had been taken over by historical materialists, who were better equipped, as in Thomson (along with figures such as Christopher Caudwell and Jack Lindsay, who drew out the implications for cultural theory in general) than the Cambridge ritualists to exploit the method fully, explaining the relation of cultural changes to the growth of the monetary economy, and arriving by these means at a "labor theory of culture."[61]

Ironically, Thomson had graciously written in the Preface to the first edition of *Aeschylus and Athens*: "The books to which I owe most are, in my special field, the works of Jane Harrison and [William] Ridgeway, and the earlier works of Cornford, and more generally Morgan's *Ancient Society*, Engels' *Origin of the Family*, and Caudwell's *Illusion and Reality*."[62] No doubt shocked at being included among such a group of thinkers, including none other than Engels himself, Cornford struck out against Thomson, claiming that he had falsely accused Plato of proposing the "poisoning" of the minds of Greek citizens in his plans for an authoritarian state.[63] The debate on Greek antiquity was thus muddied with Cornford's accusations that Thomson and others were contaminating the analysis with their reductionist Marxism. The obvious goal was one of ostracizing figures such as Thomson and Farrington from the core spheres of influence within British classical studies.

Faced with Cornford's attack on him and others for referring to Plato's "noble lie," a quite literal translation, and Comford's replacement of this with the phrase "convenient fiction," Thomson hit back in *The First Philosophers* with a lengthy explanation of the terms of translation preceded by the statement: "It is regrettable that so fine a scholar would have lent his name to this perversion of the Greek."[64] But the state of British classical studies was such that subsequent translations have tended to follow Cornford, with similar apologies, defending Plato at all costs, though the nature of his argument in *The Republic* (and *The Laws*) cannot be disguised. Still, there can be no doubt that Epicurus was right in pointedly referring to Plato, with an allusion to his famous parable, as "the golden man." Plato's opposition to materialism and defense of idealism was so strong that, according to ancient testimony, he wanted Democritus's works burned.[65]

Thomson, like Farrington, laid stress on Epicurus's concept of justice as a historical and materialist phenomenon, with its real roots in the principle of reciprocity, but distorted with the development of the city-state and its laws. He highlighted Epicurus's principle that conditions of justice necessarily change with changing historical conditions, and related this to Marx's later materialist conception of history. Epicurus's swerve was recognized by Thomson as the origin of a materialist conception of free will, and as a precondition for a world that was not fully determined, but rather subject to resistance. Nothing could be more objectionable to Cornford, who ended his essay on Marxism and ancient philosophy by denying the relevance of class concepts in the analysis of the great minds of antiquity. Plato and Epicurus, he contended, could not be seen as class actors.[66]

Perhaps the greatest insight that Thomson was to have with respect to Epicureanism in his *The First Philosophers* was to dispatch the then conventional idea that it had simply a static or circular view of the world and to highlight Lucretius's reference to "progress," varying according to historical conditions and between "different peoples."[67] As Epicurus stated in his historical-anthropological analysis: "Again we must suppose that nature too had been taught and forced to learn many various lessons by the facts themselves, that reason subsequently develops what it has thus received and makes fresh discoveries, among some tribes more quickly, among others more slowly, the progress thus made being at certain times and seasons, greater, at others, less."[68] This was to be understood, not simply as progress in the means of production but more importantly in social relations. For these reasons, Thomson declared that "the philosophy of Epicurus is the culmination of ancient philosophical materialism. His sense of dialectics, revealed in his conception of the interdependence of necessity and chance, of the relation between man and nature, and of the uneven development of human progress, invites comparison with the intuitive dialectics of Ionian materialism, which culminated in Herakleitos." Thomson was particularly impressed, like Marx, by the social-historical character of Epicurus's concept of justice.[69]

For Thomson, writing in the *First Philosophers* in 1955, Epicurus had introduced many of the propositions of historical materialism. But in contradistinction to what Farrington was later to demonstrate (and opposed to what Marx wrote in the *German Ideology* in response to Max Stirner), Epicurus, in Thomson's view, had turned away from the world. Hence, Epicureanism's main gift to the world was its materialist dialectics, yet this remained removed in the end from historical praxis.[70]

Other Marxist classicists and literary thinkers in the 1930s through the 1960s also explored the relationship of Epicureanism to Marxism. This included Caudwell, who drew on Epicurus and Lucretius in his works in his short life—he died fighting as a member of the International Brigades in the Spanish Civil War at age twenty-nine, leaving behind an extraordinary body of Marxian theory in areas extending from literary theory to biology. He translated Diogenes Laertius's passage on Epicurus and time, and made the notion of time as material change itself central to his work.[71] It was in fact Caudwell's *Illusion and Reality*, which relied heavily on the Cambridge ritualists, that had inspired Thomson's own great contributions in this respect, in which appreciation of Epicurus was to play an important part.[72]

The Australian-born Lindsay, who had been influenced by the Cambridge ritualists, was a translator of the Greek and Roman classics, including Homer, Sophocles, Catullus, and Petronius. A novelist and a contributor to scholarship in the classics, literary theory, history, Marxian theory, and the philosophy of science, he was the most prolific historical-materialist thinker of his day, writing 170 books. In his *Blast-Power and Ballistics*, written in the early 1970s, he interpreted Lucretius' *De rerum natura* as offering an Epicurean ecological critique of the creative destruction of society through its alienated relation to nature.[73]

One of the great ironies of the history of Marxist theory, from a twenty-first-century perspective, was that Engels's realistic materialist discussion of what was labeled by Sebastiano Timpanaro "the Lucretian theme of the end of the world," meaning also the eventual "end of the human race," should have been the basis of so much criticism directed against him over the years. For Engels in *The Dialectics of Nature*, the notion of the destruction of the earth and the human species was rooted in the scientific assessment by physicists in his day regarding the eventual demise of the sun (at that time thought by science to be comparatively near), as well as accelerating ecological contradictions, induced by capitalism and civilization in general. Death the immortal, affecting all but matter and motion (and all but the universe in the widest sense) is a fundamental principle of materialism, extending from Epicurus to Marx and Engels. As Timpanaro wrote *On Materialism* in 1975, "I continue, despite the smiles of many comrades, to believe that Engels was perfectly right not to consider futile the problem of the 'end of humanity,' not merely as a result of catastrophes provoked by capitalist madness, but due to 'natural causes.'"[74]

In his 1982 work, *The Sculpted Word: Epicureanism and Philosophical Recruitment in Ancient Greece*, itself a major contribution to classicism, Bernard Frischer made a strong case on historical-materialist grounds that Epicurean praxis, while driven inward, was far from nonexistent. Rather, in the context of the time Epicurus had chosen to create an "association of friends," rooted in a "philosophical community" as a "safe harbor" from worldly strife in an age where the polis, and thus public life, was no longer viable: a radical stance in the times.[75]

Epicureanism and the Second Foundation of Marxism

Marx's analysis was materialist through and through, meaning that he subscribed to materialism/realism ontologically, epistemologically, and practically, something that can already be seen in nascent form in his doctoral thesis on Epicurus and in the *Economic and Philosophical Manuscripts*. Ontologically, Marx's materialism conformed to the materialist conception of the history of natural science, in which human beings were understood to be part of the physical world existing before and beyond them, and taking the form of what is called "natural law." In this view, human beings are corporeal, sensual, and objective beings dependent on material conditions outside of themselves, which they could relate to only through their production—and in their aesthetics (the concept of beauty).[76] Epistemologically, humanity obtained knowledge primarily via the senses mediated by reason. Practically, human beings were transformative social beings, able to modify their environment and their relation to it, and thus themselves, along with their relations to others, but not entirely as they wished, but under conditions inherited from the past.[77]

If Marx's general philosophical outlook can be called dialectical-critical materialist (or dialectical-critical realist), his distinctive contribution was the materialist conception of history or historical materialism.[78] Humanity, he explained, was the self-mediating being of nature, generating itself and its social-historical process through its production. Such production took the form of the historical development of the division of labor and the rise of historical modes of production or class formations. In developing this analysis, he focused the largest part of his research on the critique of bourgeois political economy and at the attempt to discern the laws of motion of capital, and from this the possibilities for socialism.

But if classical Marxism was aimed primarily at developing the *materialist conception of history*, this rested broadly on the *materialist conception of nature* that had arisen in antiquity and had been developed further by modern science. Materialism itself, however, was divided between mechanistic materialism, which quickly became the preferred form and was to consolidate itself in bourgeois society, and a more active materialism rooted in the human sensual relation to nature, giving rise to notions of freedom as praxis. The more active, more dialectical materialism was rooted, for Marx, in the Epicurean tradition and in the work of radical French materialists who had entered into socialism. Neither the metaphysics of substance of Spinoza nor Feuerbach's genetico-critical method, then, sufficed as a basis for a genuine materialism.

Without a through materialist grounding in the material world at large, including Earth itself, historical materialism was without grounds. Hence, Marx and Engels throughout their work sought to ground their critique of bourgeois society and historical forms in the much wider context of the earthly conditions of existence. All of their texts continuously referred back to this. Nevertheless, the vast changes in natural science in the nineteenth century and the development of a crude mechanism, often accompanied by a crude idealism, forced the development (in chronological terms) of a *second foundation of Marxism*, underlying the first, that is, a materialist dialectics that would counter the prevailing mechanistic materialism. This was a task clearly recognized and taken on by both Marx and Engels. But given Marx's desperate efforts to complete his critique of political economy, which tied him down considerably, the integration of historical materialism with the materialist conception of nature via the explicit development of a dialectical naturalism fell largely to Engels in *Anti-Dühring* and his unfinished *Dialectics of Nature*.[79]

If the first foundation of classical Marxism was therefore the materialist conception of history, in which a materialist conception of nature was largely assumed, the second foundation was the development of a dialectical-natural conception of the physical world and of life as a necessary basis for moving forward. Here Engels and Marx constantly reached back to Hegelian dialectics in order to generate an active materialist philosophy of nature. But they also reached back continually to ancient materialism and to those strongly influenced by it, such as Denis Diderot.[80] Marx never ceased referring to Aeschylus, Epicurus, and the more materialist aspects of Aristotle. While Engels, for his part, saw ancient materialist philosophers—having in mind the Ionian tradition, Aristotle, and Epicurus—as "natural dialecticians."[81] When Marx, as he sometimes did, described the materialist preconditions of the world, it was always in broadly Epicurean—that is, sensual—rather than mechanical terms. This was due to the principles of *energeia* and free will that he had found in Epicurus's thought, which, in Marx's terms, formed an immanent dialectic, one that Hegel, if put firmly on his feet, only served to reinforce. Engels delighted in the return of ancient Atomism in modern chemical science, even if the brilliance of the ancient theorists, particularly Epicurus, was not fully appreciated.[82]

The second foundation of Marxism was thus a *return of*

nature and thus a dialectical integration of the materialist conception of history with the materialist concept of nature that led to major developments in cultural theory, natural science, and ecology. In the Soviet Union, a vibrant dialectical materialism formed, though in a revolutionary atmosphere, generating insights as well as contradictions, brought to an end in purges under Joseph Stalin.[83] Yet elsewhere, as in the "visible college" of red scientists in Britain, major leaps occurred. Here Epicurus was a continual reference point.[84]

In the British Isles, a heavy emphasis on the study of the classics in the elite universities meant that many of the leading cultural theorists and natural scientists on the left in the 1930s and '40s were comfortable reading Lucretius in the original. *De rerum natura* was seen as a poetic precursor within materialist philosophy to modern natural science. Likewise, British natural scientists and cultural theorists, as a result of their early training, often had a firm knowledge of Epicurus through Diogenes Laertius. The immanent dialectic shared by Epicureanism and Marxism was thus intuitively obvious. Not only classicists like Farrington, Thomson, Lindsay, and Caudwell, and much later Bernard Frischer, but also Marxist natural scientists, like Joseph Needham, J. D. Bernal, J. B. S. Haldane, and Lancelot Hogben, found it natural to draw on Epicurus and Lucretius for inspiration in exploring materialism and dialectics.[85]

Farrington, much of whose work focused on ancient natural science—he also wrote several books on Bacon—was key to bringing Epicurus into the purview of the leading Marxist scientists. Hogben, who was a colleague of Farrington's at the University of Cape Town in the late 1920s, recalled that "Farrington awakened my interest in Greek science and the Greek atomists sufficiently to make me read everything about them—including the doctorate thesis of Karl Marx."[86]

Hogben became a deep admirer of Epicurean materialism, which he merged with his socialist outlook. In his 1938 *Science for the Citizen*, Hogben was to refer numerous times to Epicurus and Lucretius. "The revival of classical learning" in the Renaissance, he argued, had "one salutary effect" in that "it led to the study of Plato's antagonist, Epicurus, who had adopted the Atomic doctrine of Leucippus and Democritus." Although "Epicurus was not himself a scientific investigator," Hogben stated, he was engaged with the examination of social life. "Like Karl Marx (who wrote his doctorate dissertation on the Greek atomists) he regarded the teaching of natural philosophy as the proper basis of social conduct. Seeing how stupidity and cruelty . . . results from terror of the gods, he believed that human relations would become more wholesome as men learned to recognize the orderly routine of a world in which no divine dispensation gives them a natural right to keep slaves."[87] Hogben quoted Lucretius's praise of Epicurus as the figure who revealed nature's laws and trampled religion underfoot. It was his study of Epicurus, Hogben suggested, that inspired Gassendi to fight superstition regarding sorcery and witchcraft in his time.[88] Nor can there be any doubt that Hogben saw this as at one with his own lifelong fight against what Stephen Jay Gould called "the mismeasure of man," associated with biological racism and the genetic theory of racial characteristics.[89]

The great British biologist J. B. S. Haldane, one of the pioneers in the development of the neo-Darwinian synthesis and (along with the Soviet biologist A. I. Oparin) of the materialist theory of the origin of life, as well as being a leading Marxist thinker, author of *The Marxist Philosophy and the Sciences*, viewed Epicureanism as integral to dialectical materialism.[90] For Haldane it was significant that Marx had written his doctoral thesis on Epicurus, as Epicurus and Lucretius had prefigured Darwin's theory of evolution, in a theory of normalizing evolution, in which those organic forms that did not fit with the environment did not survive.[91]

A close reader of Epicurus, Haldane built his final essay, "On Being Finite" (1965), which defined his philosophical view and his view of death (he had been diagnosed with an incurable cancer), largely around Epicurus and Marx. Here he wrote: "I think . . . that we must provisionally, accept the notion that we are finite in time as we are in space, and act on that acceptance. This means that we must be, to some extent Epicureans, simply because Epicurus was the first man who did his best to work out the consequences of his finitude and act on them." To be sure, Haldane observed, we know much more about "external nature" and about "human nature" than Epicurus did in his day. Epicurus "recommended complete withdrawal from public affairs, which, in his time, when public affairs were largely wars between absolute monarchs, was sound advice." But "Epicurus taught that we should not be afraid of our own death, which amounts to being afraid of nothing." Haldane praised Epicurus's approaches to the questions of immortality, religion, and temperance in the pursuit of pleasure. Even though Lucretius's poem was characterized by "over-simplistic scientific principles," it represented an important stage in the development of materialist science. It was Marx, however, writing at the time of the Industrial Revolution and in a period of political ferment and revolution, who recognized the relation of materialist science to the development of productive forces and relations.[92]

The celebrated crystallographer J. D. Bernal, who also made critical contributions to physics and molecular biology, and who was the leading force behind the social relations of science movement in Britain in the 1930s and '40s, was no less an admirer of Epicurus. He argued in *Marx and Science* that Marx's doctoral thesis was of great significance, as it drew out the implications of

Epicurus's swerve, or "Epicurus' law of atomic deviation in which change is introduced into the rigid atomism of Democritus. The purport of this thesis was . . . by no means academic. It was to set out the liberating role of Epicurean ideas, particularly in the struggle against state-supported religion. Recent research has shown how far Epicureanism was considered a subversive philosophy in ancient Greece and Rome and how it had largely been destroyed by the efforts of the Platonic and Stoic philosophies." Because of its critique of religion, the state, and oppressive rule Epicureanism was considered a "rather dangerous school, a very materialist school."[93]

In *The Extension of Man*, Bernal explained that Epicurus had applied the atomistic materialism inherited from Democritus "to humanist ends. . . . The pleasure of Epicurus was an extremely refined kind of pleasure—he was called the Garden Philosopher. He spent his time discussing and enjoying a very simple life." In Lucretius, Bernal argued, one found a poetically and philosophically prefigured "gene theory of inheritance mixed up with the theory of atoms and, of course, the full essence of that mix-up has only been revealed to us in the last few years with the elucidation of the molecules of DNA."[94]

Among the Red Scientists in Britain in the generation that arose between the world wars, the figure who was to draw on Epicurus most fully throughout his life and work was the biologist, philosopher of science, science historian, and leading Sinologist Joseph Needham. For Needham, Epicureanism was so closely related to the method of modern science that they could be referred to interchangeably as "the Epicurean or scientific method."[95] In his introduction to *Time: The Refreshing River* (1943), he wrote: "I look back with pleasure on my enthusiasm for Epicurus and Lucretius, from which I have never seen any reason to depart."[96]

For Needham, as for Marx, among the most crucial aspects of Epicurus was the concept of the swerve, which opened the way to conceptions of contingency, organization, and free will.[97] But it was Epicurus's conception of emergence, embedded in his whole approach to Atomism, and the way that this was reflected in Marx, that was in many ways most decisive in the development of Needham's own analysis, helping to inspire his theory of integrative levels. Materialist dialectics, as "a general worldview," he explained, was "another way of expressing the fact of emergent evolution, i.e., the principle that social evolution should be understood as the continuation of biological evolution, part of the rise in organizational level that has happened throughout the development of our world."[98] The notion that the phenomenal world consisted of the organization of matter (atoms), producing various levels of existence, could be found, he argued, in Lucretius, who had written of the atoms:

> Firstly, how small the seeds which thus compose
> The feeling thing, then, with what shapes endowed,
> And lastly what *positions* they assume
> What *motions*, what *arrangements*. . . .[99]

Needham was particularly impressed by Mikhail Shirokov's *A Textbook of Marxist Philosophy*, which drew on both Epicurus and Marx (as well as Hegel) in developing the materialist philosophy of emergence.[100]

In his studies of science and civilization in China, Needham was to stress the close correlation between Epicureanism in ancient Greece and Rome and Daoism developing in the Warring States period in China. Both emphasized the organic material connections of life and a philosophy of self-sufficiency. Reflecting a modern age where ecology was becoming ever more important,

Needham argued, "Today we are all Taoists and Epicureans."[101] For Needham, Marxism both in its most authentic materialist-scientific version in the West, emerging out of Epicureanism, and in the ways that it had been creatively transformed in the East, when placed in contact with traditional Chinese civilization, particularly Daoism, expressed the cross-civilizational affinity of classical organic philosophies—an affinity rooted in material life itself.[102]

The Negation of Materialism

"Perhaps the sole characteristic common to virtually all contemporary varieties of Western Marxism," Timpanaro wrote in *On Materialism*,

> is their concern to defend themselves against the accusation of materialism. Gramscian or Togliattian Marxists, Hegelian-Existentialist Marxists, Neo-Positivizing Marxists, Freudian or Structuralist Marxists, despite the profound dissensions which otherwise divide them, are at one in rejecting all suspicion of collusion with "vulgar" or "mechanical" materialism; and they do so with such zeal as to cast out, together with mechanism or vulgarity, materialism *tout court*. . . . It is true that in itself polemics against vulgar materialism in no way constitutes an idealist deviation from Marxism, but rather, as is well known, form part of the original nucleus of its doctrine. . . . But it cannot be overlooked that what . . . [some now call] "mechanical materialism" is simply *any* materialism whatsoever.[103]

The Western Marxist philosophical tradition was defined primarily by the rejection of Engels's "dialectics of nature," seen as constituting a break with Marx, and the intrusion of positivist views into Marxism. As Jean-Paul Sartre wrote, "In the historical and social world . . . there *really* is a dialectical reason; by transferring it to the 'natural' world, and forcibly inscribing it there, Engels stripped it of its rationality: there was no longer a dialectic which man produced by producing himself; and which, in turn, produced man; there was only a contingent law, of which nothing could be said except *it is so* and not otherwise."[104]

But once the dialectic was no longer seen as applying to nature, but only to history, that is, to the social world apart from external nature, then a materialist conception of nature could be dropped altogether. It was increasingly seen as irrelevant to the social process and relegated to the realm of science and positivism, at most entering social analysis by way of the consideration of technology. Sartre's position on materialism was presented most explicitly in his famous essay "Marxism and Revolution," which was a polemic against French Marxist philosopher Roger Garaudy and what Sartre vituperatively called "Neo-Stalinist Marxism."[105] With respect to the materialist conception of nature, he was abundantly clear, writing: "It is obvious that the notion of *natural history* is absurd," since the only history is human history. Engels's claim that Charles Darwin's evolutionary theory pointed to a dialectics of nature was, Sartre declared, equally absurd, since Darwin was simply a "mechanical" thinker. Materialism, Sartre wrote, "has the advantage of offering a crude myth about the origin of the species whereby the more complex forms of life proceed from the simpler ones." Viewing natural science as a form of positivism, Sartre separated dialectics from natural science, arguing that "science is, by reason of its inmost concerns, its principles, and its methods, the opposite of dialectics," that is, positivist in nature.[106]

In his criticism of the then dominant tradition of Marxism associated with the French Communist Party, Sartre claimed that its whole object was the conquest of nature: "The Marxist expression for designating the society of the future is *antiphysis*. This means that Marxists want to set up a human order whose laws will constitute the negation of natural laws," generating an "anti-Natural" order aimed at "finality."[107] He was later to argue for a counter-finality stemming from external nature itself, representing ecological contradictions, in a manner similar to Engels's argument on the "revenge" of nature. Here Sartre appears to have been concerned with countering what he saw as the finality of Soviet productivism, rather than altering his negative positions on materialist ontology and the dialectics of nature.[108]

Sartre, however, did not stop with the rejection of the materialist conception of nature as lacking any ontological value. He went on from there to argue that *practical materialism*, divorced from materialist ontology and epistemology, was the real intellectual basis of revolutionary movements. But absent any real scientific standing, it was materialism as "myth" that fulfilled the necessary ideological requirement justifying revolution.[109]

Sartre's approach to materialism as a *myth*, supporting revolution, was illustrated in the case of Epicurus. As "the first and the most naïve of the great materialists," Epicurus was unable to come up with anything but "an infinite number of equally valid explanations" for phenomena. Here Sartre provided a very questionable extrapolation from Epicurus's approach to meteorological questions, lying beyond what could be ascertained by the senses. Naturally, this did not apply to Epicurus's philosophy as a whole. But if Epicurus was thus taken to stand for the failure of materialism in explaining reality, he was nonetheless portrayed as having played a crucial role in promoting materialism as myth, thus serving the end of revolutionary praxis. Thus, Sartre explained: "The first man who made a deliberate attempt to rid men of their fears and bonds, the first man who tried to abolish slavery within his domain, Epicurus, was a materialist."[110] For Marx, Epicurus was the Enlightenment figure of antiquity who opened up the way to both materialist natural science and free will. For Sartre, in contrast, representing the tradition of Western Marxism, Epicurus stood not for materialism as *science* but as revolutionary *myth*. The materialist conception of nature was considered to be invalid, along with the dialectics of nature. All that was left was materialism as a myth of Prometheus conducive to revolution.

Sartre subsequently identified more fully with Marxism in his *Search for a Method* and in his *Critique of Dialectical Reason*. Yet he continued to reject the concept of the dialectics of nature and to distance himself from materialism philosophically, apart from purely *historical* materialism. Marx's definition of materialism, he wrote in *The Search for a Method*, was limited to his political-economic perspective, in which "the mode of production of material life dominates the development of social, political, and historical life."[111] Yet interpreting Marx's materialism in this way denied any deeper ontological materialism, arising from the fact that human beings were corporeal, sensuous beings, and thus part of nature. Although Sartre's work was distinctive, it can also be seen as standing for the general dilemma of the Western Marxist philosophical tradition in its denial of the dialectics of nature, which emptied materialism of any deep, ontological content, forcing the analysis generally in more idealist directions. Despite the enormous creativity and versatility of Western Marxism in this sense, and its complex explorations of dialectics, it became more distant from materialism itself to the point where materialism in Marxism came to mean simply a recognition of the political-economic structure of society, divorced from all other questions.

The dialectical opposite of the distorted inheritance of Marx's view evident in Western Marxism could be seen in Soviet Marxism commencing in the late 1930s, which adopted a dogmatic, often positivistic conception of dialectical materialism, in which the subjective factor was downplayed. This ideological development was accompanied by the purges of the Stalin era. Nevertheless, Soviet Marxism continued to hold on to the notions of materialism and materialist dialectics, keeping alive some key elements of Marxism, even if often in distorted form. As in Western Marxism, Soviet Marxism saw all sorts of internal struggles where thinkers sought to break out of the prevailing one-sided perspective.[112]

The result within the Western Marxist philosophical tradition was a continual thinning of the notion of materialism, sometimes taking the form of structuralism. In these terms, even the conception of Marx's materialism as *historical* was often lost. The dialectic was frequently emptied of content, leading to postmodernism and posthumanism. Marx's own explorations of the history of materialism, as in *The Holy Family*, were seldom referred to in the Western Marxist tradition. His dissertation was treated as merely a curious application of Hegelian idealism to an unimportant ancient philosophical tradition, which would have taken on real significance only if it had been incorporated, as Marx envisioned at one point, as part of a larger study incorporating the Stoics and Skeptics. In Theodor Adorno's *Negative Dialectics*, despite the fact that Marx had himself first employed the term "negative dialectics" in the context of Epicurus, the only reference to the latter figure is a contemptuous reference to "the enlightenment of Epicurus" as simply "depicting the wretched idea of disinterested divine spectators," a comment devoid of all historical context, thus a form of forgetting, of reification.[113]

The general attitude toward materialism and the dialectics of nature within Western Marxism was exemplified by Alfred Schmidt's influential *The Concept of Nature in Marx*, written originally as a dissertation under the supervision of Max Horkheimer and Adorno. The first section of Schmidt's opening chapter on "Karl Marx and Philosophical Materialism" is titled "The Non-Ontological Character of Marxist Materialism." He begins by explaining that Marx's concept of nature cannot be explained apart from the question of philosophical materialism, only to deny any ontological concept of materialism in Marx, as opposed to Engels. On the very first page Schmidt writes: "Most of the existing literature . . . fails to take into account sufficiently those aspects of Marx's thought which link him to the materialists of antiquity." After which Schmidt proceeds to say nothing on the subject. There is not a single direct mention in his book of Epicurus or Marx's doctoral thesis. Democritus is twice referred to: once in a single sentence, commenting on Engels not Marx, in which Schmidt alludes to "all the mechanical materialisms from Democritus to Holbach"; and later in an equally broad statement in a footnote where he refers to how Enlightenment thinkers discovered "the atoms of Democritus, via the physics of the Renaissance."[114]

Marx's materialism, Schmidt argues, commenced only with Feuerbach, who was not concerned with the "mechanical movements of atoms." (Here Schmidt seems unaware of Feuerbach's discussion of Gassendi in his *History of Modern Philosophy from Bacon to Spinoza*, which influenced Marx in writing his dissertation.)[115] However, "Feuerbach's man was tied to pre-human nature" and thus, Schmidt argues, to an ontological (or at least Romantic) conception of nature. In contrast, "Marx's materialism is not to be understood ontologically" at all. It cannot be ossified into an "ontological principle," Schmidt tells us, but is to be viewed simply historically and in terms of production. Marx, therefore, rejected the concept of matter of eighteenth-century materialism. "Material reality is from the beginning socially mediated."[116] The only way to speak of natural history, in Marx's sense, Schmidt tells us, is by seeing it as the product of human history: "Natural history is human history's extension backwards and is comprehended by men, as *no longer* accessible nature"—with "accessible nature" standing for nature as subsumed by society.[117]

It would be difficult, in truth, to recognize in Schmidt's idealist analysis here Marx's powerful treatment of what he called "the universal metabolism of nature" (along with the "social metabolism') which permeates his mature work. To be sure, Schmidt notes at one point in his analysis that Marx's concept of social metabolism pointed to a kind of dialectics of nature, but Schmidt later rejects that completely as a violation of dialectic itself, conceived as the identical-subject object of human relations.[118]

Schmidt's conception of nature in Marx as simply historically created nature is taken to such lengths that a genuinely ecological perspective becomes impossible. Ironically, in a work titled *The Concept of Nature in Marx* that was published in the same year as Rachel Carson's *Silent Spring*, which touched off the modern environmental movement, Schmidt produced an interpretation of Marx that has no relation whatsoever to environmental struggles. The complete absence of any mention of Epicurus or Marx's dissertation is symbolic of a work that denies the very existence of an ontological basis to Marx's materialism and that negates his concept of *material nature* itself. Much of Schmidt's book was devoted to a polemic that rejected the notion of "the reconciliation of man and nature," which Marx had adopted from Epicurus, and which was emphasized by Bertolt Brecht and Ernst Bloch.[119]

Marx's doctoral thesis on Epicurus has not, of course, been ignored altogether. There have been numerous analyses of it within Western Marxism, but almost invariably either assuming from the outset that his dissertation was Hegelian and going on from there or seeing it as supposed "proof" of Marx's Hegelian phase. It has even been suggested that Marx wrote it to prove that Epicurus was an idealist thinker. Almost invariably these analyses lack even a bare acquaintance with Epicurus's philosophy.

This dominant interpretation of the Western Marxist philosophical tradition with regard to Marx's dissertation is exemplified by the lead article by Tony Burns in the journal *Historical Materialism*. Burns is professor of political theory at the University of Nottingham and editor with Ian Fraser of *The Hegel-Marx Connection*.[120] He classifies Marx's doctoral thesis as the work of a Hegelian philosophical idealist still retaining an entirely "uncritical" view of Hegel's philosophy.[121] According to this perspective, Marx saw Epicurus's "position" as constituting a form of "philosophical idealism." Quoting Cicero (an unfriendly witness criticized as such by Marx), Burns characterizes Epicurus as an inconsistent and illogical thinker, one whose mechanical materialism was contradicted by his idealist emphasis on "free will." This view of Epicurus, and of Marx's own treatment of Epicurus, is defended as "the traditional" interpretation, said to extend as far back as Louis Althusser's *For Marx* in 1965 while including other notable figures such as Leszek Kolakowski and David McLellan.[122]

Burns claims incorrectly that modern classical scholarship still sees Epicurus as a minor figure in relation to Democritus, backing this up with the antedated and long superseded view of the British idealist philosopher A. E. Taylor from 1911, in which Epicurus is presented as offering a "blundering perversion" of Democritus's thought. For Taylor, "The wisdom of Epicurus is . . . the merest foolishness." So opposed is Taylor to Epicurus that he ends his book by siding with Plutarch in his calumnies against the Garden philosopher. Lucretius's materialist views on the eventual end of the world, which Lindsay interpreted ecologically, are dismissed by Taylor as "pathological."[123]

Indeed, Burns in his *Historical Materialism* article seems not to be troubled in the least in referring to Epicurus's "evident illogical inconsistencies" (one of which he claims is belief in both free will and causal determinism) even though this runs counter to Marx's stated view in his dissertation, where he praises Epicurus's "iron logic."[124] Burns claims, albeit with absolutely no foundation, that a more critical assessment of Epicurus was adopted by Marx in his mature work, where he is said to have reversed himself, "leaving any enthusiasm which he had once had for Epicurus behind him." Only Aristotle among ancient thinkers, we are told, exercised a lasting influence on Marx's thought.[125] It was Lenin, not the early Marx, Burns tells us, who saw Epicurus as a materialist. If Marx later explicitly declared Epicurus to be "materialist" in *The Holy Family*, this merely means he had changed his mind. The proof that Burns offers for his claim that Marx in his dissertation saw Epicurus as a proponent of "philosophical idealism" was that Epicurus had opposed strict determinism while supporting free will, something that Marx, we are told, would have seen as incompatible with philosophical materialism.[126]

What stands out in Burns's account and virtually all contemporary Marxist analyses of Marx's doctoral thesis is the almost complete absence of any demonstrated knowledge of Epicurean thought itself. In an extensive bibliography, Burns *does not include a single work that incorporates any of Epicurus's* writings. Thus, he does not cite Diogenes Laertius or any modern compendium on Epicurus (though Lucretius's *On the Nature of Things* is cited once) , while the most recent secondary source on Epicurus and Epicureanism referred to in his article is that of the idealist Taylor from *1911*. The assumption of the "traditional" view is clearly that one does not need to know anything about Epicurus directly to interpret Marx's dissertation, despite the fact that it was explicitly focused on Epicurus. Rather, it is thought to be sufficient to have a general familiarity with Hegel and with what Marx wrote in his dissertation without any more intimate knowledge of the subject. Nor is there any need to investigate contemporary Epicurean scholarship.[127]

Burns's "traditional" interpretation can be considered *traditional* only in the limited sense that Marxism is seen as confined within the narrow Western Marxist philosophical tradition, as this arose first in the 1920s. Here Marxism is viewed as opposed to materialist and dialectical conceptions of nature, while Marx is considered primarily a radical Hegelian in his overall philosophical view. Marxist perspectives that conflict with this are rendered virtually invisible. Thus, despite the fact that some of the leading classicists and scholars on Epicurean philosophy in the twentieth century, figures like Farrington and George Thomson, were also Marxist theorists, their extensive, expert analyses have no place within the so-called traditional interpretation of Marx's dissertation and are scarcely ever mentioned.[128]

The Return of the Garden

The publication in 1967 of Farrington's *The Faith of Epicurus*, marking a turning point in the Marxist theory of Epicurus, in which the *political* and *historical* nature of Epicureanism was highlighted for the first time, coincided with the publication in the same year of David J. Furley's landmark *Two Studies in the Greek Atomists*. In that work Furley was to revolutionize the understanding of Epicurus's swerve, by explaining that it did not accompany every voluntary action, as Bailey and others had supposed, but simply set the stage for voluntary action by introducing *the possibility of freedom*. Since the emphasis was on the psychology of freedom, Furley argued that Epicurus's swerve played a largely "negative part," opening up but not determining. As a result, "The peculiar vulnerability of Epicurean freedom [as previously interpreted]—that it seems to fit random actions, rather than deliberate and purposive ones—is a myth, if this explanation is correct."[129]

With Furley's argument before it, which depended on a recognition of a much more intimate relation between Aristotle and Epicurus's philosophies of freedom than previously conceived, and with the research into and translation of Epicurus's Book 25 of *On Nature*, first uncovered by Gomperz, a great debate on freedom, determinism, and emergence in Epicurus's philosophy arose. Consequently, over the last half-century and more, Marx's doctoral thesis on Epicurus has become more and more relevant to contemporary debates and is increasingly recognized in Epicurean scholarship. The profound dialectical nature of Marx's conception of Epicurus's materialism, including its relation to human freedom, historical change, emergent evolution, and to the identity-in-difference of naturalism and humanism increasingly came to the fore in Epicurean studies themselves.

In 1968, Bloch published *On Karl Marx*, with its chapter near the end on "Epicurus and Karl Marx." Bloch, a leading critical theorist fluent in the classics, had no doubt about the significance of Epicurus's materialist dialectic for Marxism. If Marx approached Epicurus initially from an idealist direction, the encounter with Epicurean materialism transformed him so that we see "materialism germinating within him." What was most significant, according to Bloch, was the "energizing principle," the "effective beginning," which Marx obtained from Epicurus's countermove against fatalism, rigid determinism, idealism, and skepticism alike.[130] The emphasis on the freedom of self-consciousness that Marx found in Epicurus he saw as *bringing philosophy into the world*, despite the more limited political practice of Epicureanism, which demanded a kind of "withdrawal" responding to the social collapse of the polis in his time. The very definition of pleasure in Epicurean philosophy, Thomson had noted, seen "as the absence of pain," reflected "the social desperation of the age" in which the Garden arose.[131]

The dialectical complexity of Epicurus was immediately obvious to Bloch, who wrote of Marx's fascination with Epicurus's swerve: "A true evaluation of living forces (here the subjective factors) never occurs without a true evaluation of determination by the factors of objective conditioning in which the subjective element can alone develop—and, O Epicurus, vice versa, in mutuality."[132] In *The Principle of Hope* Bloch observed, with Marx also in mind, that "Epicurus , the materialist, for Lucretius becomes the same in science as Prometheus was in myth."[133] In Lucretius's words, Epicurus was "the first to shatter the imprisoning bolts of the gates of nature."[134]

In 1970 and 1972, the Dutch theologian and philosopher Arend Th. van Leeuwen presented a series of Gifford Lectures, later published under titles of the *Critique of Heaven* (1972) and *Critique of Earth* (1974) on the development of Marx's philosophical views, at the core of which was Marx's relation to Epicurus. Van Leeuwen's thesis was that "in a sense," throughout Marx's *Notebooks on Epicurean Philosophy* and his dissertation, "Epicurus acts as Marx's double. Every time the name of Epicurus is mentioned, we are to think of Marx reflecting his own problems in the mirror of Greek philosophy." Via Epicurus, Marx believed in the end that he had penetrated to the "inner sanctum" of philosophy and arrived at the question of praxis.[135] Epicurus recognized how the contradiction between matter and form generated the phenomenal world, the world of appearance, the counterpart of essence (atom and void). Time was merely *change in form*, reflecting death the immortal.

For Van Leeuwen, "the real hero" of Marx's dissertation, as Marx himself suggested in his Foreword, "seems to be" Aeschylus's "Prometheus in the guise of Epicurus. The hitherto unsolved problem of philosophy which Marx sought out to solve appears to have more than intellectual dimensions. It is the problem of Prometheus."[136] Here the reference is to the Prometheus who defied the gods and brought light (in the form of fire) to humanity, the ancient symbol of Enlightenment. But "if Epicurus in the guise of Prometheus" was the "real hero" of Marx's thesis, van Leeuwen points out, then philosophy cannot be different than activity, for not only does it require a critique of heaven, but also a critique of earth. Although Epicurus inspired Marx, what Marx really wanted was a more active, more revolutionary Epicurus. Nevertheless, Van Leeuwen contends that "Epicurus remained Marx's life-long companion, and in a sense, his double." Even though he appears infrequently in Marx's later work, he remained ever-present, mole-like, "beneath the surface," representing a subversive materialism, a humanity no longer in contradiction with nature, the world, and itself.[137] Moreover, for Van Leeuwen, echoing Marx and Farrington, Epicureanism had its defiant, radical aspects: "Epicurus had the nerve, as a lone apostate, to repudiate the ancient religious cult of the celestial bodies," putting himself in conflict with the state religion of his time.[138]

In 1977, French philosopher Jean Fallot brought out a new, expanded Italian edition of his masterpiece, *Pleasure and Death in the Philosophy of Epicurus*, first published in French in 1950.[139] At the time he wrote the first French edition of his book, as Fallot later explained, he was something of a left materialist, but not yet a Marxist. The later Italian edition, however, provided a more Marxist reading of Epicurus's work.

As Timpanaro says, Fallot was too good a historian of ancient philosophy "to make Epicurus the 'Marx of Antiquity.'"[140] At the same time, the areas of overlap between Epicurus and Marxism, due in part to the influence that the former had exercised on the latter, were emphasized, including Epicurus's egalitarianism and focus on friendship, even if these were seen as removed from the public life of the citizen in the polis. Fallot went so far as to suggest that to understand Epicurus you have to be his friend. An important part of his treatment of Epicurus's relation to Marx was aimed at securing the "materialist meaning" of his dialectic. However, all mythological notions of an abstract "free will" completely divorced from materialism needed to be avoided. Based on an understanding of Epicurus and Marx, Fallot emphasized that human beings were first organic beings, connected to external nature, and from this productive beings, and social relations beings. Thus, the material base is always present and related to the formation of revolutionary subjects.

Nevertheless, what seemed to point toward a potential confluence of Marxian analysis of Epicurus in the late 1960s and early 1970s, with new developments in the understanding of Epicurus's materialist philosophy of materialism, freedom, and emergence within classical studies, never came to fruition. Although the rediscovery of Epicurus on the part of classicists, reinforced by translations from *On Nature*, continued within classical studies, the vital research of Farrington, Thomson, Bloch, Van Leeuwen, and Fallot received relatively little attention in Marxist circles, in the context of the general crisis of Marxism in the 1980s and '90s, and the continued dominance of Western Marxism, which increasingly drained into postmodernism and posthumanism. With the crisis of Marxism the more orthodox tradition, associated with Marx's materialist dialectical method, was diminished, and the ascendancy of anti-materialist views was for a time largely unquestioned.

However, a renewed interest in the significance of Epicurus's materialism for Marxism was gradually to arise as a result of two unrelated theoretical developments: (1) Althusser's conception of "aleatory materialism" based on Epicurus; and (2) research in Marx's ecology, which led to investigations of the roots of his materialist conception of nature (as well as history), leading back to this doctoral thesis on Epicurus.

Althusser's analysis of Epicurus did not rely on Marx's doctoral thesis in any way, which he saw as Hegelian in substance as well as form.[141] More important, he dismissed the standard treatments of Epicurus, including that of Marx, as "perverted into an idealism of freedom," in which the swerve was seen as pointing to "the existence of human freedom even in the realm of necessity."[142] Seeing all of this as distorted, Althusser, drawing almost exclusively (aside from references to Epicurus's concept of death) on Lucretius's description of the swerve in his treatment of Epicurean natural philosophy, argued that the *clinamen*/swerve introduced an "aleatory encounter" between atoms, and thus a theory of the origin of the world, which pointed to "transcendental contingency of the world." There was no anterior meaning, no teleology, simply the facticity, in which the swerve was a "given."[143] The answer to how the world began was that it began simply with a fortuitous encounter generated by the swerve, with no anterior meaning, and merely aggregated from there.[144]

Althusser's emphasis in this late phase of his thought was thus on the arbitrary and contingent basis of material existence, or the phenomenal world introduced by Epicurus's materialism, with no relation to Epicurus's philosophy as a whole or to Marx's writings on Epicurus. This then set up a "subordination of necessity to contingency" and a transcendence of the great philosophical questions. "Every encounter . . . is contingent, and necessarily contingent."[145] Marx was seen as caught between "the aleatory of the Encounter" and "the necessity of Revolution."[146] Epicurus thus was the beginning of what Althusser characterized as an "underground current of the materialism of the encounter," which he idiosyncratically saw as manifested in Epicurus, Spinoza, Hobbes, Jean-Jacques Rousseau, Marx, and Martin Heidegger.[147] Reference to "a materialism, of the encounter," Althusser wrote, was "only for convenience." Thus, it broke with all traditional materialisms in that it "includes Heidegger and eludes the classical criteria of every materialism." Despite the references to Epicurus and Marx, this view was radically divorced from notions of the individual subject or of human freedom, much less materialism as historically conceived. Rather Althusser's aleatory materialism was defined as "*a process without a subject*." Nevertheless, it represented "the primacy of the friends of the Earth, over the friends of the Forms," that is, Epicurus over Plato.[148]

Aleatory materialism, or the philosophy of the encounter, in Althusser's conception was based on the selection of one aspect of Epicurus's argument on the swerve (the mere declination from the straight line), which was then extended to the interpretation of Marx; while ignoring all of the rest of Epicurean thought, even most of the analysis of the swerve. The hundreds of pages of analysis that Marx devoted to the analysis of Epicurean philosophy play no role in Althusser's argument, including Marx's own treatment of the swerve. As the terminus of this "underground current of the materialism of the encounter" Althusser oddly presented Heidegger's irrationalist philosophy, focusing on the notion of the merely "given."[149] The emphasis was on fortuitousness, while eliminating the individual subject, human freedom, and historical necessity, along with humanism, thus making any meaningful historical-materialist analysis impossible. It is best seen as the collapse of a rational worldview. Althusser's later philosophy, as Antonio Negri contended in a somewhat different context (related to Althusser's writings on Niccolo Machiavelli), can be conceived as "completely reversed" in relation to his earlier thought or, more accurately, elevates the dialectical opposite of his earlier structuralist Marxism.[150] The emphasis of Althusser on the swerve as random was, as Thomas Nail, the author of *Marx in Motion*, has pointed out, a gross error: "Read Marx's dissertation. He doesn't think it [the swerve] is random. He says that it is about the swerve and the repulsion. It's matter moving within itself; against itself; transforming itself. It's a constant immanent dialectic. Importantly, an immanent dialectic."[151]

Nevertheless, given Althusser's previous celebrity, his turn to Epicurus as a forerunner of Marx was to have considerable influence in bringing Epicurus's philosophy back into Marxist discussions. Thus, Diego Fusaro states, though incorrectly, in his *Marx, Epicurus, and the Origins of Historical Materialism* (2017): "Only Louis Althusser with his elaboration of 'aleatory materialism' has insisted on the Epicurean roots of Marx's philosophy."[152] Althusser's close associate Etienne Balibar, influenced by Althusser (and following the lead of Constanzo Preve), broke with the traditional notion of the three sources of Marxism, represented by Hegelian dialectics, French Enlightenment materialism, and British political economy, arguing that this has to be extended to include "four masters": "*Epicurus* . . . for the materialism of freedom, given metaphorical expression in the doctrine of the *clinamen* or random 'swerving' of atoms; *Rousseau*, who supplies the idea of egalitarian democracy . . . ; *Adam Smith*, from whom the idea that the basis of property is labour is taken . . . ; and lastly, *Hegel* . . . a constant inspiration and adversary to Marx in his work on 'dialectical contradiction' and historicity."[153] It was the addition of Epicurus, now seen as representing the "materialism of freedom" (a view, however, in stark contrast to that of Althusser), that marked the main innovation here.

A much more direct and significant *Return to the Garden* within Marxism was to emerge as a result of research in Marxian ecology, aimed at recovering Marx's dialectical naturalism, in response to the contemporary ecological crisis and the need for more revolutionary solutions. This commenced at the outset of the twenty-first century and has developed rapidly in the quarter-century since.[154] By the end of the twentieth century, when it was recognized that Marx had provided a powerful critique of ecological crisis, now known as the theory of metabolic rift, the question of Marx's larger analysis of nature/ecology arose. The answer, it was discovered, lay in the nature of Marx's materialism, particularly the relationship of his materialist conception of history to the materialist conception of nature.[155]

But materialism, in this sense, had ironically been left far behind within Western Marxism, along with the dialectics of nature. For an understanding of Marxism's relation to philosophical materialism, embracing both ontology and epistemology, and connected to the development of natural philosophy and natural science, it was necessary to go back to the origins of his worldview, as reflected in his treatment of Epicurus's philosophy of nature and its implications. This, however, constituted a very rich beginning in that Marx, having mastered Hegel's dialectical method, immersed himself in the work of the greatest of the materialist philosophers of antiquity, absorbing Epicurus's critical materialism, which, as Bloch explained, played a crucial role in "germinating" Marx's own materialist-dialectical worldview, which was soon to emerge. Marx's materialism did not arise in an instant, fully formed, without a struggle, like Athena from the head of Zeus. Rather, Marx, a child of the Enlightenment (particularly the French Enlightenment) had entered into the study of Hegel with hesitation, viewing his philosophy as the "enemy." No sooner had he captured the essence of the Hegelian dialectic than he turned to a study of ancient materialism (reflecting an interest in Epicurus that he had evinced early on), focusing explicitly on Hegel's error with respect to the understanding of Epicurus, which revealed a level of incoherence in Hegel's own philosophy. In the process, Marx discovered a materialism in Epicurus, which was non-mechanical, rooted in sensation, that emphasized the unity of nature and humanity, pointed to human freedom, and encompassed a principle of *energeia*, extending to human action. The egalitarianism and social materialism of Epicurus, evident in his concept of justice and the social contract, were also crucial to Marx.

Marx did not travel this road alone but, in a sense, was accompanied all along by Feuerbach, who was moving in a similar direction. As Van Leeuwen wrote in the *Critique of Heaven*, "There runs a line from Epicurus via Gassendi and Feuerbach to Marx."[156] Marx not only studied Gassendi on Epicurus, but also Feuerbach on Gassendi's Epicurus, in the process of writing his dissertation, and was aware of Feuerbach's discovery of a more sensual materialism. The influence of Epicurus through Gassendi on Feuerbach was profound, and this complex inheritance was integral to Marx's own favorable response to Feuerbach's later philosophy.

However, Feuerbach's materialism was ultimately too abstract, confined mainly to a simple inversion of Hegel's idealist perspective, while missing the essential *content* of Hegel's philosophy, which encompassed the concept of labor, even if in idealized form. Moreover, Feuerbach's recognition of the sensual basis of Epicurus's materialism, which he was to adopt as his own, did not reach down to the deeper philosophical aspects of this. Thus, Epicurus, in Marx's view, had made the distinction between matter and form the core of his philosophy evident in his concept of time, manifested as the alienation of appearance from essence. His atomism had led to a concept of the organic body, and to mortality, death the immortal, as the phenomenal form of human existence. Human beings were corporeal beings always existing in relation to nature, even in the context of the development of society. It was this corporeal character of human beings—the materialist conception of nature as it applied to human existence—that set up the problem of human needs and human production.

Epicurus, in the very limited conditions of his time, had dealt with these issues in terms of human self-sufficiency rather than the expansion of production (a view scarcely available to antiquity). His concern with the reconciliation of humanity with nature had to do with the disruption of the social and ecological world around him in the time of the declining polis and the wars of the Diadochi. The answer was to create communities of friends, relying on self-sufficiency in relation to objective needs, expanding the realm of freedom through sociability—distinct from the political alienation of the polis. This was criticized at the time as a plebeian philosophy, since directed at the population and *ataraxia*. Although defying the forms of class rule and state-religion (particularly the cult of the astral gods), Epicureanism was revolutionary in an inward, if not an outward, form. In contrast, Marx, in the modern age, saw the material, corporeal, sensuous existence of human beings as requiring the *revolution of production*, not simply in terms of the expansion of productive forces, but even more in terms of revolutionary relations of production, which would turn the state upside down, and with it, class relations, thereby allowing for sustainable human development in relation to both nature and society. If Epicurus provided Marx with a materialist basis for understanding the world (even extending to anthropology and history in Lucretius's Book 5), the object from then on was the forward movement of revolutionary praxis, in which the more limited world of the ancients was left behind, but not forgotten.

In Marxian ecology the exploration of Marx's *Notebooks on Epicurean Philosophy*, his dissertation on Epicurus, and his later treatment of the relation of Democritus and Epicurus to Enlightenment materialism have all opened up the way to a deeper understanding of Marx's relation to such varied materialist thinkers as Feuerbach, Darwin, and Lewis Henry Morgan.[157] It has also provided crucial insights into Marx's ecological (as well as economic) critique of political economy. Marx's recognition of Epicurus's "immanent dialectic" and the emergentism in his materialist philosophy has pointed to the possibility of a synthesis between Western Marxism and scientific Marxism, by bringing the dialectics of nature and a throughgoing materialism, rooted in Marx's notion of the metabolism of nature and society, back into the picture. Here long neglected scientific and cultural figures associated with the Second Foundation of Marxism, such as Bernal, Needham, Haldane, Hogben, Farrington, Thomson, and Lindsay, all of whom merged Epicurus and Marx into their analysis, come back to the fore, allowing for the further development of Marxism as a science, critical theory, and a revolutionary praxis. The importance of the Second Foundation of Marxism, in this sense, is clearly evident in the work of thinkers in our time such as Stephen Jay Gould, Richard Levins, and Richard Lewontin, all of whom emphasized a dialectical evolutionary theory embracing contingency and punctuated change.

Epicurus's philosophy anticipated the very essence of modern materialism. In the words of Boris Hennig, professor of ancient philosophy at Ryerson University in Toronto, commenting on the close relation of the Epicurean notion of the circular character of reality to Marx's materialist notion of production and reproduction within processes of mutual exchange, "All human activity is a sort of metabolic exchange with and within nature. . . . If human life is a form of circular, metabolic movement, it makes sense to think of alienation as a disruption or distortion of this movement. . . . Capitalism is, as it were, a cancerous epicycle of social metabolism" and metabolic rifts.[158] Nail, in his *Marx and Motion*, has made a similar connection, comparing Lucretius's ancient discussion of fermentation to the modern approach to metabolism as articulated by Marx.[159] The sense of environmental crisis, as Lindsay explained, is present in both Epicurus/Lucretius and Marx, and takes the form of the disruption of the elemental forces connecting humanity to nature.[160]

It is no accident that Arthur Tansley in introducing the concept of ecosystem in 1935 referred to Lucretius.[161] Epicurus and Lucretius's notion of *simulacra* (the Latin term that Lucretius introduced to refer to Epicurus's *eidola*), consisted of woven images/effusions, that, in Marx's words, constituted "natural bodies which, as surfaces, as it were, detach themselves like skins" and "stream constantly forth," permeating the world and underlying our sensual perceptions of material forms. This was a deeply ecological conception in which nothing was in reality isolated, everything interpenetrated everything else. It has been seen by Nail in his *Lucretius II: An Ethics of Motion*, as providing a fundamentally ecological vision of the web of life, which undoubtedly affected Marx's own views.[162]

It would be a critical mistake, as Fallot's approach to Epicurus suggested, to Marxify Epicurus, as has sometimes been done, by overenthusiastic left proponents of his ideas.[163] But if it is necessary to avoid historical anachronisms, it is also essential to understand the radical nature of Epicurean philosophy *in its time*, and its significance for *our own time*, necessarily mediated by more contemporary materialist perspectives. Epicurus's analysis, though limited by the conditions of antiquity in which it arose, was crucial in the formation of Enlightenment thought, in the development of Marx's views, and for the evolution of later Marxist theory, specifically with respect to materialist dialectics.

For Marxian ecology this is particularly evident. Constantine Skordoulis, professor of epistemology and dialectical methodology at the National and Kapodistrian University of Athens, usefully remarked in 2007 in "Science and Worldview in the Marxist Tradition":

> The study of Epicurus provides a way of understanding Marx's materialism in natural philosophy. Marx's study of ancient and early modern materialism brought him inside the scientific understanding of the natural world in ways that influenced all of his thought, since it focused on evolution and emergence, and made Nature, not God, the starting point.
>
> Moreover, Marx's encounter with Hegel has to be understood in terms of the struggle that Marx was carrying on regarding the nature of materialist philosophy and science. Epicurus, not Hegel, emerges as the pivotal figure in Marx's early development. Marx's doctoral dissertation assumes special weight in this account, marking a significant rupture with Hegel. Rather than contained within the idealist philosophy of the Hegelian system, Marx's thesis aimed at formulating an anti-teleological materialism that incorporated the "activist element" of Hegelianism. Building on Epicurus, Marx's emergent materialism denied neither the objectivity of nature, as Hegel did, nor humans' active relation to nature and to each other. . . .
>
> Epicurus believed that perception through the senses is only possible because it expresses *an active relation to nature*—and indeed, of nature to itself. Even more significant for Marx's thinking was Epicurus's notion that material existence was only evident

> through change, that is, evolution. For Marx, dialectical reasoning can be considered as a necessary element of our cognition, arising from the emergent, transitory character of reality. Marx developed a "dialectical naturalism" that admits a dialectical approach to the study of nature as well as society.[164]

It is difficult to exaggerate the significance of these propositions for the development of a dialectical-ecological materialism. For Marx, the critique of heaven led to the critique of earth. Marx's materialism, germinating in his encounter with Epicurus, was followed by his entry into the critique of political economy, first as editor of the *Rheinische Zeitung*. From the beginning, then, Marx's materialism could be said to have two sides: the ecological and the economic. This was later manifested in his development in *Capital* of his theory of the metabolic rift. To understand the full dialectical character of his thought, his underlying materialist conception of nature is as vital as the materialist conception of history: there is, in the end, only *one materialism*.

Today we are faced with a series of anthropogenic rifts in the biophysical cycles of the Earth System, generating a planetary ecological crisis, of vast and multivarious dimensions. The answer is combating a social system of capitalism devoted to the accumulation of capital, primarily for a very few, a system for which nothing is ever enough. It is all the more important, therefore, to hold on to a philosophy of enough in the material sense, compatible with sustainable human development. As Epicurus wrote, criticizing the society of acquisition already visible in the money economy of his time: "Nothing is enough for someone for whom enough is little."[165] The Earth and our relation to it cannot be one of conquest or radical preservation, it has to be one of self-sufficiency and sustainable human existence/development, of which Epicurus's Garden stands as a humanistic and naturalistic reminder.

However, this emphasis on the reconciliation of humanity and nature within Marxian treatments of Epicurus today has led to a relative de-emphasis on the equally important aspect of Epicurus's philosophy, and the one most central to Marx's dissertation: the swerve away from all rigid determinism/fatalism, making possible voluntary human action. Here Epicurus's materialist concept of freedom, which so inspired Marx, remains absolutely vital. Marxian scholarship in this realm needs to catch up with developments within contemporary Epicurean studies, arising out of the translation of Book 25 of Epicurus's *On Nature*, the first efforts at the analysis of which originated with Gomperz in the late nineteenth century. The rejection of mechanism, fatalism, and teleology, along with the notion that, despite limits imposed by objective material conditions, in the end it is in many ways "up to us," is needed now more than ever.[166] The emergence of new relations to nature and society is possible.

Crucial to the conception of an irreducible world in which causal determinism also allows for free will and agency, and in which there is also no transcendental God governing things, is the notion of emergence or integrated levels. As Alfred North Whitehead wrote in his *Nature and Life* with respect to the organization of material reality: "One conclusion is the diverse modes of functioning which are produced by diverse modes of organization. The second conclusion is the aspect of continuity between these different modes. . . . A third conclusion is the difference in the aspects of Nature as we change the scale of observation." This conception of material reality as subject to levels of organization, which encompassed complexity and diversity, directed us, in Whitehead's view, all the way to the emergence of mind.[167]

However, it was Needham in his theory of integrative levels, as bears repeating, who best summed up this perspective, which he traced to Epicurus and saw as developed in the work of Marx and Engels:

> Marx and Engels were bold enough to assert that it [the dialectical process] happens actually in evolving nature itself, and that the undoubted fact that it happens in our thought about nature is because we and our thoughts are a part of nature. We cannot consider nature otherwise than as a series of levels of organisation, a series of dialectical syntheses. From the ultimate particle to atom, from atom to molecule, from molecule to colloidal aggregate, from aggregate to living cell, from cell to organ, from organ to body, from animal body to social association, the series of organisational levels is complete. Nothing but energy (as we now call matter and motion) and the levels of organisation (or the stabilised dialectical syntheses) at different levels have been required for the building of our world.[168]

For Marx and Engels, it was this same process of emergence that lay at the core of the materialist dialectic, not unrelated to Epicurus's own immanent dialectic that pointed to the creation of new forms and new powers as a result of changes in social organization, as well as to the possibility of crisis and extinction.[169] "In emergence generally," Roy Bhaskar stated in *Dialectic: The Pulse of Freedom*, "new beings (entities, structures, totalities, concepts) are generated out of pre-existing material from which they could have been neither induced nor deduced. There is a quantum leap, or nodal line, of (one feels like saying) the materialized imagination. . . . This is matter as creative, as autopoietic. It seems . . . to yield a genuine ontological analogue of Hegelian preservative determinative negation."[170] But in a materialist worldview, as opposed to Hegel's entelechy, emergence is accompanied by *disemergence*, as in Book 6 of Lucretius's *On Nature*, in which whatever was created in the phenomenal world is faced with the prospect of eventual annihilation, raising issues of both change and sustainability.[171]

The degree to which a dialectical-naturalist perspective was already embodied in Epicureanism and was integral to its conception of material evolution, contingency, historical change, human freedom, and emergent levels of reality is remarkable. Here we can recall Sedley's statement, quoted in chapter 2, that Epicurus "almost uniquely among Greek philosophers . . . arrived at what is nowadays the unreflective assumption of almost anyone with a smattering of science, that there are truths at the microscopic level of elementary particles and further very different truths at the phenomenal level." Ontologically, "the status of phenomenal properties, states of mind, etc.," is that of accidental properties of groups of atoms, which, however, are subject to organization, and the creation of new forms. Epicurus thus pointed to "the modern notion of 'emergence.'"[172]

In the words of Lucretius's great poem:

> But since many first beginnings of things in many ways,
> propelled by infinite blows from infinite time up to
> the present day
> and impelled by their own weight, have been used to being
> borne along,
> and to meet in all sorts of ways and to try all combinations,
> whatever they are able to create when brought together
> among themselves,
> therefore it happens that, circulating for a great quantity of time,
> by trying out every type of meeting and motion,
> at last these assemble which, when suddenly brought
> together, often become the beginnings of great things
> of the world, sea, sky, and the race of living creatures.[173]

This perspective of material emergence also applied to the mind itself. In Book 25 of *On Nature*, Epicurus provided a view of the human psyche that focused on the internal "productions" or "developments" of the mind based on an "original constitution." In this way, he accounted for the growth of individual human capacities, including the ability to choose different courses of action that were not at all predetermined. As he explained in Book 25, the "preconception of our responsibility," or of "our own agency," reflected the reality of human freedom. The mind itself was an emergent property of the material world and of human development, and its exercise, and the actions chosen, were "up to us."[174]

Naturally "to comprehend human agency as a causally . . . irreducible mode of matter," as Bhaskar wrote, "is not to posit a distinct substance 'mind' endowed with reasons for acting apart from the causal network, but to credit intentional embodied agency with distinct (emergent) causal powers from the biological matter out of which agents were formed, on which they are capable of reacting back (and must, precisely as materially embodied causally efficacious agents, do so, if they are to act at all)."[175]

What we find in Epicurus, according to Sedley in his treatment of Book 25 of *On Nature*, is a radical emergentism opposed to all forms of reductionism and to all transcendent causes. The implications, moreover, go far beyond the body-mind connection to the question of nature and human production. What Marx added to this was a clearer conception of human beings as the makers (*homo faber*) of history, who could change the world, but not entirely as they chose, but based on material conditions—both natural and social—inherited from that past.[176]

Epicurean philosophy can be seen as "Promethean" in character, but only in the revolutionary sense presented in Aeschylus's great tragedy, the basis of Marx's identification of Epicurus with Prometheus. Here Prometheus as "the renegade of heaven" brought Enlightenment to humanity, in defiance of the gods, passing on "all manner of arts" to human beings, and thus provided them with the power to transform both the natural world and the human relation to it.[177] But for Epicurus, as opposed to the modern conception of Prometheanism as mechanistic productivism, the goal was not production for its own sake, or the endless pursuit of wealth, both of which he explicitly rejected, but a community based on *enough*, geared to self-sufficiency and contentment (*ataraxia*), rooted in relations of friendship and reciprocity.[178]

The "preconception of our responsibility" that was to be found in each and every human being, according to Epicurus, stood for the possibility of human freedom within an otherwise determinant existence. It is therefore necessary to *break the bonds of fate* in the struggle to create a more human and social world, one that remains in accord with nature.

Notes

Preface

1. Marx to Ferdinand Lassalle, December 21, 1857, in Karl Marx and Frederick Engels, *Collected Works* (New York: International Publishers, 1975), vol. 40, 226.
2. This book is still in process.

Introduction

1. Epigraph: Diog. Laert. 10.93, translation according to Marx and Engels, *Collected Works* (New York: International Publishers, 1975), vol. 1, 421.
2. Lucr. 2.25, trans. Marx and Engels, *Collected Works*, vol. 1, 49, 416.
3. Karl Marx and Frederick Engels, *Collected Works*, vol. 30, 62–63; Karl Marx, *Eighteenth Brumaire of Louis Bonaparte* (New York: International Publishers, 1963), 15.
4. Roy Bhaskar, *Dialectic: The Pulse of Freedom* (London: Verso, 1993), 50.
5. Walter Englert, "Introduction," in Lucretius, *On the Nature of Things*, trans. Walter Englert (Indianapolis: Hackett Publishing, 2003), xv.
6. Epicurus, *On Nature*, Book 25, in A. A. Long and David N. Sedley, *The Hellenistic Philosophers* (Cambridge: Cambridge University Press, 1987), vol. 1, 102–4; Sedley, "Epicurus's Refutation of Determinism," *Syzetesis, studi sull' epicureismo greco e romano offerti a Marcello Gigante* (Napoli: G. Macchiaroli, 1983), 21, 23–24.
7. Marx and Engels, *Collected Works*, vol. 5, 141.
8. Long and Sedley, *The Hellenistic Philosophers*, vol. 1, 102.
9. The chaos at the end of an empire is something that has repeated itself numerous times in world history. The term here is taken from Samir Amin, *Empire of Chaos* (New York: Monthly Review Press, 1992).
10. Plut., *Mor.* (*Reply to Colotes*), 1097, 1127.33, translation according to Einarson and Lacy in *Plutarch, Moralia*, vol. 14, trans. Benedict Einarson and Philip H. De Lacy (Cambridge, MA: Harvard University Press, 1967), 311, 313 (Loeb Classical Library).
11. Lucr. 2.71-80, translation according to Englert (Hackett), 33.

12. Epicurus, *The Epicurus Reader*, trans. and ed., Brad Inwood and L. P. Gerson (Indianapolis: Hackett Publishing, 1994), 39 (Vatican Saying, no. 68).
13. On the relation of these concepts of "social metabolism," the "universal metabolism of nature" and the metabolic rift within Marx's analysis, see John Bellamy Foster, *Capitalism in the Anthropocene* (New York: Monthly Review Press, 2023), 41–61.
14. Marx described his approach to Epicurus as a "genetic exposition." In his *Science of Logic* Hegel associated "genetic exposition" with "objective logic" and "the dialectical movement of substance." Marx and Engels, *Collected Works*, vol. 1, 505; Georg Wilhelm Friedrich Hegel, *The System of Logic* (Amherst, NY: Humanity Books, 1969), 577; Jason Devine, "How Hegelian Was Marx?," Links.org, August 4, 2023, https://links.org.au/how-hegelian-was-marx-contribution-history-marx-and-young-hegelianism/.
15. Karl Marx, *Capital*, vol. 3 (London: Penguin, 1981), 959; John Bellamy Foster, *The Return of Nature* (New York: Monthly Review Press, 2020), 16–21.
16. Diog. Laert. 10.7–8. Epicurus singled out Plato at times, referring to him as the "golden man" and engaged in criticisms of the Academy in fragments from *On Nature*. Benjamin Farrington, *Science and Politics in the Ancient World* (London: George Allen and Unwin, 1939), 98; Eleni Kechagia, *Plutarch Against Colotes: A Lesson in History of Philosophy* (Oxford: Oxford University Press, 2011).
17. The well-known conflict between Epicureanism and Stoicism was confined to the later Roman Age.
18. The Academy under Arcesilaus, sometimes seen as the beginning of the New Academy, is also referred to as the Second or Middle Academy to distinguish it from both the First or Old Academy of Plato and the Third or "New Academy" of Carneades founded in 155 BCE. However, from Arcesilaus on the Academy was strongly associated with Skepticism. James Allen, "Carneades," *Stanford Encyclopedia of Philosophy* (2020), https://plato.stanford.edu/entries/carneades/; John Hazel, *Who's Who in the Ancent Greek World* (London: Routledge, 2000). 27, 51–52.
19. The emphasis on critique can easily be seen from the list of Epicurean titles. See Diog. Laert. 10.24–30; Tiziano Dorandi, "Epicurus and the Epicurean School," in *The Oxford Handbook of Epicurus and Epicureanism*, ed. Phillip Mitsis (Oxford: Oxford University Press, 2020),19–21; Norman Wentworth DeWitt, *Epicurus and His Philosophy* (Minneapolis: University of Minnesota Press, 1954), 95. Arcesilaus did not become head of the Academy (Middle Academy) until several years after Epicurus's death, but presumably his influence was dominant even before that. Epicurus may therefore have reacted against Arcesilaus's philosophy. But the main Epicruean critque was to come with Colotes's *On the Point that Conformity to the Doctrines of the Other Philosophers Actually Makes It Impossible to*

Live. See Einarson and De Lacy, Introduction in *Plutarch*, *Moralia*, 153–54; Tiziano Dorandi, "Chronology," in *Hellenistic Philosophy* (Cambridge: Cambridge University Press, 2005), 44.

20. David Sedley, "Epicurean Theories of Knowledge from Hermarchus to Lucretius and Philodemus,' *Lexicon Philosophicum*," Special Issue (2018): 108–9.
21. Marx and Engels, *Collected Works*, vol. 1, 457.
22. Marx and Engels, *Collected Works*, vol. 1, 457; Kechagia, *Plutarch Against Colotes*, 300.
23. Marx and Engels, *Collected Works*, vol. 1, 35.
24. Diog. Laert. 10.9; Norman Wentworth DeWitt, *Epicurus and His Philosophy* (Minneapolis: University of Minnesota Press, 1954), 328–31.
25. Dorandi, "Epicurus and the Epicurean School," 22–30; DeWitt, *Epicurus and His Philosophy*, 333–34.
26. Lucian, *Selected Satires*, ed. and trans. Lionel Casson (New York: W. W. Norton, 1962), 280–81.
27. Dorandi, "Epicurus and the Epicurean School," 32.
28. DeWitt, *Epicurus and His Philosophy*, 328, 333–36.
29. Martin Bernal, *Black Athena: The Afroasiatic Roots of Classical Civilization* (New Brunswick, NJ: Rutgers University Press, 1987).
30. Christopher I. Beckwith, *Greek Buddha: Pyrrho's Encounter with Early Buddhism in Central Asia* (Princteon: Princeton University Press, 2015). Pyrrhonism, the major skeptical tradition inspired by Pyrrho's thought, did not arise until several centuries after his death.
31. Bernard Frischer, *The Sculpted Word: Epicureanism and Philosophical Recruitment in Ancient Greece* (Los Angeles: University of California Press, 1982), 42.
32. DeWitt, *Epicurus and His Philosophy*, 3.
33. Ibid., 329.
34. Cic., *De Fin*., 5.1.3, translation according to Frischer, *The Sculpted Word*, 87; Frischer, *The Sculpted Word*, 87–96.
35. Clem. Al., *Strom*., 1.11; Marx and Engels, *Collected Works*, vol. 5, 142. In his *Notebooks on Epicurean Philosophy*, Marx quotes Clement of Alexandria directly and says: "This passage is now better understood, and it is known that Paul had all of philosophy in mind." There is no doubt from Clement's statement that Epicureanism was singled out for criticism, and Marx dropped his reference to all philosophy being criticized when he returned to this passage from Clement in *The German Ideology* a few years later. See Marx and Engels, *Collected Works*, vol. 1, 488.
36. Giambattista Vico, *The New Science*, trans. Thomas Goddard Bergin and Max Harold Frisch (Ithaca, NY: Cornell University Press, 1948), 85; Gino Bedani, *Vico Revisited* (Oxford: Berg, 1989), 132.
37. Samir Amin, *Eurocentrism* (New York: Monthly Review Press, 2009), 13, 109, 115, 121, 143–46, 212–13. Amin does not place an emphasis

on Epicureanism in the Hellenistic period but on the Neo-Platonism of Plotinus (119-22).

38. Joseph Needham, *Within the Four Seas: The Dialogue of East and West* (Toronto: University of Toronto Press, 1969), 91; Joseph Needham, *Time: The Refreshing River* (London: George Allen and Unwin, 1943), 55–56. For a more detailed discussion of Needham and the close correlation of Epicureanism and Daoism/Confucianism (and the relation of each to ecology) see John Bellamy Foster, *The Dialectics of Nature* (New York: Monthly Review Press, 2024), 171–84.

39. For contemporary analyses of the Axial Age, primarily written in idealist, culturalist, and religious terms, see Robert N. Bellah and Hans Joas, eds., *The Axial Age and Its Consequences* (Cambridge, MA: Harvard University Press, 2012); S. N. Eisenstadt, ed., *The Origins and Diversity of Axial Age Civilizations* (Albany: State University of New York Press, 1986).

40. Amin, *Eurocentrism*, 136, 213.

41. In an essay that relies on extreme culturalism, Kiran Pizarro Mansukhani argues that Marx's "dissertation," merely because it focused on the Greek and Roman classics and reflected a German education in the classics, was "enclosed in an epistemology so Eurocentric that it produces structurally racist arguments." However, lacking any concrete evidence of actual Eurocentrism (the view of Europe as the universal culture) in Marx's dissertation, Mansukhani simply pronounces that Marx's thesis *had to be Eurocentric* since Marx had been educated in a racist environment in Germany, and thus inevitably carried the taint of "white, European man" that was incorporated into all German analyses, from Alexander Humboldt to Hegel (thinkers with whom Marx, of course, had major differences). Moreover, Marx is condemned for having presented what Mansukhani calls a "condescending view of Hellenistic thought," since he went so far as to acknowledge the historical fact that Hellenistic philosophy was unable to continue to move forward, and eventually died out over the centuries (in the case of Epicureanism due to the growth of Christianity). Ironically, in a final desperate effort to provide some substantial basis for his argument, Mansukhani ends up citing, as the leading example of the work of "Marx's critics" in this regard, Amin's *Eurocentrism*, one of the great works of contemporary historical materialism. Here it is alleged that Amin provided a "critique of the 'historical' aspect of historical materialism" for its Eurocentrism, extending this criticism to Marx himself. Yet Amin provides nothing but praise in his book for Marx's views on the ancient Greeks. At no point does Amin, any more than Marx, resort to *culturalist*, as opposed to *historical-materialist*, arguments. Indeed, his entire book is a condemnation of the former. Kiran Pizarro Mansukhani, "The Anti-Radical Classicism of Karl Marx's Dissertation," in *Critical Ancient World Studies: The Case for Forgetting the Classics*, ed. Mathura Umachandran and Marchella Ward (London: Routledge, 2023), 234–51; Amin, *Eurocentrism*, 119, 169, 212–13.

42. Marx and Engels, Collected Works, vol. 5, 141.
43. Marx, *Early Writings* (London: Penguin, 1974), 348–49.

Chapter One: Epicurus and Hellenistic Athens

1. Diog. Laert. 10.1–4; Norman Wentworth DeWitt, *Epicurus and His Philosophy* (Minneapolis: University of Minnesota Press, 1954), 36–42. The Gargettus deme was in northeast Attica just south of Mt. Pentelikos. For a map of the demes see A. W. Gomme, *The Population of Athens* (Oxford: Oxford University Press, 1933).
2. Graham Shipley, *A History of Samos, 800–188 BC* (Oxford: Oxford University Press, 1987), 141–43; Alfonso Moreno, "The Attic Neighbor: The Cleruchy in the Athenian Empire," in *Interpreting the Athenian Empire*, ed. John Ma, Nikolas Papazarkadas, and Robert Parker (London: Duckworth Pres, 2009), 211–21; G. L. Cawkwell, "Notes on the Failure of the Second Athenian Confederacy," *Journal of Hellenic Studies* 101 (1981): 40–55.
3. Shipley, *A History of Samos*, 132–33, 146.
4. Ibid., 135–37.
5. Ibid., 138–43; A.W. Pickard-Cambridge, *Demosthenes and the Last Days of Greek Freedom, 384–322* (New York: G. P. Putnam's Sons, 1914), 58.
6. Stephen Ruzicka, "Epaminondas and the Genesis of the Social War," *Classical Philology* 93, no. 1 (January 1998): 60–69; Shipley, *A History of Samos*, 156–58; Pickard-Cambridge, *Demosthenes*, 109–11.
7. Pickard-Cambridge, *Demosthenes*, 412.
8. "The World of Alexander," British Museum, https://www.britishmuseum.org/collection/galleries/world-alexander.
9. Mehdi K. Nakosteen, Robert Browning, "Education in Classical Cultures: Athens," Britannica, https://www.britannica.com/topic/education/Education-in-classical-cultures; Duncan Howitt-Marshall, "The Education System in Ancient Greece," Greece Is, September 14, 2023, https://www.greece-is.com/the-education-system-in-ancient-greece/; De Witt, *Epicurus and His Philosophy*, 42–45.
10. Clarence A. Forbes, "Teachers' Pay in Ancient Greece," University of Nebraska Studies, *Studies in the Humanities 2* (May 1942), https://digitalcommons.unl.edu/cgi/viewcontent.cgi?article=1040&context=univstudiespapers; DeWitt, *Epicurus and His Philosophy*, 40–42.
11. Diog. Laert. 10.3–4; Victor Ehrenberg, *The People of Aristophanes* (Oxford: Basil Blackwell, 1943), 262. Until recently it was believed that the inscription by Diogenes of Oenoanda included a letter from Epicurus to his mother. But this is now assumed to be a letter by Diogenes himself. Diog. Oen., fr. 125–126, *The Epicurean Inscription*, https://www.english.enoanda.cat/the_inscription.html/.
12. Plut., *Mor.*, 1098.
13. Hes. *Theog.*, 115–20; Sext. Emp., Adv. Math. 10.18–19; Diog. Laert.

10.2–4; Norman Wentworth DeWitt, *St. Paul and Epicurus* (Minneapolis: University of Minnesota Press, 1954), 4; DeWitt, *Epicurus and His Philosophy*, 42–43; David Konstan, *A Life Worthy of the Gods: The Materialist Psychology of Epicurus* (Las Vegas: Parmenides Publishing, 2008), 63.

14. Cic. *Nat. D.*, 1.71–73; DeWitt, *Epicurus and His Philosophy*, 43–48.
15. Diod. Sic., 18.8.2–5.
16. Arist., *Const. Ath.*, 42; Benjamin Farrington, *The Faith of Epicurus* (London: Weidenfeld and Nicolson, 1967), 5.
17. Pickard-Cambridge, *Demosthenes*, 472–86; ; François Chamoux, *Hellenistic Civilization* (Oxford: Blackwell, 2002), 41–42; John Hazel, *Who's Who in the Greek World* (London: Routledge, 2000), 76–80 ("Demosthenes"); Britannica, "Lamian War," https://www.britannica.com/event/Lamian-War; DeWitt, *Epicurus and His Philosophy*, 50.
18. Diog. Laert. 10.1–2; R. M. Errington, "Samos and the Lamian War," *Chiron* 5 (1975): 51–58.
19. Diog. Laert. 10.–4–6; DeWitt, *Epicurus and His Philosophy*, 53–54.
20. Plut. *Mor.*, 1126; Diog. Laert. 10.28; DeWitt, *Epicurus and His Philosophy*, 78.
21. Diog. Laert. 4; Hazel, *Who's Who in the Greek World*, 254 ("Xenocrates"); De Witt, *Epicurus and His Philosophy*, 50–51.
22. Jonathan Barnes, ed., *Early Greek Philosophy* (London: Penguin 2001), 40–47 (Xenophanes); James Lesher, "Xenophanes," Stanford Encyclopedia of Philosophy, (May 19, 2023), https://plato.stanford.edu/entries/xenophanes/; Glen A. Most, "The Poetics of Early Greek Philosophy," in *The Cambridge Companion to Early Greek Philosophy*, ed. A. A. Long (Cambridge: Cambridge University Press, 1999), 337–39.
23. DeWitt, *Epicurus and His Philosophy*, 61–62; Hazel, *Who's Who in the Greek World*, 163; Jacques Brunschwig, "Pyrrhon," in *Greek Thought: A Guide to Classical Knowledge*, ed. Jacques Brunschwig and Geoffrey E. R. Lloyd (Cambridge, MA: Harvard University Press, 2000), 739–44; Richard Bett, "Pyrrho," *Stanford Encyclopedia of Philosophy* (September 15, 2022), https://plato.stanford.edu/entries/pyrrho.
24. A few passages of Nausiphanes on rhetoric can be found in Philodemus but nothing on Nausiphanes's epistemology.
25. Diog. Laert. 10.14.; DeWitt, *Epicurus and His Philosophy*, 64–65.
26. Diog. Laert. 10, 11–12; Anaxagoras, fragments, in Barnes, ed., *Early Greek Philosophy* (London: Penguin, 2001), 185–200; George Thomson, *The First Philosophers* (London: Lawrence and Wishart, 1961), 308–10; Daniel W. Graham, "Empedocles and Anaxagoras: Responses to Parmenides," in Long, ed., *The Cambridge Companion to Early Greek Philosophy*, 163–64; Benjamin Farrington, *The Faith of Epicurus*, 48–51; Hazel, *Who's Who in the Greek World*, 15.
27. André Laks, "Epicurus," in Brunschwig and Lloyd, ed., *Greek Thought*, 586–87; Phillip de Lacy, "Review of [1] Filodemo, Agli Amici di Scuola

(PHerc 1005), by Anna Angeli, [2] Demetrio Lacone, Aporie Testuali, ed. Esegtiche in Epicuro (PHerc 1012) by Enzo Puglia, [3] Demetrio Lacone, La Poesia (PHerc 188 e 1014) by Constatina Romeo; and [4] Carneisco Il Secondo Libro del Filista (PHerc 1027) by Mario Capasso," *American Journal of Philology*, vol. 111, no. 4 (Winter 1990): 575. Aristotle's exoteric works were mainly dialogues directed at the general populace, none of which have survived. In contrast, the esoteric works were primarily lectures delivered at the Lyceum, which make up Aristotle's surviving corpus.

28. Diog. Laert. 10.24–25; Tiziano Dorandi, "Epicurus and the Epicurean School," in *The Oxford Handbook of Epicurus and Epicureanism*, ed. Phillip Mitsis (Oxford University Press, 2020), 20; DeWitt, *Epicurus and His Philosophy*, 70–77.
29. Ellen Meiksins Wood and Neal Wood, *Class Ideology and Ancient Political Theory* (Oxford: Basil Blackwell, 1978), 249–53; Ian Worthington, *Athens After Empire* (Oxford: Oxford University Press, 2021), 34; Hans Volkmann, "Antigonus I Monopthalmus," *Britannica.*
30. https://www.britannica.com/biography/Antigonus-I-Monophthalmus#ref 238215. Farrington, *The Faith of Epicurus*, 50–52.
31. Plut., *Mor.*, 1097, 1126; DeWitt, *Epicurus and His Philosophy*, 78–79, 85; Stanley M. Burstein, "Lysimachus and the Greek Cities of Asia: The Case of Miletus," *The Ancient World: A Scholarly Journal for the Study of Antiquity* 3, no. 3–4 (1980): 73–79.
32. DeWitt, *Epicurus and His Philosophy*, 80–81; Hazel, *Who's Who in the Greek World*, 133.
33. Cic. *Pis.*, 26.63; Cic. *De Finibus*, 2.21, 2.68, Diog. Laert. 10.5, 10.25–26.
34. Diog. Laert. 10.23–25; Dorandi, "Epicurus and the Epicurean School," 19; DeWitt, *Epicurus and His Philosophy*, 81, 94.
35. Dorandi, "Epicurus and the Epicurean School," 20.
36. DeWitt, *Epicurus and His Philosophy*, 82–83.
37. Diog. Laert. 10.4–11.
38. Worthington, *Athens After Empire*, 47–51; DeWitt, *Epicurus and His Philosophy*, 89–90; M. Rostovtzeff, *The Social and Economic History of the Hellenistic World* (Oxford: Oxford University Press, 1941), vol. 1, 14–15.
39. Worthington, *Athens After Empire*, 5, 79–80.
40. Plu., *Vit.* 34, Worthington, *Athens After Empire*, 83–90.
41. Paus. 1.26.1; Hazel, *Who's Who in the Greek World*, 18, 72–74, 150, 208–10, 216–17; Worthington, *Athens After Empire*, 96–101; Chamoux, *Hellenistic Civilization*, 58–60; "Wars of Alexander's Successors (Diadochi), Heritage History, https://www.heritage-history.com/index.php?c=resources&s=war-dir&f=wars_diadochi.
42. Diog. Laert. 10.152–54, translation according to R. D. Hicks (Loeb Classical Library).
43. Us.221, trans. according to DeWitt, *Epicurus and His Philosophy*, 67; see also "Selected Fragments from Epicurus," trans. by Peter-Saint-Andre, https://

monadnock.net/epicurus/fragments.html, (numbering according to Herman Usener); "Epicurea: Selections from the Classic Compilation of Hermann Usener," https://newepicurean.com/introduction/documents/3B4CA8326F201AD3508F9B168E0287DDCD7E941C.html; Diog. Laert. 10.12–13.

44. Demetrius of Phalerum got his "revenge" on Athens by convincing Ptolemy I to set up the massive Museum and Library in Alexandria, which was to lead to Alexandria displacing Athens as the intellectual capital of the Greek world. Hazel, *Who's Who in the Greek World*, 72; Alice Bennett, "10 Reasons the Ancient City of Alexandria Was an Intellectual Powerhouse," *The Collector*, December 5, 2020, https://www.thecollector.com/ancient-city-alexandria-intellectual-powerhouse/.

45. Diog. Laert. 10.10; Plut. *Adv. Col.*, 1127; Chamoux, *Hellenistic Civilization*, 203; Farrington, *The Faith of Epicurus*, 2–4; "Colophon," Britannica, https://www.britannica.com; Richard Stillwell et al., "Colophon Ionia, Turkey," Princeton Encyclopedia of Classical Sites, https://www.perseus.tufts.edu. Tiziano Dorandi, "The Schools and Texts of Epicurus in the Early Roman Empire," in *Plotinus and Epicurus*, ed. Angelo Longo and Daniela Patrizia Taormina (Cambridge: Cambridge University Press, 2016), 42.

46. Us.189, translated in "Epicurea: Selections from the Classic Compilation of Hermann Usener"; Diskin Clay, "Sailing to Lampsacus: Diogenes of Oenoanda, New Fragment 7," Greek, Roman, and Byzantine Studies 14, no. 1 (1973): 49–59; Wim Nijs and Ku Leuven, "The Wise Man and the Sea: Epicureans on Seas Storms, Shipwrecks, and Chance," *Greece and Rome* 70, no. 2 (2023): 245; DeWitt, *Epicurus and His Philosophy*, 184.

47. Mogens Herman Hansen, *The Athenian Democracy in the Age of Demosthenes* (Oxford: Blackwell, 1991),

48. Gomme, *The Population of Athens*, 26; Ellen Meiksins Wood, *Peasant-Citizen and Slave: The Foundations of Athenian Democracy* (London: Verso, 1988), 43–44. The actual number of slaves in 323 in the census conducted by Demetrius of Phalerum as quoted by Athenaeus at the beginning of the third century CE listed 400,000 slaves, but historians and demographers have regarded this as a mistake of transcription: the number given by Gomme is only 104,000. See Gomme, *The Population of Athens*, 18.

49. Norma Miller, Introduction to Menander, *Plays and Fragments* (London: Penguin, 1987), 3–17; Ehrenberg, *The People of Aristophanes*; Edith Hamilton, *The Greek Way* (New York: W. W. Norton, 1943), 77–97; Worthington, *Athens After Empire*, 43–45.

50. De Witt, *Epicurus and His Philosophy*, 52–53, 330, 376.

51. Ibid., 90–93.

52. Cic. *De Fin.*, 1.20.65, translation according to Farrington, *The Faith of Epicurus*, 125.

53. Elizabeth Asmis, "Epicurean Economics," in *Philodemus and the New Testament World*, ed. John T. Fitzgerald, Dirk Obbink, and Glenn S. Holland (Boston: Brill, 2004), 137.

54. Sen. *Ep*., 21; translation according to Seneca, *Episulae Morales* I, Books 1–4 (Cambridge, MA: Harvard University Press, 1917), 147 (Loeb Classical Library).
55. Farrington, *The Faith of Epicurus*, 12; DeWitt, *Epicurus and His Philosophy*, 90–93; "Don" (anonymous), "Where Was the Garden of Epicurus?: Evidence from the Ancient Sources and Archaeology," https://www.epicureanfriends.com/wcf/filebase/download/94//.
56. Plut. *Vit*., *Dem*., 34.2; DeWitt, *Epicurus and His Philosophy*, 193.
57. Plut., *Mor*., 1097.
58. Epic., *Sent. Vat*., 21; trans. Brad Inwood and L. P. Gerson, *The Epicurus Reader* (Indianapolis: Hackett Publishing 1994), 37.
59. Diog. Laert. 10.25–28; Dorandi, "Epicurus and the Epicurean School," 16, 18; DeWitt, *Epicurus and His Philosophy*, 111–20.
60. Cic. *Tusc.* 1.23.55; Seneca, *Epis. Mor.* 79.15–16; Lactant, *Div. Inst.* 3.25; De Witt, *Epicurus and His Philosophy*, 42, 96; Farrington, *The Faith of Epicurus*, 106–7; Benjamin Farrington, *Science and Politics in the Ancient World* (London: George Allen and Unwin, 1939), 230–32; Wood and Wood, *Classical Ideology and Ancient Political Theory*, 119–252.
61. Bernard Frischer, *The Sculpted World: Epicureanism and Philosophical Recruitment in Ancient Greece* (Berkeley: University of California Press, 1982), 52–54.
62. Diog. Laert. 10.3, 10.9, 10.18, 10.21; Gomme, *The Population of Athens*, 26; George Thomson, "Ancient Greek Materialism," *Labour Monthly* 19, no. 2 (February 1937): 121–23.
63. G. E. M. de Ste. Croix, *The Class Struggle in the Ancient Greek World* ((London: Duckworth, 1981), 98–103; Wood and Wood, *Class Ideology and Ancient Political Theory*, 49–52; Ehrenberg, *The People of Aristophanes*, 177, 193, 201–2.
64. Plut., *Mor.* 1097, translation according to Einarson and De Lacy in Plutarch, *Moralia*, vol. 14, trans. Benedict Einarson and Phillip H. De Lacy (Cambridge, MA: Harvard University Press, 1967), 89 (Loeb Classical Library).
65. Diog. Laert. 10.5, 10.25–28; Cic. *De Fin* 2.21, translation according to Rackam in Cicero, *De Finibus Bonorum et Malorem*, trans. H. Rackham (New York: G. P. Putnam's Sons, 1931), 157; Cic. *Piso*. 26.63; Lactant. *Div. Inst.* 3.25; Pamela Gordon, *The Invention and Gendering of Epicurus* (Ann Arbor: University of Michigan Press, 2012), 85.
66. Gordon, *The Invention and Gendering of Epicurus*, 84–85.
67. Diog. Laert. 10.4–7; PHerc. 1005, fr. 117, col. 6; Us, frag. 414; Gordon, *The Invention and Gendering of Epicurus*, 101–102; Frischer, *The Sculpted World*, 62; DeWitt, *Epicurus and His Philosophy*, 95–97.
68. Diog. Laert. 10.4–6, Cic. *Nat. D.*, 1.91–93, Gordon, *The Invention and Gendering of Epicurus*, 83–84.
69. Pliny, *HN*., 35.36.79–81, trans. John Bostock, Perseus.tufts.edu,; Diog.

Laert. 10. 4-6, 10.18-20, 10.22-24; Plut., *Mor.*, 1098, Pliny quoted by Gordon, *The Invention and Gendering of Epicurus*, 108-9.

70. Cic., *De Fin.*, 1.20.65-70; Epic. *Sent. Vat.* 23, 52, 66, trans. according to DeWitt, *Epicurus and His Philosophy*, 101-5, 307.
71. DeWitt, *Epicurus and His Philosophy*, 102.
72. Diog Laert., 10.150-52, trans. according to Inwood and Gerson, 35-36; Lucr. 5.1020-1025, 5.1145-50.
73. *PHerc* 1005, col. 4.9-14; Konstan, *A Life Worthy of the Gods*, xi-xii (Epicurus quoted), 151-52.
74. DeWitt, *Epicurus and His Philosophy*, 51-52, 192.
75. Diog. Laert. 10.11, 10.130-33, trans. according to Inwood and Gerson, *Epicurus Reader*, 39.
76. Diog. Laert., 10.123-24; Philodemus, *On Piety: Critical Text with Commentary*, ed. Dick Obbink (Oxford: Oxford University Press, 1996), 157; Karl Marx and Frederick Engels, *Collected Works* (New York: International Publishers 1975), vol. 1, 51; A. A. Long and D. N. Sedley, *The Hellenistic Philosophers*, vol. 1 (Cambridge: Cambridge University Press,1975), 145-49. Farrington, *The Faith of Epicurus*, 63-87; A. J. Festugière, *Epicurus and His Gods* (Cambridge, MA: Harvard University Press, 1956); John Bellamy Foster, Brett Clark, and Richard York, *Critique of Intelligent Design* (New York: Monthly Review Press, 2008), 49-64.
77. Lucr. 5.835-880; trans. according to Latham in Lucretius, *On the Nature of the Universe*, trans. R. E. Latham and John Goodwin (London: Penguin, 1994), 149-51; David Sedley, *Creationism and Its Critics in Antiquity* (Berkeley: University of California Press, 2007); A. A. Long, "Evolution vs. Intelligent Design in Antiquity," November 2006, 3-5, https://townsend-center.berkeley.edu/sites/default/files/publications/nov-dec_06_nl.pdf.
78. Luc. 1.150, translated according to Englert (Hackett).
79. Diog. Laert. 10.13-16, translation according to Inwood and Gerson, *Epicurus Reader*, 4.
80. Diog. Laert. 10.9, translation according to Inwood and Gerson, *Epicurus Reader*, 4; Dorandi, "Epicurus and the Epicurean School," 13; DeWitt, *Epicurus and His Philosophy*, 29-31, 33-35, 328-53.

Chapter Two: Epicurus's Materialist Philosophy

1. Diog. Laert. 10.30, Diogenes Laertius, *Lives of the Eminent Philosophers*, trans. R. D. Hicks (Cambridge, MA: Harvard University Press, Loeb Classical Library, 1931).
2. Diog. Laert. 10.37-40; Philodemus, *On Methods of Inference: A Study in Ancient Empiricism*, ed./trans. Phillip Howard De Lacy and Estelle Allen De Lacy (Philadelphia: American Philological Association, 1941).
3. Jonathan Barnes, *The Presocratic Philosophers* (London: Routledge and Keagan Paul, 1981), 43-44; Cyril Bailey, *The Greek Atomists and Epicurus* (New York: Russell and Russell, 1964), 9-27.

4. Barnes, *The Presocratic Philosophers*, 427; Gaston Javier Basile, "The Early Greek Prose-Writing Tradition: Bridging the Myth-History Divide," *Dialogues D'Historie Ancienne* 45, no. 2 (2019), https://www.cairn.info/revue-dialogues-d-histoire-ancienne-2019-2-page-81.htm.
5. Barnes, *The Presocratic Philosophers*, 305; C. C. W. Taylor, "The Atomists," in *The Cambridge Companion to Early Greek Philosophy*, ed. A. A. Long (Cambridge: Cambridge University Press, 1999), 183.
6. George Thomson, *Aeschylus and Athens* (London: Lawrence and Wishart, 1946), 369–70.
7. Immanuel Kant, *Logic* (New York: Dover, 1988), 34; Hegel, *Lectures on the History of Philosophy* (Lincoln: University of Nebraska Press, 1995), vol. 2, 281, 293, 296.
8. Cyril Bailey, *The Greek Atomists and Epicurus* (Oxford: Oxford University Press, 1928), 252.
9. Plato, *Meno*, 80d-e, trans. G. M. A. Grube in Plato, *Meno* (Indianapolis, Indiana: Hackett Publishing, 1976); Gisela Striker, "Epistemology," in *The Oxford Handbook of Epicurus and Epicureanism*, ed. Phillip Mitsis (Oxford: Oxford University Press, 2020), 43, 47; A. A. Long and David N. Sedley, *The Hellenistic Philosophers: Translation of the Principal Sources with Philosophical Commentary*, vol. 1 (Cambridge: Cambridge University Press, 1987), 89.
10. Democr. fr.s B 8, B 125 and fr. B 117, trans. in Jonathan Barnes, ed., *Early Greek Philosophy* (London: Penguin, 2001), 209, 224; Striker, "Epistemology," 47; Taylor, "The Atomists," 191–92.
11. Hegel, *Lectures on the History of Philosophy*, vol. 2, 281.
12. Striker, "Epistemology," 44.
13. Diog. Laert. 10.30-32, trans. Hicks (Loeb Classical Library).
14. Diog. Laert. 10.34, 10.146, trans. Hicks (Loeb Classical Library); Sext. Emp., *Math*, 7: 205–12; Striker, "Epistemology," 51; Bailey, *The Greek Atomists and Epicurus*, 253–55.
15. Diog. Laert. 10.146.
16. Sext. Emp., *Math*, 7:205–12; Diog. Laert. 10:34-35; Lucr. 4:353–63.
17. Bailey, *The Greek Atomists and Epicurus*, 233, 253, 267.
18. Protagoras quoted in Barnes, *The Presocratic Philosophers*, 541–45, 644, translation altered in accord with Ellen Meiksins Wood and Neal Wood, *Class Ideology and Ancient Political Theory* (Oxford: Basil Blackwell, 1978), 134–37.
19. Plato, *Meno*, 80d–81e, trans. G. M. A. Grube in Plato, *Meno* (Indianapolis: Hackett Publishing, 1976).
20. Diog. Laert. 10.32-34; Long and Sedley, *The Hellenistic Philosophers*, vol. 1, 88–89.
21. Arist., *An post.*, 1.3.
22. Long and Sedley, *The Hellenistic Philosophers*, vol. 1, 89.
23. Diog. Laert. 10.38, translated according to Long and Sedley, *The Hellenistic*

Philosophers, 87; André Laks, "Epicurus," in *Greek Thought: A Guide to Classical Knowledge*, ed. Jacques Brunschwig and E. R. Lloyd (Cambridge, MA: Harvard University Press, 2000), 591.

24. Julia Annas, "Epicurus on Agency," in *Passions and Perceptions: Studies in the Hellenistic Philosophy of Mind*, ed. Jacques Brunschwig and Martha C. Nussbaum (Cambridge: Cambridge University Press, 2009), 54.
25. Diog. Laert. 10:34–35.
26. Laks, "Epicurus," 589; Striker, "Epistemology," 48.
27. Elizabeth Asmis, "Psychology," in Mitsis, ed., *The Oxford Handbook on Epicurus and Epicureanism*, 193–94. Aristotle's approach to naturalism, while insisting on the non-rational character of animals, was in many ways similar to Epicureanism. See Christine M. Korsgaard, *Fellow Creatures* (Oxford: Oxford University Press, 2018).
28. Diog. Laert. 10.38, Epicurus, "Letter to Herodotus," translated according to Long and Sedley, *The Hellenistic Philosophers*, vol. 1, 87.
29. Diog. Laert. 10.34; Long and Sedley, *The Hellenistic Philosophers*, vol. 1, 9192; Striker, "Epistemology," 52–56.
30. Diog. Laert. 10.37-38, trans. Long and Sedley, *The Hellenistic Philosophers*, vol. 1, 87.
31. Lucr. 1.329–45, 1.418–30; Sex. Emp., *Math*, 7.1.211–13; David Konstan, "Atomism," in Mitis, ed., *The Oxford Handbook of Epicurus and Epicureanism*, 61; Elizabeth Asmis, "Epicurean Epistemology," in *The Cambridge History of Hellenistic Philosophy*, ed. Keimpre Algra, Jonathan Barnes, Japp Mansfeld, and Malcolm Schofield (Cambridge: Cambridge University Press, 2005), 283; Striker, "Epistemology," 53–55.
32. On the Epicurean theory of signs, see Elizabeth Asmis, *Epicurus' Scientific Method* (Ithaca, NY: Cornell University Press, 1984), 175–96.
33. Cic., *Fat.*, 37; Cicero, *Nat. D.*, 68–70; David Sedley, "Epicureanism. 12. Free Will," *Routledge Encyclopedia of Philosophy* (2005), https://www.rep.routledge.com/articles/thematic/epicureanism/v-1/sections/free-will#; R. J. Hankinson, "Determinism and Indeterminism," in Algra, ed., *The Cambridge History of Hellenistic Philosophy*, 517–22.
34. David Sedley, *Creationism and Its Critics in Antiquity* (Berkeley: University of California Press, 2007), 141.
35. Striker, "Epistemology," 57–58.
36. Benjamin Farrington, *The Faith of Epicurus* (London: Weidenfeld and Nicolson, 1967), 7–8.
37. Farrington, *The Faith of Epicurus*, 8.
38. Konstan, "Atomism," 61.
39. Diog. Laert. 10.40–42.
40. The ancient sources appear to conflict over whether Democritus saw weight as a primary characteristic of the atom, though the sources that are most explicit on this issue say he did not. See, for example, Euseb., *Praep. evang.*, 14.749b-c. This has generated some controversy in modern discussions,

but the literature overall still leans toward the notion that weight was derivative of size for Democritus. A classic discussion of the whole issue was provided by Marx in his doctoral thesis. See Karl Marx and Frederick Engels, *Collected Works* (New York: International Publishers, 1975), vol. 1, 54–57.

41. Epicurus uses the notion of the "assemblage" of atoms in Book 25 of *On Nature*, where he says that a particular thing can be referred to as a *qua* "assemblage but also, [as] *qua* atoms and *qua* moving atoms or assemblage." Quoted in Annas, "Epicurus on Agency," 59. See also Diog. Laert. 10.61–63.
42. Democritus, fr. B125, translated by Jonathan Barnes, ed., *Early Greek Philosophy*, 210, 224; David Furley, "Democritus," in *Greek Thought*, 576–80; Bailey, *The Greek Atomists and Epicurus*, 128–37; Barnes, *The Presocratic Philosophers*, 365-67. Lucretius introduced the term *simulacra* in Latin in translating *eidola*. Lucr. 4.35.
43. Aëtius quoted in Furley, "Democritus," 578.
44. Furley, "Democritus," 578; Bailey, *The Greek Atomists*, 128, 132–33.
45. Diog. Laert. 9.45, translated according to Hicks (Loeb Classical Library).
46. Euseb., *Praep. evang.*, I, p. 23d, trans. Karl Marx and Frederick Engels, *Collected Works*, vol. 1, 81.
47. Cic., *Fat.*, 10, trans. Marx and Engels, *Collected Works*, vol. 1, 81; Arist. *Gen. an.* 5.8.789b.
48. Thgn.1.425–27; Diog. Laert. 10.127–28, 133–34, trans. Hicks (Loeb Classical Library).
49. Diog. Laert. 10.59–61; Lucr. 2.225–262; Sext. Emp. *Math.*, 10.220–24.
50. Lucr. 2.235–39; Marx and Engels, *Collected Works*, vol. 1, 57; Lane Cooper, *Aristotle, Galileo, and the Tower of Pisa* (Ithaca, NY: Cornell University Press, 1935), 49. Ludwig Feuerbach, *History of Modern Philosophy from Bacon to Spinoza*, trans. Tim Newcomb (Stuttgart: Newcomb Livaria Press, 2023), 70.
51. Diog. Laert. 10.56–10.57; Euseb., *Praep. evang.*, 23.773b; Long and Sedley, *The Hellenistic Philosophers*, vol. 1, 3944, Konstan, "Atomism," 63–70.
52. Lucr. 3.288–322, 4.26–32, 4.45–58, 4.794–806; A. A. Long, *Hellenistic Philosophy: Stoics, Epicureans, and Sceptics (*Berkeley: University of California Press, 1986), 52–56; Walter Englert, "Voluntary Action and Responsibility," in Mitsis, ed., *The Oxford Handbook of Epicurus and Epicureanism*, 23; W. H. D. Rouse and Martin F. Smith, translators' note to Lucretius, *On the Nature of Things* (Cambridge, MA: Harvard University Press, 1992), 278–79 (Loeb Classical Library). In Epicurus, as distinct from Democritus, the process of sensuousness, reflected in the atomic films of the eidola/simulacra, was the process, as Marx put it, of "accidentals in sensuous perception," and so the unfolding of time itself. Marx and Engels, *Collected Works*, vol. 1, 65.

53. Diog. Laert. 10.42–10.44; Attraction and repulsion are evident in Lucretius's treatment of magnetism, which is used to point to wider principles. Lucr. 6.910–16, 6.1042–47, while Galen attributes this directly to Epicurus. Galen, *Nat. Fac.*, 1.14–15; Taylor, *Pleasure, Mind and Soul*, 184–85.
54. Lucr. 2.225–238.
55. Englert, "Voluntary Action and Responsibility," 222; Basil Evangellidis, "Lucretius's Argument on the Swerve and Free Action" (2019), https://philpapers.org/rec/EVALAO. Cicero's treatment of Carneades's argument on Epicurus's swerve had taken on great importance in today's treatments of Epicurus's theory. Moreover, it is significant that Carneades was writing in the late third/early second century BCE.
56. Lucr., 2.51–93, 2.216–50.
57. Lucr. 2.25, translation according to Marx and Engels, *Collected Works*, vol. 1, 49, 416.
58. Philoponus. *Phys.* 3.494.19–25; Taylor, "The Atomists," 188; C. C. W. Taylor, *Pleasure, Mind and Soul: Selected Papers in Ancient Philosophy* (Oxford: Oxford University Press, 2008), 1989. In contrast to Taylor, who, along with Marx, sees attraction and repulsion as integral to Democritus (and by implication Epicurus), and to Immanuel Kant, who interpreted the motion of atoms in Epicurus as one of attraction and repulsion, David Konstan states that Epicurus "did not know the . . . ideas of attraction and repulsion among atoms." David Konstan, "Epicurus," *The Stanford Encyclopedia of Philosophy* (Fall 2022), https://plato.stanford.edu/archives/fall2022/entries/epicurus/; Immanuel Kant, *Cosmogony* (New York: Greenwald, 1968), 12–13. Nevertheless, there is substantial evidence of the origin of the concepts of attraction and repulsion in antiquity. See Dragoslav Stoiljkovic, "Attraction and Repulsion as the Essence of Matter—From Ancient Philosophy to Contemporary Science," *Annals of the Branch of Sanu in Novi Sad* (Serbian Academy of Sciences and Arts, Branch in Novi Sad), 11 (2015): 58–69, https://www.researchgate.net/publication/300230119_ATTRACTION_AND_REPULSION_AS_THE_ESSENCE_OF_MATTER_-_FROM_ANCIENT_PHILOSOPHY_TO_CONTEMPORARY_SCIENCE/.
59. Marx and Engels, *Collected Works*, vol. 1, 51.
60. Marx and Engels, *Collected Works*, vol. 1, 46.
61. Marx and Engels, *Collected Works*, vol. 1, 53, 61–62.
62. Sedley, "Epicureanism. 12. Free Will."
63. Walter Scott, *Fragmenta Herculanensia: A Descriptive Catalogue of the Oxford Copies of the Herculanean Rolls* (Oxford: Oxford University Press, 1885), 1; Joseph Jay Deiss, *Herculaneum: Italy's Buried Treasure* (Los Angeles: Getty Publications, 1985), 68; John Hazel, *Who's Who in the Greek World* (London: Routledge, 2000), 186; David Blank, "Philodemus," *Stanford Encyclopedia of Philosophy* (January 16, 2019), https://plato.stanford.edu/entries/philodemus/#NapHerVilPap.

64. Scott, *Fragmenta Herculanensia*, 5.
65. Theodor Gomperz, *Essays und Erinnerungen* (Stuttgart: Deutsche Verlags-Anstalt, 1905), 43–48, translation by Anita Mage; Gomperz quoted by Tiziano Dorandi, in Introduction to Theodor Gomperz, *Eine Auswhal herkulanischer kleiner Schriften (1864–1909)*, ed. Tiziano Dorandi (Leiden: E. J. Brill, 1993), xiv–xv. See also Kirk Summers, Review of Tiziano Dorandi, ed. *Theodor Gomperz: Eine Auswahl herkulanisher kleiner Schriften (1864–1909)*, *Bulletin of the American Society of Papryologists* 32, no. 3/4 (1995): 207–8; Scott, *Fragmenta Herculanensia*, 6, 11; David Sedley, "Epicurus, On Nature, Book XXVIII," *Cronache Ercolanesi* 3 (1973): 7.
66. Gomperz, *Essays und Erinnerungen* (Stuttgart: Deutsche Verlags-Antalt, 1905), 43–48, translation by Anita Mage.
67. W. Brent Seales and Christy Chapman, "Technology and the Quest to Unlock the Secrets of the Herculaneum Scrolls," in *Buried by Vesuvius: The Villa dei Papiri at Herculaneum*, ed. Kenneth Lapatin (Los Angeles: Getty Publications, 2019), 125.
68. Dorandi, Introduction to Gomperz, *Eine Auswhal herkulanischer kleiner Schriften*, translated by Anita Mage; Scott, *Fragmenta Herculanensia*, 62–64. It is notable that Gomperz's intensive study of the papyri fragments of Book 25 of *On Nature*, on which all later studies depended, is seldom mentioned in the literature, while his actual conclusions seem to be long forgotten. For a rare, brief acknowledgment see David Sedley, "Epicurus On Nature, Book 28," *Cronache Ercolanesi* 3 (1973): 7.
69. Gomperz, *Eine Auswhal herkulanischer kleiner Schriften (1864–1909)*, 78–89, translation by Anita Mage. Although Gomperz was to become a follower of John Stuart Mill, he had studied philosophy under the young Hegelian Franz Thomas Bratranek. He was a strong anti-slavery backer of the North at the time of the U.S. Civil War and promoted various workers' organizations. He prided himself on being a "critical" thinker, in the German tradition of *critique*. Gomperz, *Essays und Erinnerungen*, 43–48; Dorandi, Introduction to Gomperz, *Eine Auswahl herkulanischer kleiner Schriften*, xiii; Scott, *Fragmenta Herculanensia*, xiii.
70. Gomperz, *Eine Auswhal herkulanischer kleiner Schriften (1864–1909)*, 102–6.
71. Compatibilism was advanced in the seventeenth to nineteenth centuries in England by Thomas Hobbes, David Hume, and John Stuart Mill. Michael McKenna and D. Justin Coates, "Compatibilism," *Stanford Encyclopedia of Philosophy* (November 26, 2019), https://plato.stanford.edu/entries/compatibilism/; Paul Russell, "Hume on Free Will," *Stanford Encyclopedia of Philosophy* (May 27, 2020), https://plato.stanford.edu/entries/hume-freewil/.
72. Epicurus, *On Nature*, Book 25, in Long and Sedley, *The Hellenistic Philosophers*, vol. 1, 103.
73. Long and Sedley, *The Hellenistic Philosophers*, vol. 1, 104.

74. Diog. Laert. 10.134–35, trans. Hicks (Loeb Classical Library).
75. Gomperz, *Eine Auswhal herkulanischer kleiner Schriften (1864–1909)*, 78–89; Epicurus, *On Nature*, Book 25, in Englert, "Voluntary Action and Responsibility," 228; Long and Sedley, *The Hellenistic Philosophers*, vol. 1, 102; Simon Laursen, "The Later Parts of Epicurus, On Nature, 25th Book," *Cronache ercolanesi* 27 (1997): 51; Tim O'Keefe, "The Reductionist and Compatibilist Argument of Epicurus' 'On Nature,' Book 25," *Phronesis* 47, no. 2 (2002): 164; J. M. Rist, *Epicurus: An Introduction* (Cambridge: Cambridge University Press, 1972), 96; Suzanne Bobzien, *Determinism, Freedom, and Moral Philosophy* (Oxford: Oxford University Press, 2021), 176.
76. Epicurus, *On Nature*, Book 25, in Long and Sedley, *The Hellenistic Philosophers*, vol. 1, 103.
77. Diog. Laert. 10.133–34, trans. Long and Sedley, *The Hellenistic Philosophers*, vol. 1, 102.
78. Long and Sedley, *The Hellenistic Philosophers*, 106.
79. Simon Laursen, "The Early Parts of Epicurus *On Nature*, 25th Book," *Cronache ercolanesi* 25 (1995): 39–41.
80. Lucr. 2.16–93.
81. David Sedley, "Epicurus' Refutation of Determinism," *Syzetesis*, studi sull' epicureismo Greco e romano offerti a M. Gigante (Naples: G. Macchiaroli, 1983): 11–51; David Sedley, "Epicurean Anti-Reductionism," in *Matter and Metaphysics: Fourth Symposium Hellenisticum*, ed. Jonathan Barnes and Mario Mignucci (Naples: Bibliopolis, 1988), 295–327; Tim O'Keefe, "The Reductionist and Compatibilist Argument of Epicurus' 'On Nature,' Book 25," *Phronesis* 47, no. 2 (2002): 153–86; Tim O'Keefe, "Action and Responsibility," in *The Cambridge Companion to Epicureanism*, ed. James Warren (Cambridge: Cambridge University Press, 2009), 142–57; Tim O'Keefe, *Epicurus on Freedom* (Cambridge: Cambridge University Press, 2009).
82. Sedley, "Epicurus' Refutation of Determinism," 11–12.
83. PhHerc, *Sign.*, 36.10–20, trans. in Philodemus, *On Methods of Inference*, trans. and ed. Lacy and Lacy.
84. Sedley, "Epicurus' Refutation of Determinism," 18.
85. Epicurus, *On Nature*, Book 25, in Long and Sedley, *The Hellenistic Philosophers*, vol. 1, 102–4; Sedley, "Epicurus's Refutation of Determinism," 21.
86. Sedley, "Epicurus's Refutation of Determinism," 23–24; Englert, "Voluntary Action and Responsibility," 228.
87. Lucr. 4.472, translation according to Sedley, "Epicurus's Refutation of Determinism," 26.
88. Sedley, "Epicurus's Refutation of Determinism," 30–33.
89. Ibid., 34–35.
90. Ibid., 14.

91. Ibid., 39.
92. Ibid., 39, 42–44.
93. Lucr. 2.1021–25, translated according to Englert (Hackett). See also Lucr. 2.688–99 and 1.192–98.
94. Compare Bertrand Russell, *Human Knowledge: Its Scope and Its Limits* (London: George Allen and Unwin, 1948), 41.
95. Sedley, "Epicurus's Refutation of Determinism," 48; Bobzien, *Determinism, Freedom, and Moral Responsibility*, 173–74.
96. Cic., *Fat.*, 23; Sedley, "Epicurus' Refutation of Determinism," 49–50.
97. Sedley, "Epicurean Anti-Reductionism," 299, 327; C. D. Broad, *Mind and Its Place in Nature* (London: Kegan Paul, Trench, Trubner, and Co., 1925), 58, 69. Ironically, while Sedley cites Broad in support of an "emergent vitalism," to which the latter referred to a number of times in his book, Broad's *The Mind and Its Place in Nature* is best known for advancing what he was the first to refer to as "emergent materialism," and which was very much in line with Epicurus's analysis. Broad's work inspired the emergentist materialism of Roy Wood Sellars, *The Philosophy of Physical Realism* (New York: Macmillan, 1932), and later the work of Mario Bunge, *Scientific Materialism* (Dordrecht, Holland: D. Reidal Publishing Company, 1981) and that of John Searle, *Minds, Brains, and Science* (Cambridge, MA: Harvard University Press, 1984), in which Searle introduced his notion of "biological naturalism." Sedley's own analysis of Epicurus is closest to the approach of a thinker like Searle, which rose out of the explorations of emergentist materialism. See also Richard C. Vitzthum, *Materialism: An Affirmative History and Definition* (Amherst, MA: Prometheus Books, 1995); Attila Németh, *Epicurus on the Self* (London; Routledge, 2017), 82–83. Sedley's reference to an emergent vitalism should not be confused with the neo-vitalistic tendencies in the interpretation of Lucretius as in Deleuze's *The Logic of Sense*. As Thomas Nail rightly notes, "This kind of neo-vitalist reading [of the swerve] is textually insupportable." Gilles Deleuze, *The Logic of Sense* (New York: Columbia University Press, 1990), 266–79; Thomas Nail, *Lucretius II: An Ethics of Motion* (Edinburgh: Edinburgh University Press, 2020), 213.
98. On the early twentieth-century discussions of the concept of emergence see John Bellamy Foster, *The Return of Nature* (New York: Monthly Review Press, 2020), 317–22, 401–12. For a contemporary analysis of emergentist materialism within a dialectical frame see Roy Bhaskar, *Dialectic: The Pulse of Freedom* (London: Verso, 1993), 49–56, 397.
99. Joseph Needham, *Time: The Refreshing River* (London: George Allen and Unwin, 1943), 259.
100. O'Keefe, "The Reductionist and Compatibilist Argument of Epicurus' 'On Nature,' Book 25," 153, 155–56; O'Keefe, *Epicurus on Freedom*, 2, 68–69. Despite its presence in the title to his "Reductionist and Compatibilist" article O'Keefe does not address the issue of "compatibilism" except to say in

a footnote at the beginning of his article that "I believe that Epicurus . . . is not a compatibilist." Seemingly contradicting himself, he states later in his article that Epicurus's response to Democritus "is the sort of reply offered by a compatibilist." O'Keefe, "*The Reductionist and Compatibilist Argument of Epicurus' 'On Nature,' Book 25*," 154, 169. In *Epicurus on Freedom* O'Keefe opens the book with references to Epicurus's "incompatibilism," but without much in further clarification.

101. O'Keefe, "The Reductionist and Compatibilist Argument of Epicurus' 'On Nature,' Book 25," 155, 159–60.
102. O'Keefe introduces the term "eliminativist" to take up much what is normally conceived of as crude reductionism. At the same time, he argues that reductionism is consistent with a certain degree of emergentism. The central issue raised by reductionism, that is, whether all of reality at every level can be reduced to *mere* physical terms (matter, atomic motion), thereby excluding emergent powers resulting from qualitative transformations in organization, is thus largely obscured in his treatment of Epicurus as a "reductionist." His approach seems to presuppose that materialism/physicalism and reductionism are the same thing, excluding the possibility of a non-reductionist emergentist materialism of the sort common in science. See O'Keefe, "The Reductionist and Compatibilist Argument of Epicurus' 'On Nature,' Book 25," 155–60, 170. For a view in line with O'Keefe's characterization of Epicurus as a reductionist, see Englert, "Voluntary Action and Responsibility," 224.
103. O'Keefe, "Action and Responsibility," 153.
104. Needham, *Time: The Refreshing River*, 14–15.
105. This can be seen as related to the matter-form distinction in Aristotle, and his insistence on the specificity of form, on which Hegel's criticism of mechanism can be said to rest. Form raises the issue of qualitatively different organization, just as in Aristotle's distinction in his four causes, the *formal cause* in the construction of a house (that is, the organizational shape) differs from the *material cause* (the material means) that underlies it.
106. O'Keefe, "Action and Responsibility," 142.
107. O'Keefe, *Epicurus on Freedom*, 10–25.
108. O'Keefe, "The Reductionist and Compatibilist Argument of Epicurus' 'On Nature,' Book 25," 176.
109. O'Keefe, *Epicurus on Freedom*, 94.
110. Needham, *Time: The Refreshing River*, 182–83.
111. O'Keefe, "The Reductionist and Compatibilist Argument of Epicurus' 'On Nature,' Book 25," 184.
112. Long and Sedley, *The Hellenistic Philosophers*, vol. 1, 102.
113. Lucr. 1.910-914, translated according to Englert (Hackett). In Lucretius *ligna* and *ignus* in English translations since at least H. A. J. Munro have often rendered *ligna* (wood) as "firs" to create the near homonyms.
114. Cyril Bailey, *The Greek Atomists and Epicurus*, 319–23, 433–37; Walter

Englert, "Voluntary Action and Responsibility," in Mitis, ed., *Oxford Handbook of Epicurus and Epicureanism*, 223; Elizabeth Asmis, "Free Action and the Swerve: Review of Walter G. Englert, *Epicurus on the Swerve and Voluntary Action*," *Oxford Studies in Ancient Philosophy* 8 (1990): 276–77.

115. Lucr. 2.61–83.
116. David Furley, *Two Studies in the Greek Atomists* (Princeton: Princeton University Press, 1993), 232–33; Asmis, "Free Action and the Swerve," 276.
117. Sedley, "Epicurus's Refutation of Determinism," 48–49; Julia Annas, *Hellenistic Philosophy of Mind* (Cambridge: Cambridge University Press, 1992), 184–85; Bobzien, *Determinism, Freedom, and Moral Responsibility*, 168, 174.
118. Diog. Laert. 10.133, trans. Epicurus, *The Epicurus Reader*, trans. and ed. Brad Inwood and L. P. Gerson (Indianapolis: Hackett Publishing, 1994), 31.
119. O'Keefe, "Action and Responsibility," 143.
120. Epicurus, in Long and Sedley, ed., *The Hellenistic Philosophers*, 103.
121. Suzanne Bobzien, *Determinism, Freedom, and Moral Philosophy*, 156; Gomperz, *Eine Auswhal herkulanischer kleiner Schriften (1864–1909)*, 78–89, trans. Anita Mage.
122. Here it should be noted that though O'Keefe places supreme importance on Epicurus's rejection of the principle of bivalence with respect to future contingents, this is also seen as crucial in Sedley's interpretation. Sedley, "Epicurus' Refutation of Determinism," 46.
123. Németh, *Epicurus on the Self*, 82.
124. Ibid., 100.
125. Needham, *Time: The Refreshing River*, 15, 183.
126. Ibid., 259. The recent debate has centered on what Németh, *Epicurus on the Self*, 82, has termed the "key sentence" in the fragments of Book 25, which he translates (following Laursen) as: "Thus, whenever something is produced (ἀπογεννηθῇ [τ]ι) [i.e. an occurrent mental state] that takes on some otherness from the atoms according to some differentiating mode (τρόπον διαληπτικόν), not in the way as from another distance, it gets the cause out of itself; then it immediately gives it on to the first natures and somehow makes the whole of it one." Sedley, *Epicurus' Refutation*, 39, for "differentiating mode (τρόπον διαληπτικόν)" prefers a "'transcendent (literally 'separative') kind, not just a difference of scale." While O'Keefe in "The Reductionist and Compatabilist," 172, renders the phrase "in a way that allows for a distinction (κατά τ[ινα]ν τρόπον διαληπτικόν), not the one as from another distance." See also Laursen, "The Later Parts of Epicurus, *On Nature*, Book 25," 49–52.

The difference between "transcendent" and mere "distinction" neatly captures the "emergentist" as opposed to "reductionist" understanding, while Németh's "differentiating mode" takes a neutral position. It is at the least amusing to note that Google Translate's machine translation, Modern Greek to English, gives "dialectical" for διαληπτικον.

127. A. A. Long, "Evolution vs. Intelligent Design in Classical Antiquity," https://townsendcenter.berkeley.edu/sites/default/files/publications/nov-dec_06_nl.pdf (November 2006), 3–5; A. A. Long, *From Epicurus to Epictetus: Studies in Hellenistic and Roman Philosophy* (Oxford: Oxford University Press, 2006), 155–77.
128. Diog. Laert. 10.93, trans. Marx and Engels, *Collected Works*, vol. 1, 421.
129. A. A. Long, *Hellenistic Philosophy* (Berkeley: University of California Press, 1986), 49–52.
130. Diog. Laert. 10.124.26, translated according to Hicks (Loeb Classical Library).
131. Lucr. 3.869.
132. Sex. Emp., *Math*, 10.219–27; Long and Sedley, ed., *The Hellenistic Philosophers*, 34–35.
133. Lucr. 1.459–63, trans. Englert (Hackett).
134. Diog. Laert. 10.126–28, trans. Hicks (Loeb Classical Library).
135. Németh, *Epicurus on the Self*, 1–10.
136. Diog. Laert. 10.129–33.
137. Epicurus, *Sent. Vat.*, 18, trans. Inwood and Gerson (Hackett).
138. Epicurus, *Sent. Vat.*, 25, 67, 68; trans. Inwood and Gerson (Hackett).
139. Diog. Laert, 10.144, trans. Inwood and Gerson (Hackett); Elizabeth Asmis, "Epicurean Economics," in *Philodemus and the New Testament World* (Boston: Brill, 2004), 143–49.
140. Richard Seaford, "Ancient Greece and Global Warming," Classical Association Presidential Address, 2009 (London: The Classical Association, 2009); Richard Seaford, *Money and Early Greek Mind: Homer, Philosophy, Tragedy* (Cambridge: Cambridge University Press, 2004).
141. Diog. Laert., 10.141.
142. Epicurus, *Sent. Vat.*, 23, trans. Inwood and Gerson (*The Epicurus Reader*, Hackett).
143. Ibid., 52.
144. Farrington, *The Faith of Epicurus*, 103.
145. Diog. Laert. 10.149–50, trans. Inwood and Gerson (Hackett).
146. Diog. Laert. 10.150–52, trans. Hicks (Loeb Classical Library).
147. Diog. Laert. 10.153, trans. Hicks (Loeb Classical Library).
148. Jan Maximilian Robitzsch, *Epicurean Justice: Nature, Agreement, and Virtue* (Cambridge: Cambridge University Press, 2024), 161.
149. John D. Barrow and Frank J. Tippler, *The Anthropic Cosmological Principle* (Oxford: Oxford University Press, 1986), 34.
150. Lucr. 5.836–76.
151. Lucr. 5.821–1160.
152. Lucr. 5.1130–35, translation according to Englert (Hackett).
153. Diog. Laert. 10.88–89.

154. Several of the paragraphs that follow draw on John Bellamy Foster, Brett Clark, and Richard York, *Critique of Intelligent Design* (New York: Monthly Review Press, 2008), 49–64.
155. David Sedley, *Creationism and Its Critics in Antiquity* (Berkeley: University of California Press, 2007), 78.
156. Xen., *Mem.*, 1.4.1–11, trans. according to Xenophon, *Conversations of Socrates*, trans. Hugh Tredennick and Robin H. Waterfield (London: Penguin, 1990), 90–91.
157. Xen., *Mem*, 1.4.1–11, 4.3, trans. Tredennick and Waterfield (Penguin).
158. Pl., *Ti*, 29–31, 39–40, 68–69, Pl., *Leg.*, 888–92; Benjamin Farrington, *Science and Politics in the Ancient World* (London: George Allen and Unwin, 1939), 131–32; Farrington, *The Faith of Epicurus*, 73.
159. Gomperz, *Eine Auswhal herkulanischer kleiner Schriften*, xiii (Dorandi introduction), 51.
160. Sedley, *Creationism and Its Critics in Antiquity*, 155–66.; Long and Sedley, *The Hellenistic Philosophers*, vol. 1, 37–44.
161. A. J. Festugière, *Epicurus and His Gods* (Cambridge, MA: Harvard University Press, 1956), 73–89; Farrington, *The Faith of Epicurus*, 76–85, 93–104.
162. Pl. Leg., 12.960–69.
163. Diog. Laert. 10.142–43, trans. Inwood and Gerson (Hackett).
164. Laks, "Epicurus," 74–75.
165. Diog. Laert. 10.93, trans. Marx and Engels, *Collected Works*, vol. 1, 69.
166. Lucr. 1.63–70, trans. Englert (Hackett).
167. Pl., *Rep*, 3.415; Diog. Laert., 10.08, translation according to Epicurus, *The Extant Epicurus,* trans. Cyril Bailey (New York: Limited Editions Club, 1947), 9; Benjamin Farrington, *Science and Politics in the Ancient World* (London: George Allen and Unwin, 1939), 98.
168. Diog. Laert., 10. 150–52; Wood and Wood, *Class Ideology and Ancient Political Theory*, 139–42.
169. Benjamin Farrington, "Karl Marx—Scholar and Revolutionary," *Modern Quarterly* 7, no. 2 (Spring 1952): 92.
170. Marcello Gigante, *Philodemus in Italy: The Books from Herculaneum*, trans. Dirk Obbink (Ann Arbor: University of Michigan Press, 1995), 10, 67, 69, 72. The fact that Philodemus's work was focused in part on the Hellenistic kings seems to receive added credence by the statues and wall portraits of these kings, notably Demetrius Poliorcetes (Besieger of Cities), found in Herculaneum, 47, 55. Piso, the original owner of the villa of the papyri and the patron of Philodemus, was the Roman governor of Macedonia in 57–55 BCE. The prominence given to Demetrius Poliorcetes, standing for the Antigonid dynasty, in the Herculaneum statues and portraits may have been related to that. Jeffery Fish, "Lucius Calpurnius Piso Caesonius: A Philosophical Statesman of the Late Roman Republic," in Lapatin, ed., *Buried by Vesuvius*, 6. However, the view of Demetrius the Besieger offered

in the finds in Herculaneum is hardly complimentary and may have reflected Epicurus's view and that of Philodemus. Next to the bust of Demetrius was found a sculpture of Pan, half-human, half-goat, copulating with a she-goat, the horns on Pan's head conspicuous. The bust of Demetrius also has small horns protruding from his brow. Although the horns on Demetrius Poliorcetes's statue may have originally signified something else, this was quite likely meant as a humorous pairing of statues next to each other, symbolizing Demetrius's well-known licentiousness. Francesco Sirano, "Looking to the Future, Starting from the Past," in Lapatin, ed., *Buried by Vesuvius*, 202–5.

171. Lucr. 5.999–1000, 5.1117–50.
172. Diog. Laert. 7.6–10; Hazel, *Who's Who in the Greek World*, 176.
173. Luc., *Alex*, 25–26, 43–48, translated in Lucian, *Selected Satires*, trans. Lionel Casson (New York: W. W. Norton, 1962); John Hazel, *Who's Who in the Greek World*, 13.
174. Farrington, *The Faith of Epicurus*, 133.

Chapter Three: Marx and Epicurus

1. Stephen Greenblatt, *The Swerve* (New York: W. W. Norton, 2011), 81–86; P. J. Parsons, "Waste Paper City," The Oxyrhynchus Papyri, Oxford University, https://oxyrhynchus.web.ox.ac.uk/waste-paper-city/; G. W. F. Hegel, *Lectures on the History of Philosophy*, vol. 3 (Lincoln: University of Nebraska Press, 1995), 109–10.
2. Greenblatt, *The Swerve*, 109.
3. Charles L. Stinger, *Humanism and the Church Fathers: Ambrogio Traversari (1386–1439) and Christian Antiquity in the Italian Renaissance* (Albany: State University of New York Press, 1977), 36; Ada Palmer, "Humanist Dissemination of Epicureanism," in *The Oxford Handbook of Epicurus and Epicureanism*, ed. Philip Mitsis (Oxford: Oxford University Press, 2020), 621–26. Vernacular translations of Diogenes were published in the mid-sixteenth century, about a century prior to vernacular translations of Lucretius. Diogenes Laertius's text, in which Epicurus appeared only in Book 10, was treated as less dangerous in the religious climate of the time than Lucretius, which was a purely Epicurean text.
4. Robert Hugh Kragon, *Atomism in England from Hariot to Newton* (Oxford: Oxford University Press, 1966); Howard Jones, *The Epicurean Tradition* (New York: Routledge, 1992), 166–85; Alfred Cobban, *In Search of the Humanity: The Role of the Enlightenment in Modern History* (New York: George Braziller, 1960), 75; John Bellamy Foster, *Marx's Ecology* (New York: Monthly Review Press, 2000), 39–51; Greenblatt, *The Swerve*, 261–62.
5. Foster, *Marx's Ecology*, 27–28; Greenblatt, *The Swerve*, 233–41.
6. Greenblatt, *The Swerve*, 253–56.
7. Francis Bacon, *Philosophical Works*, ed. John M. Robertson (Freeport, NY: Books for Libraries Press, 1905), 471–72. Bacon added: "Democritus and

Epicurus when they proclaimed their doctrine of atoms, were tolerated by some of the more subtle wits; but when they proceeded to assert that the fabric of the universe itself had come together through the fortuitous concourse of atoms, without a mind, they were met with universal ridicule."

8. Bacon, *Philosophical Works*, 754–55; Diog. Laert. 10.123–24, trans. Hicks (Loeb Classical Library). See also Reid Barbour, *English Epicures and Stoics: Ancient Legacies in Early Stuart Culture* (Amherst: University of Massachusetts Press, 1998), 79–91.
9. Lucr. 6.1–5. Benjamin Farrington, *Philosopher of Industrial Science* (New York: Collier Books, 1961), 30; Benjamin Farrington, *Francis Bacon: Pioneer of Planned Science* (New York: Frederick A. Praeger, 1963), 35; Benjamin Farrington, "The Christianity of Francis Bacon," *Baconiana: Journal of the Francis Bacon Society*, 48, no. 165 (October 1965): 15–33, https://archive.org/details/1965-baconiana-no.-165/mode/2up/.
10. Karl Marx and Frederick Engels, *Collected Works* (New York: International Publishers, 1975), vol. 4, 126.
11. Jones, *The Epicurean Tradition*, 42–43; Pierre Gassendi, *Epicurus: His Life and Doctrine*, in Thomas Stanley, *History of Philosophy*, vol. 3 (London: Humphrey Mosely, 1660).
12. It is claimed that Locke drew on Gassendi more than any other thinker. J. M. Robertson, *A Short History of Free Thought, Ancient and Modern* (London: Watts and Co., 1906), 114.
13. David Hume, *Enquiries Concerning Human Understanding and Concerning the Principles of Morals* (Oxford: Oxford University Press, 1975), 132–42.
14. Peter Gay, *The Enlightenment* (New York: Alfred A. Knopf, 1966), vol. 1, 102–3.
15. Denis Diderot, *Diderot: Interpreter of Nature; Selected Writings*, ed. Jonathan Kemp (New York: International Publishers, 1963), 343.
16. Paul-Henry Thiry, Baron d'Holbach, *The System of Nature* (New York: Garland Publishing, 1984), vol. 1, 138.
17. Gay, *The Enlightenment*, 105.
18. Denis Diderot, *Rameau's Nephew and D'Alemberts' Dream* (London: Penguin, 1966), 181.
19. Catherine Wilson, *Epicureanism and the Origins of Modernity* (Oxford: Oxford University Press, 2008), 162–65.
20. Immanuel Kant, *Cosmogony* (New York: Greenwood, 1968), 12–13; James W. Ellington, "Kant, Immanuel," *Dictionary of Scientific Biography*, vol. 7 (New York: Charles Scribner's Sons, 1973), 224–35.
21. Immanuel Kant, *Critique of Pure Reason* (Cambridge: Cambridge University Press, 1997), 702.
22. Immanuel Kant, *Logic* (New York: Dover, 1988), 34, 36.
23. Hermann Samuel Reimarus, *The Principal Truths of Natural Religion Defended and Illustrated, in Nine Dissertations: Wherein the Objections of Lucretius, Buffon, Maupertuis, Rousseau, Le Mettrie, and Other Ancient and*

Modern Followers of Epicurus Are Considered, and Their Doctrines Refuted (London: B. Law, 1766), 117–20, 152, 220. Paragraph adapted from John Bellamy Foster, Brett Clark, and Richard York, *Critique of Intelligent Design* (New York: Monthly Review Press, 2008), 87–88.

24. Georg Wilhelm Friedrich Hegel, *Lectures on the Philosophy of Religion* (Berkeley: University of California Press, 1988), 262–63.
25. Georg Wilhelm Friedrich Hegel, *Lectures on the History of Philosophy*, vol. 2 (Lincoln: University of Nebraska Press, 1995), 279, 281.
26. Hegel, *Lectures on the History of Philosophy*, vol. 1, 14.
27. Hegel, *Lectures on the History of Philosophy*, vol. 2, 300.
28. Hegel, *Lectures on the History of Philosophy*, vol. 2, 297–98, 300.
29. Tony Burns, "Materialism in Ancient Greek Philosophy and the Writings of the Young Marx," *Historical Materialism* 7 (Winter 2000): 24.
30. Michael Heinrich, *Karl Marx and the Birth of Modern Society* (New York: Monthly Review Press, 2019), 36, 77; Doug Enaa Greene and Harrison Fluss, "Marx and the Communist Enlightenment," *Left Voice*, August 2, 2020.
31. David McLellan, *Karl Marx: His Life and Thought* (New York: Harper and Row, 1973), 2, 7, 15–16; Heinrich, *Karl Marx and the Birth of Modern Society*, 36, 90–91; M. Kovalevsky, "Meetings with Marx," in *Reminiscences of Marx and Engels*, ed., Institute of Marxism-Leninism (Moscow: Foreign Languages Publishing House, n.d.), 298.
32. Marx and Engels, *Collected Works*, vol. 1, 639, Heinrich, *Karl Marx and the Birth of Modern Society*, 103. The Young-Hegelian critique of religion was launched with David Strauss's *Life of Jesus* in the same year that Marx's gymnasium paper on "The Union of Believers with Christ" was written.
33. Heinrich, *Karl Marx and the Birth of Modern Society*, 283.
34. Marx and Engels, *Collected Works*, vol. 1, 18–19.
35. Ludwig Feuerbach, *History of Modern Philosophy Bacon to Spinoza* (Stuttgart: Newcomb Livraria Press, 2023), 73–74.
36. James White, *Karl Marx and the Intellectual Origins of Dialectical Materialism* (London: Palgrave Macmillan, 1996), 122–23.
37. Marx and Engels, *Collected Works*, vol. 1, 73.
38. Marx and Engels, *Collected Works*, vol. 5, 141–42.
39. Marx and Engels, *Collected Works*, vol. 1, 102.
40. White, *Karl Marx and the Intellectual Origins of Dialectical Materialism*, 42.
41. Heinrich, *Karl Marx and the Birth of Modern Society*, 295; Marx and Engels, *Collected Works*, vol. 1, 504.
42. Marx and Engels, *Collected Works*, vol. 1, 416. Marx had already addressed the swerve in his first notebook, but it seems that it took on a much greater significance as he engaged with the whole material–sensual and anti-teleological character of Lucretius's poem. He was to engage with Lucretius's use of the swerve to address human freedom.

43. Marx and Engels, *Collected Works*, vol. 5, 27.
44. Diog. Laert. 10.31–34; Marx and Engels, *Collected Works*, vol. 1, 405–6.
45. Clem. Al., *Strom.*, 2.3, translation according to Marx and Engels, *Collected Works*, vol. 1, 487.
46. Diog. Laert. 10.34–35; translation according to Marx and Engels, *Collected Works*, vol. 1, 406.
47. Arist. *De An.* 3.3 (also 2.2); translation according to Aristotle, *De Anima*, trans. Hugh Lawson-Tancred (London: Penguin, 1986), 197–98 (also 159–60); Marx and Engels, *Collected Works*, vol. 5, 142. See also Marx, *Collected Works*, vol. 1, 505.
48. Aristotle, *Metaph.*, A4.985.18–21; Marx and Engels, *Collected Works*, vol. 1., 435; Frederick Copleston, *A History of Philosophy*, vol. 1, *Greece and Rome*, part 1 (New York: Doubleday, 1962), 88.
49. Marx and Engels, *Collected Works*, vol. 1, 413, 425.
50. Marx and Engels, *Collected Works*, vol. 1, 447–48, 458.
51. Marx and Engels, *Collected Works*, vol. 1, 428–29.
52. Lucr. 3.865–69; Diog. Laert. 10.139; Marx and Engels, *Collected Works*, vol. 1, 30, 62, 407, 478; Karl Marx, *The Poverty of Philosophy* (New York: International Publishers, 1963), 110, 228.
53. Diog. Laert. 10.134, trans. in Marx and Engels, *Collected Works*, vol. 1, 408.
54. Marx and Engels, *Collected Works*, vol. 1, 409–10.
55. Diog. Laert. 10.154, translation according to Brad Inwood and L. P. Gerson, *The Epicurus Reader*, trans. and ed., Inwood and Gerson (Homewood, IL: Hackett Publishing, 1994), 36. See also George Thomson, *The First Philosophers: Studies in Ancient Greek Philosophy* (London: Lawrence and Wishart, 1972), 312.
56. Marx and Engels, *Collected Works*, vol. 8, 327–28.
57. See Marx and Engels, *Collected Works*, vol. 5, 141–42.
58. Marx and Engels, *Collected Works*, vol. 1, 413–16; Thomas Nail, *Marx in Motion* (Oxford: Oxford University Press, 2020), 21–27.
59. Marx and Engels, *Collected Works*, vol. 1, 423–24, 431, 469.
60. Marx and Engels, *Collected Works*, vol. 1, 59, 412, 415–16.
61. Marx and Engels, *Collected Works*, vol. 1, 64.
62. Marx and Engels, *Collected Works*, vol. 1, 416.
63. Lucr. 2.251–62, translation according to Marx and Engels, *Collected Works*, vol. 1, 49, 416 ("breaks" in the translation on page 49 substituted for "snaps" on page 416).
64. Georg Wilhelm Friedrich Hegel, *Philosophy of Nature* (Oxford: Oxford University Press, 2004), 44, 60–62; Georg Wilhelm Friedrich Hegel, *Phenomenology of Spirit*, trans. A. V. Miller (Oxford: Oxford University Press, 1957), 104, 113.
65. Marx and Engels, *Collected Works*, vol. 1, 416.
66. Diog. Laert. 10.93; Marx and Engels, *Collected Works*, vol. 1, 40, 69, 421–23, 507.

67. Marx and Engels, *Collected Works*, vol. 1, 419–21.
68. Karl Marx, *Early Writings* (London: Penguin, 1974), 244–45. See also Arend Th. van Leeuwen, *The Critique of Heaven* (New York: Charles Scribner's Sons, 1972); Arend Th. van Leeuwen, *The Critique of Earth* (New York: Charles Scribner's Sons, 1974).
69. Marx and Engels, *Collected Works*, vol. 1, 423–24.
70. Alexi Mikailovich Voden, "Talks with Engels," in Institute of Marxism-Leninism, ed. *Reminiscences of Marx and Engels* (Moscow: Foreign Languages Publishing House, n.d.), 332.
71. Benedict Einarson and Phillip H. De Lacy, "Introduction" to "That Epicurus Actually Makes a Pleasant Life Impossible," in Plutarch, *Moralia*, vol. 14, trans. Einarson and De Lacy (Cambridge, Massachusetts: Harvard University Press, 1967), 3 (Loeb Classical Library).
72. David Sedley, "Epicurean Theories of Knowledge from Hermarchus to Lucretius and Philodemus," *Lexicon Philosophical*, Special Issue (2018): 108–10.
73. Plut., *Moralia*, 1096.14, translated according to Einarson and De Lacy (Loeb Classical Library).
74. Pl., *Resp.*, 9.585–86; Einarson and De Lacy, Introduction to *Plutarch*, "Reply to Colotes," in *Plutarch*, *Moralia*, vol. 14, 172.
75. Plut., *Mor.*, 1108.
76. Marx and Engels, *Collected Works*, vol. 1, 457. On what Marx meant by Socrates's historical position see Ellen Meiksins Wood and Neal Wood, *Class Ideology and Ancient Political Theory* (Oxford: Basil Blackwell, 1978), 81–115.
77. Marx and Engels, *Collected Works*, vol. 1, 457.
78. Plut., *Moralia*, 1109.4; Hegel, *Phenomenology of Spirit*, 60–65, 123–26.
79. Hegel, *Lectures on the History of Philosophy*, vol. 2, 328–29.
80. Hegel, *Lectures on the History of Philosophy*, vol. 2, 329.
81. Marx and Engels, *Collected Works*, vol. 1, 458.
82. Marx and Engels, *Collected Works*, vol. 1, 458.
83. Marx and Engels, *Collected Works*, vol. 1, 468, 472.
84. Marx and Engels, *Collected Works*, vol. 1, 61, 472–73.
85. Marx and Engels, *Collected Works*, vol. 1, 473.
86. Marx and Engels, *Collected Works*, vol. 1, 475.
87. Marx and Engels, *Collected Works*, vol. 1, 505, 508–9.
88. Marx and Engels, *Collected Works*, vol. 1, 510–14.
89. Hegel, *Philosophy of Nature*, 45–46, 61; Immanuel Kant, *Prolegomena* and *Metaphysical Foundations of Natural Science* (London: George Bell and Sons, 1883), 172, 183–85; Marx and Engels, *Collected Works*, vol. 1, 46.
90. Editors' Notes, in Marx and Engels, *Collected Works*, vol. 1, 734–35; Heinrich, *Karl Marx and the Birth of Modern Society*, 300–302; Norman D. Livergood, *Activity in Marx's Philosophy* (The Hague: Martinus Nijhoff, 1967).
91. Elizabeth Asmis, "A Tribute to a Hero: Marx's Interpretation of Epicurus

in His Dissertation," in *Approaches to Lucretius*, ed. Donncha O'Rourke (Cambridge: Cambridge University Press, 2020), 241–58.

92. Marx and Engels, *Collected Works*, vol. 1, 30.
93. Aesch., *PV*, 964–70; translation according to Marx and Engels, *Collected Works*, vol. 1, 31. See also White, *Karl Marx and the Origins of Dialectical Materialism*, 122–23.
94. Louis Althusser, *For Marx* (New York: Vintage, 1969), 35.
95. Engels quoted in Voden, "Talks with Engels," 332–33.
96. Marx and Engels, *Collected Works*, vol. 40, 269.
97. Marx and Engels, *Collected Works*, vol. 1, 29–30.
98. Marx and Engels, *Collected Works*, vol. 1, 34–36.
99. Cyril Bailey, "Karl Marx on Greek Atomism," *Classical Quarterly* 22, no. 3/4 (July–October 1928): 205–6.
100. Diog. Laert. 10.56–10.57; Euseb., *Praep. Evang.*, 23.773b; Long and Sedley, *The Hellenistic Philosophers,* vol. 1, 39–44; David Konstan, "Atomism," in *The Oxford Handbook of Epicurus and Epicureanism*, ed. Philip Mitsis (Oxford: Oxford University Press, 2020), 63–70.
101. Marx and Engels, *Collected Works*, vol. 1, 50, 473.
102. Lucr. 2.254; translation according to Marx and Engels, *Collected Works*, vol. 1, 49, 64, 416.
103. Marx and Engels, *Collected Works*, vol. 1, 38–39, 45.
104. Marx and Engels, *Collected Works*, vol. 1, 58–62; van Leeuwen, *Critique of Heaven*, 204.
105. Marx and Engels, *Collected Works*, vol. 1, 473.
106. Pseudo-Plut, *Placita Phil*, 1.25, translation according to Marx and Engels, *Collected Works*, vol. 1, 81; Diog. Laert. 10.133–34, trans. Hicks (Loeb Classical Library); Marx and Engels, *Collected Works*, vol. 1, 81–82.
107. Marx and Engels, *Collected Works*, vol. 1, 50.
108. Marx and Engels, *Collected Works*, vol. 1, 473.
109. Marx and Engels, *Collected Works*, vol. 1, 52.
110. Marx and Engels, *Collected Works*, vol. 1, 46, 52, 61–62.
111. Marx and Engels, *Collected Works*, vol. 1, 39, 62, 79, 89.
112. Marx and Engels, *Collected Works*, vol. 1, 50–53.
113. Cic. *Nat. D.*, 1.20; Marx and Engels, *Collected Works*, vol. 1, 43, 420.
114. Seneca, *Ep.*, 12, translation according to Marx and Engels, *Collected Works*, vol. 1, 56, 82.
115. Seneca, *Ep.*, 8, trans. Marx and Engels, *Collected Works*, vol. 1, 41, 80.
116. Marx and Engels, *Collected Works*, vol. 40, 269.
117. Long and Sedley, *The Hellenistic Philosophers*, vol. 1, 102–03.
118. Diog. Laert. 10.38–39; Lucr. 1.199–249, 78–802; Marx and Engels, *Collected Works*, vol. 1, 63–64.
119. Marx and Engels, *Collected Works*, vol. 1, 64–65; Diog. Laert. 10.51–52; Epicurus, *The Extant Remains*, trans. Cyril Bailey (Oxford: Oxford University Press, 1926), 29, 198–99.

120. Marx and Engels, *Collected Works*, vol. 1, 448, 458.
121. Marx and Engels, *Collected Works*, vol. 1, 65.
122. Diog. Laert. 10.44–46; Lucr. 4.26–323; Marx and Engels, *Collected Works*, vol. 1, 65; Thomas Nail, *Lucretius II: An Ethics of Motion* (Edinburgh: Edinburgh University Press, 2020), 147–66; Amanda Jo Goldstein, *Sweet Science: Romantic Materialism and the New Logic of Life* (Chicago: University of Chicago Press, 2017), 212–14. As Nail points out, once seen as opposed to modern physics, the broad Epicurean conception of the *eidola/simulacra* is no longer seen as incompatible with the latest developments, e.g., the Epicurean theory of *simulacra* is "not inconsistent" with the role of photons in contemporary optics, leading to its revival in contemporary philosophy. Nail, *Lucretius II: An Ethics of Motion*, 153–54.
123. Marx and Engels, *Collected Works*, vol. 1, 431.
124. Marx and Engels, *Collected Works*, vol. 1, 66.
125. Marx and Engels, *Collected Works*, vol. 1, 51.
126. Diog. Laert. 10.63–7.
127. Plut., *Mor.*, 14.1101–1103; Marx and Engels, *Collected Works*, vol. 1, 30, 102, 446.
128. Diog. Laert. 10.143, trans. Inwood and Gerson, *The Epicurus Reader*, 33.
129. Marx and Engels, *Collected Works*, vol. 1, 85.
130. Marx and Engels, *Collected Works*, vol. 1, 73.
131. Here Marx is referring to the "energizing principle" that characterized Epicurus's materialism as opposed to that of Democritus. See Franz Mehring, *Karl Marx: The Story of His Life* (Ann Arbor: University of Michigan Press, 1979), 31; Ernst Bloch, *On Karl Marx* (New York: Herder and Herder, 1971), 156.
132. Marx and Engels, *Collected Works*, vol. 1, 73; Aryeh Kosman, *The Activity of Being* (Cambridge, MA: Harvard University Press, 2013), vii–xiii; Marx and Engels, *Collected Works*, vol. 5, 139. David Bradshaw argues that while Aristotle's "*energeia*" should normally be translated as "activity" it is in the sense of the "exercise of a capacity." David Bradshaw, *Aristotle East and West: Metaphysics and the Division of Christendom* (Cambridge: Cambridge University Press, 2004), 1–4.
133. Lucr. 2.1115–1174, translation according to Rouse and Smith in Lucretius, *On the Nature of Things*, trans. W. H. D. Rouse and Martin F. Smith (Cambridge, MA: Harvard University Press, 1982) (Loeb Classical Library); Lucr. 5.786–809; 5.837–54.
134. Lucr. 1.208–24, Lucr. 5.1361–79.
135. Lucr. 5.855–77.
136. Marx and Engels, *Collected Works*, vol. 1, 498.
137. Vanessa Christina Williams, *Marx's Ethical Vision* (Oxford: Oxford University Press, 2024), 104.
138. Marx and Engels *Collected Works*, vol. 1, 29.

139. Heinrich, *Karl Marx and the Birth of Modern Society*, 297. Tony Burns mistakes the significance of Marx's translation of Aristotle in the context of his work on his dissertation by mistakenly pushing the date back to 1842, after the dissertation. Tony Burns, "Materialism in Ancient Greek Philosophy and in the Writings of the Young Marx," *Historical Materialism* 7 (Winter 2000): 26.
140. Arist., *De Anima*, 403a, translation according to Benjamin Farrington, *The Faith of Epicurus* (London: Weidenfeld and Nicolson, 1967), 100.
141. Farrington, *The Faith of Epicurus*, 97–99; André Laks, "Epicurus," in Brunschwig and Lloyd, eds., *Greek Thought*, 586–87; Phillip de Lacy, Review of (1) Filodemo, Agli Amici du Scuola (Pherc 1005), by Anna Angeli, (2) Demetrio Lacone, Aporie Testuali, ed. *Esegtiche in Epicuro* (Pherc 1012) by Enzo Puglia, (3) Demetrio Lacone, La Poesia (Pherc 188 e 1014) by Constatina Romeo Carnesico, and (4) Il Secondo Libro del Filista (Pherc 1027) by Mario Capasso, *American Journal of Philology* (Winter 1990): 575. Epicurus is sometimes characterized as "post-Aristotelian." See Bernard Frischer, *The Sculpted Word: Epicureanism and Philosophic Recruitment in Ancient Greece* (Berkeley: University of California Press, 1982), 34. Although this is obviously true in chronological terms, and while the Peripatetic School obviously exerted an influence on Epicurus, his philosophy is too independent of Aristotle to be usefully characterized in that way.
142. Bloch, *On Karl Marx*, 154.
143. Heinrich, *Karl Marx and the Birth of Modern Society*, 317–21.
144. Marx and Engels, *Collected Works*, vol. 2, 360–66.
145. Jason M. Wirth, "Review: The Return of the Repressed: Schelling, Kierkegaard, and Nachträglichkeit in the Legacy of German Idealism," *Research in Phenomenology* 41, no. 1 (2011): 134–47; Marx and Engels, *Collected Works*, vol. 2, 607.
146. Leeuwen, *Critique of Heaven*, 84; Douglas Moggach, "Bruno Bauer," Stanford Encyclopedia of Philosophy, February 7, 2022, https://plato.stanford.edu/entries/bauer/.
147. Heinrich, *Karl Marx and the Birth of Modern Society*, 318–19.
148. Marx and Engels, *Collected Works*, vol. 1, 379.
149. "Karl Friedrich Bachmann," https://de.wikipedia.org/wiki/Karl_Friedrich_Bachmann; Sven-Eric Liedman, *A World to Win: The Life and Works of Karl Marx* (London: Verso, 2018), 68.
150. Marx W. Wartofsky, *Feuerbach* (Cambridge: Cambridge University Press, 1977), 146; Charles T. Wolfe and Cá Foscari, "Medical Materialism, Early Modern," in *Encyclopedia of Early Modern Philosophy and the Sciences*, ed. D. Jalobenau and Charles T. Wolfe (Cham, Switzerland: Springer Cham, 2022), 1–6, https://link.springer.com/referenceworkentry/ 10.1007/978-3-319-20791-9_299-2/. Marx saw Cabanis as representing the more mechanist tradition coming out of Descartes. Marx and Engels, *Collected Works*, vol. 5, 125–26.

151. Wartofsky, *Feuerbach*, 146. It has been argued that Feuerbach's defense of Hegel was motivated by a final attempt to obtain a university position, from which he had long been blocked for political-intellectual reasons. Once he decided this was ineffectual, he changed course, leading to his 1839 "Towards a Critique of Hegel's Philosophy." See Wartofsky, *Feuerbach,* 142, 145–46; Ludwig Feuerbach, *The Fiery Brook: Selected Writings*, ed. and trans. Zawar Hanfi (Garden City, NY: Anchor Books, 1972), 53–96.
152. Wartofsky, *Feuerbach*, 142–53; Warren Breckman, *Marx, the Young Hegelians and the Origins of Radical Social Theory* (Cambridge: Cambridge University Press, 1999), 126.
153. Wartofsky, *Feuerbach*, 143, 160. Wartofsky included in this statement Friedrich Dorguth, who along with Bachmann was seen as attacking Hegel from the left, and who elicited a response from Feuerbach in defense of Hegel.
154. Ibid., 143.
155. Ibid., 143–47; Dan Mihalache, "Feuerbach, Ludwig," United Architects.com, https://danassays.wordpress.com/encyclopedia-of-the-essay/feuerbach-ludwig/.
156. Wartofsky, *Feuerbach*, 152.
157. Feuerbach quoted in Breckman, *Marx, the Young Hegelians and the Origins of Radical Social Theory*, 126.
158. Frederick C. Beiser, *The Genesis of Neo-Kantianism, 1796–1880* (Oxford: Oxford University Press, 2014), 23–88.
159. Evgeny Pavlov, "The Dunghill of Servility (J. F. Fries on Hegel)," Perverse Egalitarianism, October 26, 2009, https://pervegalit.wordpress.com/2009/10/26/the-dunghill-of-servility-j-f-fries-on-hegel/; Terry Pinkard, *German Philosophy 1760–1860: The Legacy of Idealism* (Cambridge: Cambridge University Press, 2002), 199–200; Beiser, *The Genesis of Neo-Kantianism*, 55–56.
160. Terry Pinkard, *German Philosophy 1760–1860*, 199–200, 204, 208; Beiser, *The Genesis of Neo-Kantianism*, 43. All bracketed words/phrases in the original.
161. Georg Wilhelm Friedrich Hegel, *Philosophy of Right* (Oxford: Oxford University Press, 1952), 5–6, 28.
162. Hegel, *Lectures on the History of Philosophy*, vol. 3, 430, 510.
163. Georg Wilhelm Friedrich Hegel, *Science of Logic* (London: George Allen and Unwin, 1969), 52. See also Beiser, *The Genesis of Neo-Kantianism*, 19–21.
164. Charles Dudley Warner, ed., *Biographical Dictionary and Synopsis of Books Ancient and Modern* (Akron, OH: Werner Company, 1896), 353; "Heinrich Luden," Wikipedia, https://en.wikipedia.org/wiki/Heinrich_Luden.
165. Hegel, *Lectures on the Philosophy of Religion*, 262–63.
166. Schafer, Introduction in Karl Marx, *The First Writings*, ed. Paul M. Schafer (Brooklyn, NY: IG Publishing, 2006), 45.
167. Liedman, *A World to Win*, 72–73; Marx and Engels, *Collected Works*, vol. 1,

84. Bauer urged Marx to drop the strong atheistic foreword in his dissertation, lest he provide a weapon to those who would want to keep him from a professorship. Jonathan Sperber, *Karl Marx: A Nineteenth-Century Life* (New York: Liveright Publishing, 2013), 74.

168. Liedman, *A World to Win*, 73.
169. Heinrich, *Karl Marx and the Birth of Modern Society*, 259.
170. Ibid., 320.
171. Liedman, *A World to Win*, 73.
172. Ibid., 68.
173. Heinrich, *Karl Marx and the Birth of Modern* Society, 320; Marx and Engels, *Collected Works*, vol. 1, 705, 751–52.
174. Frederick Engels, *Ludwig Feuerbach and the Outcome of Classical German Philosophy* (New York: International Publishers, 1941), 21.
175. Karl Korsch, *Karl Marx* (New York: Russell and Russell, 1963), 172–73.
176. Karl Marx, *Writings of the Young Marx on Philosophy and Society*, trans. and ed., Lloyd D. Easton and Kurt H. Guddat (Garden City, NY: Doubleday, 1967), 93–95.
177. Thomas E. Wartenburg, Introduction in *Ludwig Feuerbach, Principles of the Philosophy of the Future* (Indianapolis: Hackett, 1986), xxvi.
178. Engels, *Ludwig Feuerbach*, 17–18.
179. Karl Marx, *A Contribution to a Critique of Political Economy* (Moscow: Progress Publishers, 1970), 19.
180. Marx and Engels, *Collected Works*, vol. 1, 400.
181. Marx, *Early Writings*, 244–45.
182. Feuerbach, *The Fiery Brook*, 233.
183. Ibid., 216–17.
184. Feuerbach, *History of Modern Philosophy from Bacon to Spinoza*, 71.
185. Marx and Engels, *Collected Works*, vol. 4, 125.
186. Feuerbach, *The Fiery Brook*, 172.
187. István Mészáros, *Marx's Theory of Alienation* (London: Merlin Press, 1975), 217–40.
188. Zawar Hanfi, Introduction, in Feuerbach, *The Fiery Brook*, 3–4.
189. Karl Marx, "Luther as the Arbiter Between Strauss and Feuerbach," 93–95.
190. Korsch, *Karl Marx*, 176.
191. Hanfi, Introduction, in Feuerbach, *The Fiery Brook*, 3–4.
192. Marx, *Early Writings*, 328, 355, 387.
193. Marx and Engels, *Collected Works*, vol. 1, 65.
194. Marx, *Early Writings*, 388–90, 393.
195. Diog. Laert. 10.139; Lucr. 3.865–69.
196. Marx, *Early Writings*, 399.
197. Marx, *Early Writings*, 355.
198. Marx, *Early Writings*, 322–30.
199. Epicureanism was known for its emphasis on the strong corporeal connection between human beings and animals, which were not only related in a

material, proto-evolutionary sense, but also had in common feelings of pleasure and pain. This is best exemplified by Lucretius's famous depiction of a mother cow's inconsolable grief at the loss of her calf, after it had been sacrificed on the altar of the gods. Marx was not only at one with this Epicurean view but would carry it forward in his later work and life, recognizing that objective estrangement could be extended to animals as well. Lucr. 2.350–65; John Bellamy Foster and Brett Clark, *The Robbery of Nature* (New York: Monthly Review Press, 2020), 130–51.

200. Marx, *Early Writings*, 357; István Mészáros, *Marx's Theory of Alienation* (London: Merlin Press, 1972), 162–65.
201. See Foster and Clark, *The Robbery of Nature*, 16–40; Karl Marx, *Capital*, vol. 1 (London: Penguin, 1976), 286.
202. Marx, *Early Writings*, 329–31, 356..
203. Karl Marx, *Contribution to a Critique of Political Economy* (Moscow: Progress Publishers, 1970), 19; Marx and Engels, *Collected Works*, vol. 1, 224–63.
204. John Bellamy Foster and Paul Burkett, *Marx and the Earth* (Chicago: Haymarket, 2016), 57–88.
205. Marx, *Early Writings*, 328.
206. Marx, *Early Writings*, 349–50.
207. Marx, *Early Writings*, 359–60.
208. Marx and Engels, *Collected Works*, vol. 4, 124, 126, 128.
209. Marx and Engels, *Collected Works*, vol. 4, 129.
210. Marx and Engels, *Collected Works*, vol. 4, 128.
211. Thomas Hobbes, *The Elements of Law*, ed. J. C. A. Gaskin (Oxford: Oxford University Press, 1994).
212. Hobbes, "Chapter XXV: Of Sense and Animal Motion," included in Hobbes, *The Elements of Law Natural and Politic*, 212–28.
213. Marx and Engels, *Collected Works*, vol. 4, 128–29.
214. Marx and Engels, *Collected Works*, vol. 4, 129. The title of Locke's work, which was incorrect in the *Collected Works*, has been corrected here.
215. Nicholas Jolley, *Locke's Touchy Subjects: Materialism and Immortality* (Oxford: Oxford University Press, 2015), 1. Locke alludes numerous times (with no mention of the author even though the reference is transparent) to Lucretius's well-known maxim that "no thing can be produced by divine power from nothing." However, while applying the notion that *nothing comes from nothing* in a materialist context, Locke, as a deist, generally denies it as a proof of the nonexistence of God, whose powers exceed our comprehension. John Locke, *An Essay Concerning Human Understanding*, vol. 2 (New York: Dover, 1959), 322–36; Lucr. 1.150–83.
216. John Locke, *An Early Draft of Locke's Essay Together with Excerpts From His Journals*, ed. R. I. Aaron and Jocelyn Gibb (Oxford: Oxford University Press, 1936), 122, quoted in Jolley, *Locke's Touchy Subjects*, 29.
217. Locke, *An Essay Concerning Human Understanding*, vol. 2, 195.

218. Ibid., 190–98.
219. Marx and Engels, *Collected Works*, vol. 4, 129–30.
220. Marx and Engels, *Collected Works*, vol. 4, 130.
221. Marx, *Early Writings*, 357–58.
222. Marx and Engels, *Collected Works*, vol. 4, 125; Feuerbach, *History of Modern Philosophy from Bacon to Spinoza*.
223. Marx, *Early Writings*, 357–58.
224. Marx, *Early Writings*, 421.
225. Marx, *Early Writings*, 422. Marx here uses "contemplation" in the same sense as Plutarch. See Plut., *Moralia*, 1096.
226. Plut., *Moralia*, 1096, translated according to Einarson and De Lacy (Loeb Classical Library); Diog. Laert. 10.127–28; Frischer, *The Sculpted Word*, 35.
227. In Bacon, of course, natural science itself became a means of material change.
228. Marx, *Early Writings*, 423.
229. Bloch, *On Karl Marx*, 156.
230. Marx, *A Contribution to a Critique of Political Economy*, 22.
231. Diog. Laert. 10.65–67, translation by Hicks (Loeb Classical Library); Marx and Engels, *Collected Works*, vol. 1, 59, 415.
232. Marx, *Early Writings*, 389–91.
233. Marx and Engels, *Collected Works*, vol. 5, 31. The translation here is modified in accord with Joseph Fracchia, *Bodies and Artefacts* (Boston: Brill, 2022), vol. 1, 1–2, emphases in the original.
234. Fracchia, *Bodies and Artefacts*, vol. 1., 41, 93–94.
235. Frederick Engels, "The Funeral of Karl Marx," in *Karl Marx Remembered*, ed. Philip S. Foner (San Francisco: Synthesis Publications, 1983), 39.
236. Karl Marx, *The Poverty of Philosophy* (New York: International Publishers, 1973), 147.
237. Marx and Engels, *Collected Works*, vol. 5, 449–50.
238. Stirner, *The Ego and Its Own*, 5, 324, 326. Rather that drawing directly from Epicurus, Stirner may have used this statement as a play on Goethe's poem *Vanitas, Vanitatum, Vanitas* which commences: "On nothing I have set my heart." Johann Wolfgang von Goethe, *Works*, vol. 9, https://en.wikisource.org/wiki/The_Works_of_J._W._von_Goethe/Volume_9/Vanitas,_Vanitatum_Vanitas.
239. Stirner, *The Ego and Its Own*, 25.
240. Ibid., 25–26.
241. Ibid., 25; Marx and Engels, *Collected Works*, vol. 5, 139.
242. Marx and Engels, *Collected Works*, vol. 5, 141.
243. Marx and Engels, *Collected Works*, vol. 5, 139–41; Stirner, *The Ego and Its Own*, 26; Alexander Herzen, *Selected Philosophical Works* (Moscow: Progress Publishers, 1956), 103, 205, 221–23.
244. Marx and Engels, *Collected Works*, vol. 5, 141–42.

245. Clement of Alexandria, *Stromata* [*Miscellanies*], Book 1, chap. 11 (Cologne edition, 1688), 295. Marx and Engels, *Collected Works*, vol. 5, 141–42.
246. Marx and Engels, *Collected Works*, vol. 1, 506. Hegel, *History of Philosophy*, vol. 3, 547; William Shakespeare, *Hamlet*, Act 1, sc. 5; Karl Marx, *The Eighteenth Brumaire of Louis Bonaparte* (New York: International Publishers, 1963), 121; Marx and Engels, *Collected Works*, vol 14, 656.
247. Karl Marx, *The Poverty of Philosophy* (New York: International Publishers, 1963), 110.
248. Karl Marx, *Letters to Kugelmann* (New York: International Publishers, 1931), 112.
249. Karl Marx, *Capital*, vol. 1, 323.
250. Marx, *Capital*, vol. 1, 133–34.
251. Marx, *Capital*, vol. 1, 443.
252. Marx, *Capital*, vol. 1, 172.
253. Marx, Capital, vol. 1, 103.
254. Marx and Engels *Collected Works*, vol. 1, 64.
255. Marx and Engels, *Collected Works*, vol. 4, 53.
256. Marx and Engels, *Collected Works*, vol. 1., 64.
257. Lucr. 4.472, translation according to David Sedley, "Epicurus' Refutation of Determinism," *Syzetesis, studi sull' epicureismo Greco e romano offerti a M. Gigante* (Naples: G. Macchiaroli, 1983): 26; Marx, *Capital*, vol. 1, 103.
258. Marx and Engels, *Collected Works*, vol. 40, 316.
259. Karl Marx, *Texts on Method* (Oxford: Basil Blackwell, 1975), 195.
260. Karl Marx, *Grundrisse* (London: Penguin, 1973), 488.
261. The scientific revolutions in this respect can be seen in the use of the metabolism concept to develop the first law of thermodynamics in the work of Julius Robert Mayer and in Justus von Liebig's use of the concept in his works in chemistry, particularly agricultural chemistry. See Julius Robert Mayer, "The Motions of Organisms and Their Relation to Metabolism," in *Julius Robert Mayer: Prophet of Energy*, ed. R. Bruce Lindsay (New York: Pergamon Press, 1973), 75–145; Justus von Liebig, "1862 Preface to *Agricultural Chemistry*," *Monthly Review* 70, no. 3 (July–August 2018): 146–50.
262. Roland Daniels, *Mikrokosmos: Entwurf Einer Physiologischen Anthropologie* (Frankfurt Main: Verlag Peter Lang, 1988), 49–50. Passages translated by Joseph Fracchia. Citation in square brackets to Lucretius added here by present author.
263. Lucr. 2.71–80, translation according to Englert in Lucretius, *On the Nature of Things*, trans. Walter Englert (Indianapolis: Hackett, 2003).
264. Marx, *A Contribution to a Critique of Political Economy* (Moscow: Progress Publishers, 1970), 51–52. The extent to which social metabolism was a way of understanding capital's internal regulative function is brought out by Mészáros in the concept of social metabolic reproduction. See István Mészáros, *Beyond Capital* (New York: Monthly Review Press, 1995), 39–64.
265. Marx, *Capital*, vol. 1, 133.

266. Karl Marx, *Capital*, vol. 3 (London: Penguin ,1981), 949.
267. Lucr. 1.449–63. See translations in: (1) Lucretius, *The Scheme of Epicurus (De rerum natura)*, trans. Thomas Charles Baring (London: Kegan, Paul, Trench, 1884), 21, where "fatal rift" is used; (2) Lucretius, *On the Nature of Things*, trans. Cyril Bailey (Oxford: Oxford University Press, 1910), 41–42 (where "fatal disunion" is used). Also see the translation by Englert (Hackett), 13 ("fatally harmful disintegration"). Compare to Marx, *Capital*, vol. 3, 949; *Marx*, *Capital*, vol. 1, 637.
268. Marx and Engels, *Collected Works*, vol. 4, 120–21; Marx and Engels, *Collected Works*, vol. 8, 574.
269. Marx and Engels, *Collected Works*, vol. 8, 327–28.
270. Marx and Engels, *Collected Works*, vol. 25, 470–71.
271. Marx and Engels, *Collected Works*, vol. 25, 339–40.
272. Harman Raster, "Epicurus," *The American Cyclopaedia: A Popular Dictionary*, ed. George Ripley and Charles A. Dana (New York: D. Appleton and Co., 1879), vol. 6 (Dempster-Everett), 680–81; Marx and Engels, *Collected Works*, vol. 40, 600.
273. Frederick Engels, "Letter to Friedrich Adolph Sorge, March 15, 1883," in *Karl Marx Remembered*, 28.

Chapter Four: Marxism and Epicureanism

1. Karl Marx and Frederick Engels, *On Religion* (Moscow: Foreign Languages Publishing House, 1955), 197.
2. Frederick Engels, Alexei Mikhailovich Voden, "Talks with Engels," in *Reminiscences of Marx and Engels* (Moscow: Foreign Languages Publishing House, n.d.), 332–34; Karl Marx and Frederick Engels, *Collected Works* (New York: International Publishers, 1975), vol. 1, 25–107, 413. Voden's recollection decades later of the details of his conversation with Engels, which he said was "imprinted" on his mind (and which he conveyed not long after to Georgi Plekhanov in Russia), was accurate both with respect to the details presented concerning Marx's thesis and in relation to what we know of Engels's thinking in that area. John Bellamy Foster, *Marx's Ecology* (New York: Monthly Review Press, 2000), 230; Karl Korsch, *Karl Marx* (New York: Russell and Russell, 1938), 169–70.
3. Voden, "Talks with Engels," 332–33; Friedrich Lange, *History of Materialism* (New York: Humanities Press, 1950); Immanuel Kant, *Critique of Pure Reason* (Cambridge: Cambridge University Press, 1997), 702.
4. Voden, "Talks with Engels," 326.
5. Ritter, quoted in Jean-Marie Guyau, "The Morality of Epicurus and Its Relation to Contemporary Doctrines" (1878), https://www.marxists.org/archive/guyau/1878/epicurus.htm. See also Heinrich Ritter, *The History of Ancient Philosophy*, vol. 4 (London: Henry G. Bohn, 1846) 488.
6. Eduard Zeller, *The Stoics, Epicureans, and Sceptics* (London: Longmans, Green, 1892), 418–20. Zeller presented Epicureanism as if it were a

response to Stoicism, even though Epicureanism was the older philosophy, and only in its Latin phase, centuries after Epicurus's time, could be seen as in direct conflict with Stoicism. Eduard Zeller, *Outline of the History of Greek Philosophy* (London: Routledge and Kegan Paul, 1931), 66.

7. Lange, *History of Materialism*, 142.
8. See the discussion of Gomperz's work on Book 25 of *On Nature* in chapter 2 of this book.
9. "Alexi Mikhailovich Voden," perceptionl.com.
10. Alexi Voden, "Epicurus," *Granat Encyclopedic Dictionary* 54 (1948), 401–8, https://ru.wikisource.org; V. I. Lenin, *Collected Works* (Moscow: Progress Publishers, 1960), vol. 38, 283, 291–92. One explanation for Voden not going on to explore Gomperz's work on Book 25 of *On Nature* was that the great Epicurean scholar Bailey, whom Voden had read, contended that the Book 25 fragments, while tending "in Gomperz's view, to show that Epicurus, though an opponent of fatalism, was not opposed to determinism," were still not in adequate shape to make a definite determination, and were, in effect, still in the hands of the papyrologists. "These fragments, if they could be satisfactorily restored," Bailey continued, "would throw a great deal of light on Epicurus's psychology, and so illuminate his moral theory." While Bailey thus saw the fragments from Book 25 as having a possible *future significance*, his negative judgment on their present state accounted for his failure to include them in his text on the extant remains and may well have been enough to discourage Voden from investigating the matter himself. Epicurus, *The Extant Remains*, trans. Cyril Bailey (Oxford: Oxford University Press), 392.
11. Voden, "Talks with Engels," 330.
12. Marx's comments on Spinoza were almost uniformly negative, seeing him as a representative not of materialism but of seventeenth-century metaphysics. See Marx and Engels, *Collected Works*, vol. 4, 136–37, 139.
13. V. I. Lenin, *Collected Works*, vol. 18, 25–26.
14. Alexander Herzen, *Selected Philosophical Works* (Moscow: Foreign Languages Publishing House, 1956), 201, 205, 221–33.
15. Lenin, *Collected Works*, vol. 14, 131, 474.
16. Lenin, *Collected Works*, vol. 21, 46. Although Marx's dissertation (minus the appendix and notes) was published in Stuttgart in 1902 it may have been unavailable to Lenin. A full version of the dissertation was not issued until 1927 by the Institute of Marxism-Leninism in Moscow. Marx and Engels, *Collected Works*, vol. 1, 734–35.
17. V. I. Lenin, *Collected Works*, vol. 38 (Moscow: Foreign Publishing House, 1961), 291–92, 296; Georg Wilhelm Friedrich Hegel, *The History of Philosophy*, vol. 2 (Lincoln: University of Nebraska Press, 1995), 297.
18. Marx and Engels, *Collected Works*, vol. 1, 73.
19. Lenin, *Collected Works*, vol. 38, 293–95.
20. Lenin, *Collected Works*, vol. 38, 289–97.

21. Mikhail Shirokov, *A Textbook on Marxist Philosophy* (London: Left Book Club, 1937), 91, 137, 328, 341. The text here draws on John Bellamy Foster, *The Dialectics of Ecology* (New York: Monthly Review Press, 2024), 28–29.
22. Franz Mehring, *Karl Marx: The Story of His Life* (Ann Arbor: University of Michigan Press, 1962).
23. Mehring, *Karl Marx*, 25–31.
24. Cyril Bailey, "Karl Marx on Greek Atomism," *Classical Quarterly* 22, no.3/4 (July–October 1928): 205–6; Epicurus, *The Extant Remains*, trans. Bailey; Cyril Bailey, *The Greek Atomists and Epicurus* (New York: Russell and Russell, 1964); Lucretius, *On the Nature of Things*, trans. Cyril Bailey (Oxford: Oxford University Press, 1910).
25. Francis Macdonald Cornford, *The Unwritten Philosophy and Other Essays* (Cambridge: Cambridge University Press, 195), 117–37.
26. Benjamin Farrington, "Second Thoughts on Epicurus," *Science and Society* 17, no. 4 (Fall 1953): 326–28; Cornford, *The Unwritten Philosophy*, 117; Benjamin Farrington, *Science and Politics in the Ancient World* (London: George Allen and Unwin, 1939); George Thomson, *Aeschylus and Athens* (London: Lawrence and Wishart, 1946).
27. Farrington, "Second Thoughts on Epicurus," 326, 328. Cornford's polemical attack on Farrington for being a Marxist, which he was not at the time, was all the more significant since Cornford's son, John Cornford, was a renowned poet and Communist, who died at twenty-one, fighting in the Spanish Civil War.
28. Cornford, *The Unwritten Philosophy*, 117.
29. Ibid., 131–34.
30. Plato, *Republic*, trans. Francis Cornford (Oxford: Oxford University Press, 1945), 106.
31. Farrington, "Second Thoughts on Epicurus," 327.
32. Cornford, *The Unwritten Philosophy*, 124–25, 136.
33. Farrington, "Second Thoughts on Epicurus," 328. The first published translation in English was included in Norman D. Livergood (The Hague: Martinus Nijhoff, 1967), 61–109. An earlier typewritten translation, never published, was completed in Melbourne.
34. Benjamin Farrington, "Karl Marx—Scholar and Revolutionary," *Modern Quarterly* 7, no. 2 (Spring 1952): 90–93; Farrington, *Science and Politics in the Ancient World*, 93.
35. Editorial Preface, Marx and Engels, *Collected Works*, vol. 1, xxvii. Voden, who prepared Marx's dissertation for publication, clearly thought otherwise, adopting the same position as Lenin on this.
36. Farrington, "Karl Marx—Scholar and Revolutionary," 92–93.
37. Ibid., 92; Farrington, "Second Thoughts on Epicurus," 330.
38. Farrington, "Second Thoughts on Epicurus," 332.
39. Ibid., 333.
40. Lucr. 5.1105–07, 5.1011–27, 5.1105–50, 5.1440–47; Benjamin Farrington, "Vita Prior in Lucretius," *Hermathena* 81 (May 1953): 59–62.

41. Lucr. 5.999-1001; Farrington, "Second Thoughts on Epicurus," 333.
42. Richard Seaford, *Money and the Early Greek Mind: Homer, Philosophy Tragedy* (Cambridge: Cambridge University Press, 2004), 1-20, 125-36, 147-72.
43. Dioge. Laert. 10144; Epicurus, *The Extant Remains*, trans. Bailey, 145, 161, 171.
44. Farrington, *The Faith of Epicurus*, 31.
45. Farrington, "Karl Marx—Scholar and Revolutionary," 92.
46. Lucr. 3.1014-17; Farrington, "Second Thoughts on Epicurus," 336.
47. Lucr, 3.1-93; Farrington, "Second Thoughts on Epicurus," 337 (translation according to Farrington).
48. Farrington, *Science and Politics in the Ancient World*, 125-26.
49. Farrington, "Second Thoughts on Epicurus," 338.
50. Ibid., 148-49.
51. Lucian, *Alex.*, 22-26, 43-47; trans. according to Casson in Lucian, *Selected Satires*, trans. Lionel Casson (New York: W. W. Norton, 1962), 279-82, 286-91; Farrington, *The Faith of Epicurus*, 134-35; Marx and Engels, *Collected Works*, vol. 1, 190; Marx and Engels, *Collected Works*, vol. 5, 143, 187.
52. Farrington, *The Faith of Epicurus*, 1-19.
53. Ibid., 31.
54. Free translation of Lucr. 6.1-5 in Francis Bacon, *Novum Organum* (Book 1, aphorism 129) (Chicago: Open Court, 1994), 130; translation ("re-created") used in text according to Benjamin Farrington, *Francis Bacon, Philosopher of Industrial Science* (New York: Collier Books, 1949), 31-32. See also Benjamin Farrington, "The Christianity of Francis Bacon, *Baconiana*": *Journal of the Francis Bacon Society* 48, no. 165 (October 1965): 15-33, https://archive.org/details/1965-baconiana-no.-165/mode/2up.
55. Benjamin Farrington, *Francis Bacon: Pioneer of Planned Science* (New York: Frederick A. Praeger, 1963), 35. Bacon's father had commissioned a painting that was "placed over the fireplace in the dining hall, which showed Ceres introducing to the famished race of men the art of grain-growing" (8).
56. George Thomson, *Aeschylus and Athens*, 370-71.
57. Richard Seaford, "George Thomson and Ancient Greece," *Classics Ireland* 4 (1997): 132.
58. Seaford, "George Thomson and Ancient Greece," 121, 131-32. See especially Jane Harrison, *Ancient Art and Ritual* (Bradford-on-Avon, Wilts: Moonraker Press, 1978).
59. Seaford, "George Thomson and Ancient Greece," 128.
60. Cornford, *The Unwritten Philosophy*, 118.
61. John T. O'Connor, "Jack Lindsay, Socialist Humanism and the Communist Historical Novel," *Review of English Studies*, New Series, 66, no. 274 (2014): 360. See also Charles Woolfson, *The Labour Theory of Culture* (London: Routledge and Kegan Paul, 1982).
62. Thomson, *Aeschylus and Athens*, vii.

63. Cornford, *The Unwritten Philosophy*, 131–33.
64. Thomson, *The First Philosophers*, 325–27.
65. In the 1955 Penguin translation by Desmond Lee "noble lie" is altered to "magnificent myth" with an explanation that this is to avoid the suggestion that Plato encouraged "manipulation by propaganda," which is of course exactly what Plato's dialogue did. Lee tries to get around this by saying that all three major classes in Plato's fictional account accepted the myth. This, however, is exactly what propaganda is designed to effect. Plato, *The Republic*, trans. Desmond Lee (London: Penguin, 1955), 112. According to Aristoxenus (4th century BCE) "Plato wanted the works of Demokritos burnt." George Thomson, *The Prehistoric Aegean* (London: Lawrence and Wishart, 1978), 143.
66. Cornford, *The Unwritten Philosophy*, 137.
67. Thomson, *The First Philosophers*, 312.
68. Diog. Laert. 10.75, translation according to Hicks (Loeb Classical Library).
69. Thomson, *The First Philosophers*, 312–14.
70. Ibid., 314.
71. John Bellamy Foster, *The Return of Nature* (New York: Monthly Review Press, 2020), 447.
72. Ibid., 426–27.
73. Lucr. 6.96–1281; Jack Lindsay, *Blast-Power and Ballistics: Concepts of Force and Energy in the Ancient World* (London: Frederick Muller, 1974), 379–81, 430; Foster, *The Return of Nature*, 527–30.
74. Sebastiano Timpanaro, *On Materialism* (London: Verso, 1975), 18, 98–110; Marx and Engels, *Collected Works*, vol. 25, 331–35, 460–64.
75. Bernard Frischer, *The Sculpted Word: Epicureanism and Philosophical Recruitment in Ancient Greece* (Berkeley: University of California Press, 1982), 35–42, 87–96.
76. Karl Marx, *Early Writings* (London: Penguin, 1974), 329.
77. On materialism as ontological, epistemological, and practical see Roy Bhaskar, *Reclaiming Reality* (London: Routledge, 2011), 125.
78. Dialectical-critical realism is exemplified by Roy Bhaskar, *Dialectic: The Pulse of Freedom* (London: Verso, 1993).
79. See John Bellamy Foster, *The Dialectics of Ecology* (New York: Monthly Review Press, 2024), 82–96.
80. Marx's fascination with Diderot caused him to return to him again and again. See Marx and Engels, *Collected Works*, vol. 43, 262–65.
81. Marx and Engels, *Collected Works*, vol. 25, 21.
82. Marx and Engels, *Collected Works*, vol. 25, 339–40.
83. Foster, *The Dialectics of Ecology*, 16–25.
84. Gary Werskey, *The Visible College: The Collective Biography of British Scientific Socialists of the 1930s* (New York: Holt, Rinehart and Winston, 1978); Helena Sheehan, *Marxism and the Philosophy of Science* (Atlantic Highlands, NJ: Humanities Press, 1985).

85. On left English classicists, see Henry Stead and Edith Hall, "Between the Party and the Ivory Tower: Classical Communism in 1930s Britain," in *Classics and Class: Greek and Latin Classics and the Communism at School*, ed. David Movrin Elzbieta Olechowska (Warsaw: Ljubjana, 2016), 3–18.
86. Lancelot Hogben, *Lancelot Hogben: Scientific Humanist*, ed. Adrian and Anne Hogben (London: Merlin Press, 1998), 105.
87. Lancelot Hogben, *Science for the Citizen* (New York: Alfred A. Knopf, 1938), 380–82.
88. Hogben, *Science for the Citizen,* 381–82; J. M. Robertson, *A Short History of Free Thought, Ancient and Modern* (London: Watts and Co., 1906), 192.
89. Foster, *The Return of Nature*, 337–39; Stephen Jay Gould, *The Mismeasure of Man* (New York: W. W. Norton, 1981).
90. On Haldane see Foster, *The Return of Nature*, 383–98.
91. J. B. S. Haldane, *The Marxist Philosophy and the Sciences* (New York: Random House, 1939); J. B. S. Haldane, "Eighty Years of Darwinism," December 7, 1939, Haldane Papers, University College, London, n.d., handwritten document, Reference HALDANE/2/1/47.
92. J. B. S. Haldane, *Science and Life: Essays of a Rationalist* (London: Pemberton Publishing, 1968), 196–99, 201.
93. J. D. Bernal, *Marx and Science* (London: Lawrence and Wishart, 1952), 11–12.
94. J. D. Bernal, *The Extension of Man* (Cambridge, MA; MIT Press, 1972), 85–88; Foster, *The Return of Nature*, 369.
95. Joseph Needham, *The Great Amphibium* (New York: Charles Scribner's Sons, 1932), 35.
96. Joseph Needham, *Time: The Refreshing River* (London: George Allen and Unwin, 1943), 20, 124.
97. Needham, *Time: The Refreshing River*, 124.
98. Joseph Needham, "Untitled," handwritten draft written in relation to an invitation to take part in the British Broadcasting Corporation series "A Centenary of *Das Kapital*," located in Science and Civilization China Files, Needham Research Institute in Cambridge. Quoted in Gregory Blue, "Joseph Needham, Heterodox Marxism, and the Social Background to Chinese Science," *Science and Society* 62, no. 2 (Summer 1998); Foster, *The Return of Nature*, 404.
99. Lucr. 2.894, translation according to Needham, *Time: The Refreshing River*, 259.
100. Needham, *Time: The Refreshing River*, 189.
101. Ibid., 55–56.
102. Foster, *The Dialectics of Ecology*, 171–84.
103. Timpanaro, *On Materialism*, 29, 31, 34.
104. Jean-Paul Sartre, *Critique of Dialectical Reason*, vol. 1, trans. Alan Sheridan-Smith (London: Verso, 2004), 32.
105. Sartre, *Literary and Philosophical Essays*, 185, 205. Garaudy's analysis was more than simply the "the neo-Stalinism" with which Sartre referred to it,

which can be seen in his *Marxism in the Twentieth Century* (New York: Charles Scribner's Sons, 1970), first published in 1966.

106. Jean-Paul Sartre, *Literary and Philosophical Essays*, trans. Alan Sheridan-Smith (New York: Collier Books, 1962), 191, 206, 218, 233.
107. Sartre, *Literary and Philosophical Essays*, 62, 213, 219, 234. The concept of "counter-finality" as utilized in Sartre's *Critique of Dialectical Reason* has led to a lot of confusion as to his actual meaning. The interpretation developed here is based on understanding the connection between his critique of "finality" in his "Marxism and Revolution" essay in *Literary and Philosophical Essays* and the relation of this to his notion of "counter-finality" in the *Critique of Dialectical Reason*.
108. Jean-Paul Sartre, *Critique of Dialectical Reason*, vol. 1 (London: Verso, 2004), 164; Alberto Toscano, "Antiphysics/Antipraxis: Universal Exhaustion and the Tragedy of Materiality," in *Materialism and the Critique of Energy*, ed. Brent Ryan Bellamy and Jeff Diamanti (Chicago: M-C-M′, 2018), 480–92.
109. Sartre, *Literary and Philosophical Essays*, 223.
110. Ibid., 207, 218, 222.
111. Jean-Paul Sartre, *Search for a Method*, trans. Hazel E. Barnes (New York: Vintage, 1963), 33–34.
112. Foster, *The Dialectics of Ecology*, 28–32.
113. Theodor Adorno, *Negative Dialectics* (New York: Continuum, 1973), 377.
114. Alfred Schmidt, *The Concept of Nature in Marx* (London: New Left Books, 1970), 1, 53, 220.
115. Schmidt, *The Concept of Nature in Marx*, 21. Schmidt's bibliography includes Feuerbach's philosophical works from 1842 on but excludes his *History of Modern Philosophy from Bacon to Spinoza*, which directly influenced Marx.
116. Schmidt, *The Concept of Nature in Marx*, 22, 27, 30, 33.
117. Ibid., 46.
118. Ibid., 15, 63–64, 76, 80, 88–90, 98. 139, 157, 162, 166–96.
119. Ibid., 198, 119, 149–62; Martin Jay, *The Dialectical Imagination* (New York: Little, Brown, 1973), 267–73.
120. Tony Burns, "Materialism in Ancient Greek Philosophy and the Writings of the Young Marx," *Historical Materialism* 7, no. 1 (Winter 2000): 24; Tony Burns and Ian Fraser, eds., *The Hegel-Marx Connection* (London; Palgrave-Macmillan, 2000). Another well-known advocate of the "traditional" interpretation within Western Marxism is Peter Fenves, "Marx's Doctoral on Two Greek Atomists and the Post-Kantian Interpretation," *Journal of the History of Ideas* 47, no. 3 (July–September 1986): 433–52. Fenves's article on Marx's dissertation refrains from directly citing a single sentence from Epicurus, Lucretius, or any other Epicurean philosopher, though he does so indirectly through passages from Marx's thesis and Hegel. Nor is a single secondary source on Hellenistic philosophy referred to in his article.

This leads to rather fantastic conclusions about Marx and Epicurus. For example, Fenves contends that Marx presents Epicurus as "a proto-Hegel" who "prepares the groundwork for the absolute idealism." Fenves, "Marx's Doctoral on Two Greek Atomists and the Post-Kantian Interpretation," 434–35. Similarly, George McCarthy in his *Marx in the Ancients* refers to "the idealist philosophy of nature of Epicurus" and sees Marx's own interpretation of Epicurus in those terms (in which Marx is supposed to have viewed Epicurus as a "Kantian"). Yet no actual substantive argument is provided to make the case. One can assume that this is due to lack of familiarity with the subject matter. In a whole chapter on Marx and Epicurus, there is not a single direct reference to any work by Epicurus or any Epicurean thinker, while contemporary research on Epicurean philosophy is also notable for its absence. George McCarthy, *Marx and the Ancients: Classical Ethics, Social Justice, and Nineteenth-Century Political Economy* (Savage, MD: Rowman and Littlefield, 1990), 29, 40.

121. Burns, "Materialism in Ancient Greek Philosophy and the Writings of the Young Marx," 24.
122. Ibid., 24–25, 28; Leszek Kolakowski, *Main Currents of Marxism*, vol. 1 (Oxford: Oxford University Press, 1978), 100–107; David McLellan, *Marx Before Marxism* (London: Penguin, 1970), 52–68; McCarthy, *Marx and the Ancients*. Since Burns refers to Althusser's *For Marx* as the beginning of the "traditional" interpretation of Marx's doctoral thesis, it is noteworthy that in *For Marx* Althusser's treatment of Marx's dissertation does not refer to Epicurus or even Democritus—only to Hegel. Louis Althusser, *For Marx* (New York: Vintage, 1969), 34–35, 55–56, 65. Moreover, the traditional interpretation can be seen as originating with Mehring a century ago.
123. A. E. Taylor, *Epicurus* (London: Constable, 1911), 24, 113.
124. Marx and Engels, *Collected Works*, vol. 1, 420; Burns, "Materialism in Ancient Greek Philosophy and the Writings of the Young Marx," 27.
125. Burns, "Materialism in Ancient Greek Philosophy and the Writings of the Young Marx," 22. Burns's only purported basis for Marx having reversed himself involves reading between the lines of Marx's letter to Ferdinand Lassalle (December 21, 1857) on Epicurus, where Marx, in attempting politely to convey to Lassalle that there is really no basis for many of his contentions in his recent book on Heraclitus, where he was forced to rely on a small number of extant fragments, says that he ran into similar problems in his own work devoted to Epicurus. Marx may have had some doubts about his own conclusions on Epicurus at that point, but none of this provides the slightest basis for Burns's contention that Marx reversed himself on Epicurus. In fact, the actual reading of Marx's letter to Lassalle in this way does not seem to have been carried out by Burns himself, but by Fenves, who Burns quotes. Fenves quotes a total of four lines (with ellipses) of Marx's letter on which Burns seemingly relies. Burns does not directly cite the Marx-Lassalle letter in question. Marx and Engels, *Collected Works*, vol. 40, 316; Fenves, "Marx's Doctoral Thesis

on Two Greek Atomists and the post-Kantian Interpretation," 433; Marx and Engels, *Collected Works*, vol. 40, 226.

126. Burns, "Materialism in Ancient Greek Philosophy and the Writings of the Young Marx," 25, 27, 29.

127. A similar problem to that of Burns is displayed by Gary K. Browning, professor of politics at Oxford Brookes University, who in a recent interpretation of Marx's dissertation, "Marx's Doctoral Dissertation: The Development of a Hegelian Thesis," informs us that "Marx's dissertation is a Hegelian thesis. Its Hegelian character is revealed by an analysis of its substantive focus on the natural philosophies of Epicurus and Democritus. Marx follows Hegel in taking the Epicurean philosophy as affirming abstract self-consciousness. What the dissertation provides in the detail which Marx signals as being of prime importance in intellectual history, is a decidedly Hegelian reading of the elements of Epicurean natural philosophy." Admittedly, Marx employed Hegelian concepts and methods in his dissertation, but Browning is so focused on this that he scarcely notices that in this "Hegelian reading" Marx is intent on directly challenging Hegel's own interpretation of Epicurus, and that his substantive evaluation of Epicurean philosophy is strongly opposed to that of Hegel. The reason for this is no doubt that Browning can scarcely be said to have penetrated into the substance as opposed to form of the dissertation, since his only real interest is the Hegel-Marx connection and not Epicurus's analysis itself. Thus, we find numerous references in his essay to Hegel's *Logic*, but not a single citation to the work of Democritus, Epicurus, Lucretius, or to that of any other thinker from antiquity that Marx focused on in his dissertation. Indeed, in contrast to Burns, who cites Taylor's 1911 book, there is not even a single reference in Browning's article to any modern scholarship on Epicurus and Epicureanism, other than Bailey's two-page review of Marx's dissertation. It is no wonder then that core elements of Marx's dissertation are missed altogether. Surprisingly, even Hegel's own extensive treatment of Epicurus in his *History of Philosophy* is not cited. One could perhaps argue, in Browning's defense, that he is not interested in Marx's dissertation as such, only Marx's use of Hegelian concepts. But focusing on the latter is hardly sufficient to establish the Hegelian nature of the thesis without an adequate understanding of its content. Gary K. Browning, "Marx's Doctoral Dissertation: The Development of a Hegelian Thesis," in *The Hegel-Marx Connection*, ed. Tony Burns and Ian Fraser (London: Palgrave Macmillan, 2000), 131–45.

128. See Benjamin Farrington, *The Faith of Epicurus* (London: Weidenfeld and Nicolson, 1967); George Thomson, *The First Philosophers* (London: Lawrence and Wishart, 1955); Jack Lindsay, *Blast Power and Ballistics: Concepts of Force and Energy in the Ancient World* (London: Frederick Muller, 1974), 430.

129. David J. Furley, *Two Studies in the Greek Atomists* (Princeton: Princeton University Press, 1967), 232–33.

130. Ernst Bloch, *On Karl Marx* (New York: Herder and Herder, 1971), 154–56.
131. George Thomson, "Ancient Greek Materialism," *Labour Monthly* 19, no. 2 (February 1937): 121–23.
132. Bloch, *On Karl Marx*, 156, 158.
133. Ernst Bloch, *The Principle of Hope* (Cambridge, MA: MIT Press, 1995). 3, 1291–92.
134. Lucr. 1.72 –79, translation according to Englert in Lucretius, *On the Nature of Things* (Indianapolis: Hackett Publishing, 2003), 3. See also the translation in Bloch, *The Principle of Hope*, vol. 3, 1292.
135. Arend Th. van Leeuwen, *Critique of Heaven* (New York: Charles Scribner's Sons, 1972), 74.
136. Ibid., 82–83.
137. Ibid., 203, 206.
138. Van Leeuwen, *Critique of Earth* (New York: Charles Scribner's Sons, 1974), 291.
139. Jean Fallot, *Il piacere e la morte nella filosofia di Epicuro* (Philosophy and Death in the Philosophy of Epicurus) (Turin: Giulio Einaudi, 1977).
140. The following treatment of Fallot's work is based on Sebastiano Timpanaro, Foreword, in Jean Fallot, *Il piacere e la morte nella filosofia di Epicuro*, ix–xxxi. In contrast to Fallot, Timpanaro criticizes Paul Nizan's *Les matérialistes de l'antiquité*, written in the 1930s, as going too far in seeing Epicurus as a radical egalitarian. Nevertheless, as George Thomson indicated, in line with Nizan, "The Epicurean fraternities, which sprang out of the decay of family life and the city-state were united in the pursuit of the happiness of all of their members." George Thomson, "Ancient Greek Materialism," *Labour Monthly*, vol. 19, no. 2 (February 1937): 121–23.
141. Althusser, *For Marx*, 34–35, 55–56, 65.
142. Louis Althusser, *Philosophy of the Encounter* (London: Verso, 2006), 167–69, 262
143. Ibid., 168–70, 191, 260–61. On Althusser's references to Epicurus and death see Louis Althusser, *Philosophy for Non-Philosophers* (London: Bloomsbury, 2017), 35, 195.
144. Louis Althusser, *How to Be a Marxist in Philosophy* (London: Bloomsbury, 2017), 100–101.
145. Althusser, *Philosophy of Encounter*, 170; Althusser, *How to Be a Marxist in Philosophy*, 100–101.
146. Althusser, *Philosophy of the Encounter*, 187.
147. Ibid., 168, 261.
148. Ibid., 171, 195, 264, 275.
149. Ibid., 261.
150. Antonio Negri, "Notes on the Thought of the Later Althusser," *Postmodern Materialism and the Future of Marxist Theory*, ed. Antonio Callari and David F. Ruccio (Middletown, CT: Wesleyan University Press, 1996), 54.
151. Nail, in Thomas Nail and Katerina Kolozova, "The Swerve and Ancient

Materialism," *Journal for Politics, Gender and Culture*, vol. 19, no. 1–2 (2022): 70–71. In what is clearly an error (the exchange has the look of having been transcribed), Nail refers twice in this quote to "imminent dialectic" where he clearly meant "immanent dialectic"—Marx's own phrase in referring to Epicurus. This is an easy mistake to make and hard to catch in copyediting. I have therefore taken the liberty of correcting it here.

152. Diego Fusaro, *Marx, Epicurus, and the Origins of Historical Materialism* (Oxford: Pertinent Press, 2018), 4.
153. Etienne Balibar, *The Philosophy of Marx* (London: Verso, 1995), 7.
154. John Bellamy Foster, *Marx's Ecology* (New York: Monthly Review Press, 2000).
155. Some of the key works in Marxian ecology relying on both Epicurus and Marx, include Foster, *Marx's Ecology*; John Bellamy Foster, Brett Clark, and Richard York, *The Ecological Rift* (New York: Monthly Review Press, 2010); Constantine D. Skordoulis, "Science and Worldviews in the Marxist Tradition," *Science and Education* 17, no. 6 (2008): 559–74; John Bellamy Foster and Paul Burkett, *Marx and the Earth* (Boston: Brill, 2016); John Bellamy Foster and Brett Clark, *The Robbery of Nature* (New York: Monthly Review Press, 2020); John Bellamy Foster, *The Return of Nature* (New York: Monthly Review Press, 2020); and Thomas Nail, *Marx in Motion: A New Materialist Marxism* (Oxford: Oxford University Press, 2020), 105.
156. Van Leeuwen, *Critique of Heaven*, 76.
157. See Foster, *Marx's Ecology*, chapters 2 and 6.
158. Boris Hennig, "What Sort of Kinetic Materialism Did Marx Find in Epicurus?," *Monthly Review* 72, no. 11 (April 2021): 26.
159. Nail, *Marx in Motion*, 105.
160. Lindsay, *Blast-Power and Ballistics*, 379–81, 430.
161. A. G. Tansley, "The Use and Abuse of Vegetational Concepts and Terms," *Ecology* 16, no. 3 (July 1935): 300.
162. Thomas Nail, *Lucretius II: An Ethics of Motion* (Edinburgh: Edinburgh University Press, 2020), 159–64; editors' notes in Rouse and Smith edition of Lucretius's *On the Nature of Things* (Loeb Classical Library), 278–79. The ecological character of Epicurus's *eidola* (Lucretius's *simulacra*) is well captured in Marx's discussion in his thesis. Marx and Engels, *Collected Works*, vol. 1, 66. Furley, basing himself on Lucretius, also refers to "those complicated atomic configurations that constitute *simulacra*" and which affect the mind. Furley, *Two Studies in the Greek Atomists*, 233.
163. Fusaro, *Marx, Epicurus, and the Origins of Historical Materialism*, 151–52.
164. Skordoulis, "Science and Worldviews in the Marxist Tradition," 564–65.
165. Epicurus, *The Epicurus Reader* (Indianapolis: Hackett Publishing, 1994), 39 (Vatican Sayings).
166. Long and Sedley, *The Hellenistic Philosophers*, vol. 1, 102.
167. Alfred North Whitehead, *Nature and Life* (Cambridge: Cambridge University Press, 1934), 73, 92–95; Needham, *Time: The Refreshing River*, 193.

168. Needham, *Time: The Refreshing River*, 14–15, 124. The dialectics of emergence are not altered by quantum theory. See Jim Baggot, "Quantum Dialectics," Aeon, May 23, 2024, https://aeon.co/essays/how-soviet-communist-philosophy-shaped-postwar-quantum-theory/.
169. Marx and Engels, *Collected Works*, vol. 25, 117, 331–35; Karl Marx, *Capital*, vol. 1 (London: Penguin, 1976), 443.
170. Bhaskar, *Dialectic: The Pulse of Freedom*, 49. Marx was to convey a similar conception of emergence/disemergence in *Capital*, where he wrote: "In its rational form it [the dialectic] is a scandal and an abomination of the bourgeoisie and its doctrinaire spokesman, because it includes in its positive understanding of what exists a simultaneous recognition of its negation, its inevitable destruction; because it regards every historically developed form as being in a fluid state, in motion, and therefore grasps its transient aspect as well; and because it does not allow itself to be impressed by anything, being in its very essence critical and revolutionary." Marx, *Capital*, vol. 1, 103.
171. Lucr. 6; Bhaskar, *Dialectic: The Pulse of Freedom*, 50; Lindsay, *Blast-Power and Ballistics*, 379–81, 430.
172. David N. Sedley, "Epicurus' Refutation of Determinism," *Syzetesis, studi sull' epicureismo* Greco e romano offerti a M. Gigante (Naples: G. Macchiaroli, 1983): 34–35, 39.
173. Lucr. 5.423–432, trans. Englert (Hackett).
174. Epicurus, *On Nature*, Book 25, in A. A. Long and David N. Sedley, *The Hellenistic Philosophers* (Cambridge: Cambridge University Press, 1987), vol. 1, 102–4; Sedley, "Epicurus's Refutation of Determinism," 21; Sedley, "Epicurus's Refutation of Determinism," 23–24; Walter Englert, "Voluntary Action and Responsibility," in *Oxford Handbook of Epicurus and Epicureanism*, ed. Phillip Mitsis (Oxford: Oxford University Press, 2020), 228.
175. Bhaskar, *Dialectic: The Pulse of Freedom*, 51.
176. Karl Marx, *The Eighteenth Brumaire of Louis Bonaparte* (New York: International Publishers, 1963), 15.
177. Aeschylus, *PV* (*Prometheus Bound*), https://classics.mit.edu/Aeschylus/prometheus.html.
178. Epicurus, *The Epicurus Reader*, trans. and ed. Brad Inwood and L. P. Gerson (Homewood, IL: Hackett Publishing Co., 1994), 39 (Vatican Sayings, number 68).

Names Index

Subject Index